T0351785

A National Bureau
of Economic Research
Conference Report

Measuring and Managing Federal Financial Risk

Edited by **Deborah Lucas**

The University of Chicago Press

Chicago and London

At the time this work was completed, DEBORAH LUCAS was the Donald C. Clark HSBC Professor of Consumer Finance at the Kellogg School of Management, Northwestern University. She is currently Associate Director for Financial Analysis at the Congressional Budget Office; on leave from the Sloan School of Management at the Massachusetts Institute of Technology, where she is professor of finance; and a research associate of the National Bureau of Economic Research.

The University of Chicago Press, Chicago 60637
The University of Chicago Press, Ltd., London
© 2010 by the National Bureau of Economic Research
All rights reserved. Published 2010
Printed in the United States of America

19 18 17 16 15 14 13 12 11 10   1 2 3 4 5
ISBN-13: 978-0-226-49658-0 (cloth)
ISBN-10: 0-226-49658-9 (cloth)

Library of Congress Cataloging-in-Publication Data

Measuring and managing federal financial risk / edited by Deborah Lucas.
    p. cm. — (National Bureau of Economic Research conference report)
      ISBN-13: 978-0-226-49658-0 (hardcover : alk. paper)
      ISBN-10: 0-226-49658-9 (hardcover : alk. paper) 1. Financial risk—United States—Congresses. 2. Finance, Public—United States—Congresses. I. Lucas, Deborah. II. Series: National Bureau of Economic Research conference report.
    HJ257.3.M43 2010
    352.40973—dc22   2009034562

♾ The paper used in this publication meets the minimum requirements of the American National Standard for Information Sciences— Permanence of Paper for Printed Library Materials, ANSI Z39.48-1992.

National Bureau of Economic Research

Officers

John S. Clarkeson, *chairman*
Kathleen B. Cooper, *vice-chairman*
James M. Poterba, *president and chief executive officer*
Robert Mednick, *treasurer*

Kelly Horak, *controller and assistant corporate secretary*
Alterra Milone, *corporate secretary*
Gerardine Johnson, *assistant corporate secretary*

Directors at Large

Peter C. Aldrich
Elizabeth E. Bailey
Richard B. Berner
John H. Biggs
John S. Clarkeson
Don R. Conlan
Kathleen B. Cooper
Charles H. Dallara
George C. Eads

Jessica P. Einhorn
Mohamed El-Erian
Jacob A. Frenkel
Judith M. Gueron
Robert S. Hamada
Karen N. Horn
John Lipsky
Laurence H. Meyer
Michael H. Moskow

Alicia H. Munnell
Rudolph A. Oswald
Robert T. Parry
James M. Poterba
John S. Reed
Marina v. N. Whitman
Martin B. Zimmerman

Directors by University Appointment

George Akerlof, *California, Berkeley*
Jagdish Bhagwati, *Columbia*
Glen G. Cain, *Wisconsin*
Ray C. Fair, *Yale*
Franklin Fisher, *Massachusetts Institute of Technology*
Mark Grinblatt, *California, Los Angeles*
Saul H. Hymans, *Michigan*
Marjorie B. McElroy, *Duke*

Joel Mokyr, *Northwestern*
Andrew Postlewaite, *Pennsylvania*
Uwe E. Reinhardt, *Princeton*
Nathan Rosenberg, *Stanford*
Craig Swan, *Minnesota*
David B. Yoffie, *Harvard*
Arnold Zellner (Director Emeritus), *Chicago*

Directors by Appointment of Other Organizations

Jean-Paul Chavas, *Agricultural and Applied Economics Association*
Gail D. Fosler, *The Conference Board*
Martin Gruber, *American Finance Association*
Timothy W. Guinnane, *Economic History Association*
Arthur B. Kennickell, *American Statistical Association*
Thea Lee, *American Federation of Labor and Congress of Industrial Organizations*

William W. Lewis, *Committee for Economic Development*
Robert Mednick, *American Institute of Certified Public Accountants*
Angelo Melino, *Canadian Economics Association*
Harvey Rosenblum, *National Association for Business Economics*
John J. Siegfried, *American Economic Association*

Directors Emeriti

Andrew Brimmer
Carl F. Christ
George Hatsopoulos

Lawrence R. Klein
Franklin A. Lindsay
Paul W. McCracken

Peter G. Peterson
Eli Shapiro
Arnold Zellner

Relation of the Directors to the
Work and Publications of the
National Bureau of Economic Research

1. The object of the NBER is to ascertain and present to the economics profession, and to the public more generally, important economic facts and their interpretation in a scientific manner without policy recommendations. The Board of Directors is charged with the responsibility of ensuring that the work of the NBER is carried on in strict conformity with this object.

2. The President shall establish an internal review process to ensure that book manuscripts proposed for publication DO NOT contain policy recommendations. This shall apply both to the proceedings of conferences and to manuscripts by a single author or by one or more co-authors but shall not apply to authors of comments at NBER conferences who are not NBER affiliates.

3. No book manuscript reporting research shall be published by the NBER until the President has sent to each member of the Board a notice that a manuscript is recommended for publication and that in the President's opinion it is suitable for publication in accordance with the above principles of the NBER. Such notification will include a table of contents and an abstract or summary of the manuscript's content, a list of contributors if applicable, and a response form for use by Directors who desire a copy of the manuscript for review. Each manuscript shall contain a summary drawing attention to the nature and treatment of the problem studied and the main conclusions reached.

4. No volume shall be published until forty-five days have elapsed from the above notification of intention to publish it. During this period a copy shall be sent to any Director requesting it, and if any Director objects to publication on the grounds that the manuscript contains policy recommendations, the objection will be presented to the author(s) or editor(s). In case of dispute, all members of the Board shall be notified, and the President shall appoint an ad hoc committee of the Board to decide the matter; thirty days additional shall be granted for this purpose.

5. The President shall present annually to the Board a report describing the internal manuscript review process, any objections made by Directors before publication or by anyone after publication, any disputes about such matters, and how they were handled.

6. Publications of the NBER issued for informational purposes concerning the work of the Bureau, or issued to inform the public of the activities at the Bureau, including but not limited to the NBER Digest and Reporter, shall be consistent with the object stated in paragraph 1. They shall contain a specific disclaimer noting that they have not passed through the review procedures required in this resolution. The Executive Committee of the Board is charged with the review of all such publications from time to time.

7. NBER working papers and manuscripts distributed on the Bureau's web site are not deemed to be publications for the purpose of this resolution, but they shall be consistent with the object stated in paragraph 1. Working papers shall contain a specific disclaimer noting that they have not passed through the review procedures required in this resolution. The NBER's web site shall contain a similar disclaimer. The President shall establish an internal review process to ensure that the working papers and the web site do not contain policy recommendations, and shall report annually to the Board on this process and any concerns raised in connection with it.

8. Unless otherwise determined by the Board or exempted by the terms of paragraphs 6 and 7, a copy of this resolution shall be printed in each NBER publication as described in paragraph 2 above.

Contents

Preface

The papers and commentaries that appear in this volume were prepared for a conference held at the Kellogg School of Management in February 2007. The project was funded through the generous support of the Zell Center for Risk Research, and cosponsored by the Zell Center for Risk Research and the National Bureau of Economic Research.

The conference brought together a diverse group of academics and researchers in the areas of finance, economics, public policy, and accounting, and a distinguished group of federal policymakers and budget practitioners. The aim of the project was to encourage new research directed at improving the measurement and management of federal financial costs and risks, and to foster discussion about the prospects for, and impediments to, integrating the tools of financial economics into federal accounting practices. The discussion of these issues was greatly enhanced by the formal but unpublished presentations made by Tom Allen, Daniel Crippen, Douglas Elliott, Bill Hoagland, Howell Jackson, Katherine Schipper, and Kent Smetters.

Special thanks are due to Robert Korajczyk and Deborah Brauer for Zell Center support, to the staff of the finance department at Kellogg for help with the conference, and to the many people at the Congressional Budget Office who have shaped my understanding of these issues over the years.

Any opinions expressed in this volume are those of the respective authors and do not necessarily reflect the views of the National Bureau of Economic Research or the Zell Center for Risk Research.

Introduction

Deborah Lucas

Following the collapse of US housing prices and the financial turmoil that followed, the federal government is on course to intervene in financial markets to an extent unparalleled in US history. A partial tally includes a $29 billion, no recourse loan from the Fed to rescue Bear Stearns and its subsequent interventions to restore liquidity to the money markets; the federal takeover of Fannie Mae and Freddie Mac and their exposure to the credit risk on $5 trillion of residential mortgages; loans in excess of $100 billion to insurance giant AIG; and the passage of legislation granting open-ended authority for the Treasury to purchase up to $700 billion in troubled assets from financial institutions.

Long before these extraordinary events unfolded, the US Federal Government already functioned as the world's largest financial institution. Its central role in credit and insurance markets manifests itself through such diverse activities as: guaranteeing loans for housing, agriculture, education, small businesses, and trade; making direct loans for education, housing, and rural utilities; insuring bank deposits, defined benefit pension plans, crops, and real property; providing pension benefits to federal civilian and military employees; promising Social Security and other contingent social insurance payments; implicitly or explicitly guaranteeing the obligations of government sponsored enterprises (GSEs) like the Federal Home Loan Banks and the farm credit system; and acting as a steward for environmental assets and liabilities.

A prerequisite for effective financial management—and for meaningful

At the time this work was completed, Deborah Lucas was the Donald C. Clark HSBC Professor of Consumer Finance at the Kellogg School of Management, Northwestern University. She is currently Associate Director of Financial Analysis at the Congressional Budget Office and a research associate of the National Bureau of Economic Research.

public oversight—is accurate metrics for assessing costs, benefits, and risks. This is the logic behind the increasingly stringent rules governing financial reporting for corporations and the trend toward requiring publicly traded firms to provide fair value estimates for their financial securities. Having reliable measures is arguably even more important in the public sector, where costs and risks that are not officially accounted for can be largely invisible to policymakers and to the public, or at least ignored more easily, leading to the overprovision of activities whose costs are underestimated in the budget process and other official estimates.

Despite the size and importance of federal involvement in financial markets, the costs and risks of most federal financial activities are only partially measured and are poorly understood. In important respects (e.g., the absence of capital budgets, risk adjustment, and sophisticated internal costing systems), federal accounting for financial risk and value lags well behind private-sector standards. The political process provides few incentives for improving disclosures, even when a financial crisis spurs calls for reform. Also, with a few notable exceptions, academics have devoted relatively little attention to improving the measurements of federal financial costs and risks. Programmatic complexity and the difficulty of obtaining data from federal agencies create substantial barriers to entry for researchers, and the topic has remained outside of the mainstream of economic inquiry.

The purpose of this volume is to begin filling these gaps. The chapters and discussions highlight how the rules of federal budgeting obscure the economic cost of federal financial obligations. They also provide more comprehensive estimates of the costs and benefits of a wide variety of federal financial activities and develop new methodologies to improve such measurements. The analyses encompass a broad spectrum of federal programs—housing and government sponsored enterprises, catastrophe insurance, student loans, Social Security, and environmental liabilities. Although not inclusive of the full scope of federal financial obligations, collectively, these studies demonstrate how the logic of financial economics can be informative about a broad range of federal activities and the potential for academic research to better inform public discourse on these issues.

A fundamental theme running through this volume is that market prices, or "fair value" estimates, are the best measure of the opportunity cost to society of government expenditures and that federal obligations should therefore be evaluated using them. Most economists accept the premise that using market prices (as opposed to "administrative" or "historical book" prices) is the best approach, but there is still resistance to this idea in some parts of the federal budgeting community and among many actuaries. In fact, some budget practitioners may view nonmarket estimates as natural, because federal law stipulates that credit obligations be budgeted for using risk-free rates for discounting. Whether this rule should be modified and what the effects would be are critical issues that are addressed by some of the chapters in this volume. More broadly, an aim of this book is to clearly present the case for market prices in a way that is accessible to an audience of both economists and noneconomists.

In the wake of the financial crisis and the criticisms that arose about fair value accounting for private financial institutions in distressed markets, some readers may be skeptical about the wisdom of introducing similar rules into federal accounting. Yet, these events have not invalidated the principles that are the foundations for the view that market prices are the best available measure of value. The practical resiliency of this idea and the absence of a more compelling alternative is demonstrated by several recent developments in private-sector and public-sector accounting regulation: the Federal Accounting Standards Board (FASB) continues to support fair value accounting for financial securities, albeit with new circuit breakers to mitigate problems that can arise when markets are illiquid. International accounting standards, slated to be adopted in the United States, also firmly embrace fair value principles. Most notably, federal budget agencies have recently emphasized fair value estimates for the cost of new obligations arising from the financial crisis, precisely because not adjusting for market risk produces less credible cost estimates.[1]

These basic themes are further elaborated on in chapter 3, "The Cost of Risk to the Government and Its Implications for Federal Budgeting," by Deborah Lucas and Marvin Phaup. The authors lay out the economic case for incorporating the cost of market risk in government decision making, describe how risky securities are currently accounted for in the federal budget and how this likely biases real resource allocations, and survey the results of recent research on the cost of market risk for federal obligations.

The analysis begins by addressing both the philosophical and practical impediments to incorporating the cost of risk into federal budget estimates. As noted previously, while the idea that market risk is a legitimate cost is now widely accepted in the private sector and by most academic economists, the concept has not gained such wide acceptance among policymakers nor in the federal budgeting community. The authors revisit the lively debate that took place in the late 1960s and early 1970s between the leading economists of the time over whether the risk of activities undertaken by the government should be treated as a cost. They suggest that more recent developments in financial economics support the idea, which also had considerable currency in the early debate, that systematic or market risk represents a legitimate cost to taxpayers and that this cost is best measured by market prices. Further, they make the case that the logic supporting the use of market prices

1. For instance, the legislation that authorized the Troubled Assets Relief Program (TARP) explicitly overrode the standard Federal Credit Reform Act (FCRA) practice of using the risk-free rate for discounting—it called for using risk-adjusted rates. The Congressional Budget Office has also adopted risk adjustment in accounting for the government's assumption of Fannie Mae and Freddie Mac's obligations.

is largely robust to considerations of various market frictions and market incompleteness.

The use of market prices is also justified on consistency grounds. In fact, the vast majority of expenditures are recorded in the budget at market prices. Cash transfers arising from Social Security benefits, food stamps, and so forth are accounted for at a market price; by definition—the real value of a dollar is what one gets by spending it on a consumption bundle. Federal purchases from the private sector for military hardware, the labor of the federal workforce, buildings, computers, electricity, and so on are all expenditures that occur at market prices. While the Federal Government caps certain expenditures such as Medicare reimbursements to doctors, nevertheless, the transactions occur at market prices. Thus, using market prices puts financial obligations on a consistent basis with other forms of federal spending.

Also important is that the practical alternatives to market prices—reporting historical cost or discounting expected cash flows at risk-free rates—are subject to the same criticisms. These alternatives also rely on market prices: risk-free rates are derived from the market prices of US Treasury securities, and historical book values are stale market prices. Hence, if one cannot trust markets to determine value, the leading alternatives are equally problematic.

The rules for accounting for federal financial obligations are complicated. Various categories of obligations are accounted for very differently, and distinct biases arise in each instance. Credit is accounted for on an accrual basis, whereas insurance and investments are on a cash basis. Accrual costs for credit exclude the market price of risk and also certain administrative costs. This tends to understate the full cost of credit and creates a bias toward using risky loans or loan guarantees in preference to direct grants and other forms of assistance for which cost is measured more comprehensively and at market prices. For investments in publicly traded securities (e.g., equities), a different sort of distortion arises from the use of cash basis accounting. Securities purchased at market prices entail no net transfer of resources from the government, but under cash basis accounting, such transactions appear costly, because the large initial outlays are not offset by expected dividends or interest payments in the budget window.

To illustrate the practical importance of these effects, the authors survey the existing studies estimating the size of the distortions caused by omitting the cost of risk in specific federal activities. The results suggest that the size of the omissions in many cases is sizeable; for instance, the estimate by the Congressional Budget Office (CBO) in 2005 of the present value of shortfalls for the Pension Benefit Guarantee Corporation increases from $32 billion to $63 billion when market risk is taken into account.

Catastrophic risks such as terrorism, hurricanes, earthquakes, and floods are often explicitly or implicitly insured by the Federal Government. These events, which regularly trigger billions of dollars in emergency spending, nevertheless are treated as surprises every year that require supplemental appropriations outside of the normal budget process. In chapter 4, "Federal Financial Exposure to Natural Catastrophe Risk," David Cummins, Michael Suher, and George Zanjani draw on a wide variety of government and private-sector data sources to document the size and causes of these expenditures from 1989 to 2008. Their analysis suggests that these expenses, which have been escalating rapidly, are to a large extent predictable and therefore could be better accounted for and controlled. They also make a persuasive case for the likely continuing high rate of federal spending growth for catastrophes.

One reason for the steady and protracted cost growth is the increasing value of infrastructure exposed to catastrophe. Disaster relief expenditures have been the most significant component of federal catastrophe exposure. Another driver of cost growth is the political process. While some of these obligations are explicit in the law—for instance, the Stafford Emergency Assistance and Relief Act of 1988 requires federal aid when state and local resources are overwhelmed by a major catastrophe—much of the assistance that is provided is "discretionary." However, the authors argue that the strong expectation of public assistance, combined with the ad hoc way in which the decision to grant aid is made in the legislative process, effectively means these expenditures are mandatory.

Projections of future average expenses and their probability distribution are developed using two approaches: a commercial catastrophe model and historical catastrophe loss data. Under conservative assumptions, assistance related to hurricanes, earthquakes, thunderstorms, and winter storms is projected to be about $20 billion in a normal year and could exceed $100 billion in a bad year. The $20 billion far exceeds the regular appropriations for the Disaster Relief Fund, which averaged only about $1 billion over the period from 2001 to 2005. Capitalizing the expected expenditures over the next seventy-five years, the liability to the Federal Government is estimated to be comparable in magnitude to the shortfall projected for Social Security over the same horizon.

To further the goal of increasing homeownership, federal housing policy makes extensive use of credit and tax incentives. As recent events have underscored, these activities involve substantial federal cost and risk. Chapter 5, "Housing Policy, Mortgage Policy, and the Federal Housing Administration," by Dwight Jaffee and John Quigley, reviews these programs and estimates the value of indirect and off-budget activities supporting homeownership. The analysis emphasizes the Federal Housing Administration's (FHA) mortgage insurance programs and revisits their rationale and future role in light of the rapid rise and subsequent fall of the subprime market.

Federal housing policy is executed through a complex array of institutions and programs, including the tax code, the Federal Housing Administration, the Veterans Administration (VA), and government sponsored enterprises such as Fannie Mae, Freddie Mac, and the Federal Home Loan Banks. A comprehensive look at these programs reveals that off-budget policies primarily provide subsidies for middle- and upper-income homeowners and home purchasers, whereas programs subject to Congressional budget appropriations are directed toward lower-income and rental households.

Jaffee and Quigley calculate that tax expenditures—relative to a baseline of the tax treatment of commercial real estate—represent by far the most expensive subsidies to housing. Specifically, housing services are treated asymmetrically to rental housing, and the first $0.5 million of realized capital gains is tax exempt. Depreciation, maintenance, and repairs, however, are not deductable. The net effect for 2007 is estimated to be $32.5 billion in foregone revenue from imputed rental income less expenses. The mortgage payment deduction adds another $78.1 billion in tax expenditures. The property tax exclusion represents $15 billion of cost, and the capital gains exemption represents $43 billion. Overall, tax expenditures in 2007 were about $166 billion, or about seven times the tax expenditures for all other housing programs. The value of subsidies related to the GSEs is harder to evaluate, as is their incidence. Surveying the literature that estimates the GSE subsidy, they suggest that the annual cost is on order of $10 billion.

The much less costly programs serving the low-income market have evolved from the first Public Housing Act of 1937, which financed construction aimed at the "elimination of substandard and other inadequate housing," to the current emphasis on Section 8 housing vouchers that provide rent subsidies to about 1.9 million households to obtain privately provided housing, at a reported cost of $37.7 billion in 2007.

The FHA and VA insurance and guarantee programs had their origins in the Great Depression. Mortgages at the time were short term, had low loan-to-value ratios, and required a balloon payment at maturity. The crisis left most borrowers unable to refinance and caused others to default, leading to the bankruptcy of many lending institutions. In 1934, Congress established the FHA to oversee a program of home mortgage insurance, predicated on "economically sound" self-amortizing, long-term mortgages. This led to standardization of mortgage products and underwriting procedures nationally. In its early years, the program served the vast majority of homeowners and involved little redistribution. The VA loan program came into existence near the end of World War II and grew to be a more highly subsidized benefit, providing a federal guarantee for up to 60 percent of mortgages made to eligible veterans. Over time, the FHA program evolved toward providing guarantees to low-income borrowers attracted by low down payment requirements and less stringent credit requirements.

The two programs reached their peak volume in 2003, with $165 billion and $66 billion of mortgages insured by the FHA and VA, respectively. By 2006, the volume had declined to $54 billion for the FHA and less than $25 billion for the VA in insured mortgages. The decline in the importance of these programs in terms of the share of total mortgages outstanding was more dramatic and began in the 1960s. Quigley and Jaffee show that what took their place was the (re)development of private mortgage insurance and the concurrent expansion of Fannie Mae and Freddie Mac. At the same time, FHA and VA growth was impeded by fixed nominal limits on the loans insured, and in recent years, by competition from the rapid growth of subprime lending. The higher credit quality end of FHA lending has also been increasingly captured by Fannie and Freddie, which have expanded into these riskier products. The authors argue that the fundamental reasons behind these dramatic changes include improved credit scoring models in the private sector and a philosophical shift and lack of contract innovation on the part of the FHA. The recently heightened concern about predatory lending suggests a new role for the FHA in setting standards for nonpredatory practices and perhaps in offering a higher-quality product to compete with private offerings.

In chapter 6, "Valuing Government Guarantees: Fannie and Freddie Revisited," Deborah Lucas and Robert McDonald consider some of the methodological issues surrounding estimating GSE subsidy values using a derivatives pricing approach and provide new estimates of the subsidy to Fannie and Freddie, taking these considerations into account. Existing estimates of the GSE subsidy value—made under the relatively stable market conditions of the last decade—vary enormously, ranging from $200 million to $182 billion. The wide range reduces the credibility of cost estimates and suggests the need to reconsider what is driving these differences. The takeover of Fannie and Freddie by the Federal Government and the prospect that they may remain fully federal entities for an extended time period underscore the need for improved tools to evaluate and monitor their costs and risks.

Past estimates of the GSE subsidy value are based on two broad approaches: spread based and derivatives based. The former focuses on the interest rate differential, or spread, between the borrowing rates for the GSEs versus similarly risky but unguaranteed financial firms, whereas the latter relies on the observation that a default guarantee is equivalent to a put option on the assets of the firm and hence can be valued using derivative pricing techniques. In general, spread-based analyses produce much larger estimates of subsidy value. One reason for the discrepancies is that the two approaches answer slightly different questions. The derivatives approach looks only at the cost of providing insurance against default, whereas the interest rate spread also takes into account other advantages the GSEs may have in terms of liquidity or regulatory preference that lower their cost of capital. The analysis highlights a further reason that spreads may overestimate the cost to the government: at times, insured firms have an incentive to avoid default to preserve future guarantee value, making them less likely to default than an otherwise similar uninsured firm.

To rigorously explore the question of whether and how the presence of a repeated government guarantee changes the relation between a firm's equity value and the value of its operating assets, the authors develop a theoretical valuation model. Understanding this relation is important, because in derivative-based approaches to valuing debt guarantees, the unobservable value and volatility of assets is inferred from the observable value and volatility of equity. If the presence of the guarantee changes these relations—for instance, by affecting equity dynamics—the inferences could be biased.

In the model, it is assumed that an insured firm can continue indefinitely to issue insured debt in an amount based on the value of its operating (i.e., nonguarantee) assets, as long as it comes up with sufficient cash to cover its obligations at each debt maturity date. It will do so as long as staying in business is better for equity holders than declaring bankruptcy. The theoretical analysis reveals that in fact, the presence of the guarantee does not fundamentally change the relation between the volatility of levered equity and the underlying assets, leaving intact the standard equations underlying derivatives-based pricing. It does, however, create a wedge between the value of operating assets and the market value of debt and equity equal to the present value of the future stream of income generated by the guarantee. This affects the initial conditions for derivatives-based estimates. The analysis also reveals that the spread-based approach is upwardly biased when no correction is made for the lower-predicted default rate for guaranteed firms that optimally default less often to preserve the value of future guarantees.

To provide estimates that take into account these considerations and that also incorporate potentially important complications such as jumps in underlying asset value, time-varying asset volatility, and a more complicated default policy, Lucas and McDonald calibrate and simulate a computational version of the model. They find that an insurance premium of 20 to 30 basis points on Fannie and Freddie debt would have been fair compensation for the default risk assumed by the government under the benign economic conditions of 2005. However, an asset value decline of 10 percent causes the fair premium to more than double, highlighting the sensitivity of guarantee values to changes in equity value in highly levered financial institutions, and also demonstrating the usefulness of these types of models in setting risk-based insurance premiums.

The Federal Government can support credit to target groups either through direct lending or by guaranteeing against default risk loans made by private financial institutions. Whereas most federal credit programs rely on either direct lending or on loan guarantees exclusively, the federal student loan program is unique in maintaining two large and competing programs to support higher education, one of each type—the Federal Family Educational Loan Program (guaranteed program) and the Federal Direct Loan Program (direct program). This structure provides the opportunity to compare the cost to the government of these different financing and delivery mechanisms for very similar underlying loan products. Since both programs are accounted for in the federal budget, the costs as estimated under current budgeting rules also can be compared to market value-based estimates. In chapter 7, "Guaranteed versus Direct Lending: The Case of Student Loans," Deborah Lucas and Damien Moore develop a quantitative valuation model for student loans under the rules of each program and use it to explore these issues.

After adjusting for the market cost of capital, asymmetric treatment of administrative costs, and other inconsistencies in how the programs are budgeted for, the authors find that the guaranteed program appears to be fundamentally more expensive than the direct program, with an 11 percentage point higher subsidy rate (i.e., costing $0.11 more in present value per dollar of loans originated). The differential can be attributed primarily to administrative costs associated with the structure of the guaranteed program and to the fact that guaranteed lenders are paid more than is required to induce them to lend at statutory terms. The direct program also appears to have a real cost advantage. As well as lower administrative costs, the direct program has the apparent advantage of raising funds via the Treasury rather than through private financial institutions.

In light of its cost disadvantage, a natural question is whether the guaranteed program provides offsetting benefits. In general, which method is a more efficient way to provide credit assistance depends on a variety of factors including the relative cost of capital, administrative efficiency, and the incentives to screen and monitor borrowers. Lucas and Moore point out that because student loans have categorical entitlement and an almost full credit guarantee, the value added by private intermediation is less obvious than for some other programs.

The discrepancy between budget estimates and market value estimates of subsidy rates on student loans is found to be large. Including a credit risk premium in subsidy rate estimates increases the subsidy rate by more than 15 percentage points. As a consequence, the budget cost of student loans significantly understates the cost to taxpayers. The authors also suggest that the cost understatement can distort policy choices in a way that has real effects—for instance, favoring an increase in the student loan program over other forms of assistance to students like direct grants, which have been shown to be more effective for encouraging low-income students to obtain a higher education.

The last two chapters in this volume show how the principles of financial economics can be fruitfully extended to analyze federal financial exposures that go beyond the realm of traditional financial activities. In chapter 8, "Market Valuation of Accrued Social Security Benefits," John Geanakoplos and Stephen Zeldes apply the principles of market valuation to Social Security obligations. The calculations are relevant: to assessing the size of unfunded federal liabilities, to the debate over whether and how they should be accounted for in the financial statements of the US government, to helping workers plan for retirement, for plans to privatize benefits based on the fair value of current accruals, and for considering asset allocation in the trust fund. Interestingly, this is a case where taking market risk into account has the effect of lowering the estimated cost of federal obligations relative to traditional cost estimates.

Most existing analyses project Social Security obligations forward, taking into account demographic and wage trends. They implicitly treat the projected obligations as riskless by discounting them at a riskless rate. In fact, promised benefits are correlated with long-run wages through the benefits formula, which bases lifetime annuity payments on a worker's average real wage over his or her thirty-five highest-earning years. This means that when the economy has done well, promised benefits are higher, and conversely when economic growth is low. Hence, there is systematic risk associated with Social Security obligations.

The valuation approach taken by Geanakoplos and Zeldes is to treat Social Security claims as derivatives of the stock market. Although the empirical correlation between wages and stock returns is low over short horizons, in the long-run, evidence suggests that the two are positively correlated. A risk-neutral Monte Carlo model, calibrated with historical data on stock returns, labor earnings, the risk-free rate, demographic data, and the rules governing Social Security obligations, yields an estimated market value for claims held by workers of different current ages. Aggregating across birth cohorts yields an estimate of aggregate liabilities. Adjusting for market risk has a significant effect on estimates of the present value of accrued benefits, particularly for benefits accrued for workers not yet retired. For workers under age sixty, the present value of costs, measured as the present value of accrued benefits less the current value in the trust fund, falls from $8.57 trillion to $6.05 trillion when the discount rate is risk adjusted. For retirees, the effect of market risk is minimal, since promised benefits are not affected by future shocks to the aggregate economy. Overall, taking market risk into account decreases the present value of benefits to 81 percent of the estimated value calculated using a riskless discount rate.

Failure at the federal level to account for the value of environmental assets and liabilities and to actively manage the associated risks has potentially dire consequences. In chapter 9, "Environment and Energy: Catastrophic Liabilities," Geoffrey Heal and Howard Kunreuther review the extent to which the government faces liabilities arising from its management of environmental risks and also survey estimates of the size of natural capital as an asset. They then look in detail at the Price-Anderson Nuclear Industries Indemnity Act (P-A Act) in order to assess the nature of this federal liability and to suggest ways in which it could be more effectively managed.

Valuing environmental assets and liabilities has been an active area of environmental research in the last decade, but it is a complicated undertaking that is made especially difficult by the absence of markets for many of these resources. An example given of undervaluation due to underpriced positive externalities is the New York City watershed, which provides uncompensated value in the form of clean water and the avoidance of filtration costs. Another is the cost of the gradual destruction of barrier islands in the Gulf of Mexico that partially protect New Orleans from costly storm surges. Similarly to financial transactions, the authors note that government accounting standards tend to be less stringent than those imposed in the private sector, potentially encouraging natural resource depletion. For example, mineral depletion under US generally accepted accounting principles (GAAP) must be recorded as a reduction in assets on corporate balance sheets. Under the United Nations System of National Accounts, however, depletion is not treated as a charge against national income. Data from the World Bank gives some sense of the aggregate importance of environmental assets. It shows natural capital as accounting for 26 percent of total public and private capital for low-income countries but only 2 percent for high-income Organization for Economic Cooperation and Development (OECD) countries. Even the 2 percent is a large absolute number, since many forms of natural capital are omitted, and the total size of the capital stock is large.

Nuclear power plants have a highly skewed risk profile, with a high probability of emitting no pollutants, and a very small chance of a catastrophic meltdown, as in the case of the Chernobyl reactor. The disposal of nuclear waste also entails the potential for catastrophes. Whether these risks have become more or less severe over time is hard to measure. The frequency of accidents in the United States has decreased markedly from the 1960s and 1970s, but reactors are located close to population centers that have grown larger over time, and the potential size of losses is enormous. For instance, it is estimated that the cost of a major meltdown of the Indian Point reactor located near New York City could top $1 trillion. The historical justification for the P-A Act, which was renewed in 2005, is that such exposures make it impossible for the nuclear industry to obtain private insurance. The authors review the conditions normally thought to be necessary for private insurability and conclude that the risks are in fact unique, massive, and not well understood, probably making it impossible to have a nuclear industry that relies on completely private insurance. They go on to look into the details of the P-A Act to see whether it is likely to meet goals such as mitigating moral hazard in how plants are operated and where they are sited. The conclusion is that problems such as regulatory capture by the Nuclear Regulatory Commission (NRC) and inadequate incentives for investing in safety suggest that the rules could be improved and that improvements in other catastrophe insurance programs provide some models that could be adopted in the nuclear context.

These chapters were first presented and discussed at an eponymous conference sponsored by the Zell Center for Risk Research at Kellogg and held at the Kellogg School of Management at Northwestern University in February 2007. The conference brought together scholars and policymakers from academia, research institutions, and the government. This volume includes two of the presentations made by policymakers that crystallize the central issues: a keynote address by Peter Fisher, former under secretary of Treasury and now a managing director at Blackrock, on the importance of bringing financial literacy to Washington; and a talk by Donald Marron, former acting director of the Congressional Budget Office, on how cost estimates are used in Congressional decision making and how risk might be usefully incorporated. It is my hope that the chapters and discussions in this volume will provide further impetus for work in this area that ultimately leads to better informed decision making in the public sector.

1

Bringing Financial Literacy to Washington

Peter R. Fisher

By focusing on "measuring and managing federal financial risk," you are asking the right questions about our financial future. I hope you come up with some good answers soon. The broader question you address is this: can the Federal Government become financially literate? Or, more importantly, can it learn to *behave* in a financially literate manner?

Reasonable people may conclude that the best answer to this question is "No, it cannot: abandon all hope, ye who enter here." That option is not open to me and I hope not to you. Those of us who would like to ensure that our national government's financial resources can be mobilized for our collective needs in the future *must* be concerned.

In particular, those of us who fear that we are on an unsustainable path of accumulating federal liabilities—current, contingent, and the future— bear the burden of articulating a theory of the sustainable path of federal liabilities. We bear this burden because many of our fellow citizens think we are the shepherd boy crying wolf: the Federal Government appears to have no difficulty sustaining its liabilities.

Before I get going, let me come clean: I do *not* have a theory of the sustainable path of federal liabilities. I only have a few stories and a few suggestions.

My suggestions, in summary, are as follows:

1. Do not wait for the bond market to help us out; that is not its job.
2. We need to improve the process. This is not about a single set of true numbers but about more (and more useful) information.

Peter R. Fisher is Managing Director at BlackRock, Inc.

This chapter is based on the keynote remarks given at the conference on Measuring and Managing Federal Financial Risk, Zell Center for Risk Research, Kellogg School of Management, Northwestern University, February 8, 2007.

3. It is not just about process, it is about substance: this is a very real fight over the allocation of resources.

Now for the stories.

In the fall of 2001, as a newly confirmed under secretary, my first real assignment from the White House was to persuade Congress not to enact a loan guarantee program for the airline industry following 9/11. My second assignment was to help implement the loan guarantee program that Congress enacted.

Over the following months, I found myself awkwardly defending the federal fisc from both on- and off-balance sheet attacks, including Federal Deposit Insurance Corporation (FDIC) "reform," Pension Benefit Guarantee Corporation (PBGC) "insolvency," direct lending to absorb the cost of salmon spawning during a drought, expansion plans for student loan guarantees, terrorism risk insurance, and the decaying finances of the Postal Service. With each new topic I confronted, I tried to engage my counterparts in the language of *finance, risk, and exposure* but found myself treated as if I were speaking a foreign language completely unrecognizable to the indigenous population.

So, in response, I did what every under secretary learns to do when backed into a corner: I gave a speech, somewhere out of town. In it, I compared the Federal Government to "a gigantic insurance company (with a sideline business in national defense and homeland security) which does its accounting on a cash basis—only counting premiums and payouts as they go in and out the door." For good measure, I noted: "An insurance company with cash accounting is not really an insurance company at all. It is an accident waiting to happen."

This was a clever thing to say. So clever, in fact, that a number of friends called to offer me employment in anticipation of my dismissal.

While it may have been clever at the time, it is worth asking now, some years later, whether I still think it is an accurate or useful metaphor. Upon even more sober reflection, I would say that in many ways I think it is—although in one important way it is not.

First, an insurance company with only cash accounting would not be very good at pricing and managing the exposures it takes on, as it would have little information and insufficient incentives to concern itself with risk and exposure.

Likewise, it is fair to say, I think, that the Federal Government is challenged when it comes to pricing risk. Usually, Congress intervenes, sets the price too low, and limits agency discretion to adjust price in response to risk—as the history of deposit insurance and pension benefit guarantee premiums suggests.

More troublesome than the problem of Congressional handcuffs is the problem of mental handcuffs—of financial illiteracy in action.

Consider the Pension Benefit Guarantee Corporation. For most of its history, it ran an accrual deficit. Its business of insuring the pension obligations of corporate plans with underpriced premiums meant that it did not have sufficient reserves to absorb the losses of the pension plans that it was forced to take over. While some socialization of costs like these can be accepted in principle, in this case, Congress provided no mechanism to absorb the cost—other than kicking it down the road. This is a bad business model.

Magically, in the late 1990s, the PBGC began to run surpluses that grew larger and larger as the economy (and stock market) strengthened. My friends and predecessors at the Treasury spent their time worrying not about PBGC solvency but rather about whether the PBGC's assets should be invested in indexed equity funds or ones managed on a discretionary basis. When the stock market bubble burst and the economy turned in 2000 and 2001, the PBGC's finances decayed rather quickly.

It is a shame that during the "years of plenty," more time was not spent thinking about the totality of the PBGC's balance sheet.

The PBGC is thrice exposed to the equity market. Its primary business is not as a pension fund but rather as a corporate guarantee fund. In simple form, on the liability side of its balance sheet, the PBGC is guaranteeing the bottom quintile of Wilshire 5000's pension fund's investments in the Wilshire 5000. What is the appropriate equity position to hold on the asset side of such a balance sheet? It is short, not long.

No wonder the PBGC seemed to be on such solid footing during the go-go 1990s. No wonder its finances deteriorated so quickly at the start of this decade.

The Federal Government is not a limited purpose organization; it has many objectives. But if it is going to take on the responsibility of intervening in a highly complex market of investment and actuarial exposures, it is a shame that it cannot do so with its eyes open to the financial risks and with the ability to structure its balance sheet accordingly. While it may be hard for some to imagine an instrumentality of the Federal Government shorting the American stock market, if our government is going to take on the responsibilities of an insurance company, doing so with one arm tied behind its back was bound to be expensive for taxpayers, pension plans, and retirees—as it has turned out in this case.

The second way the Federal Government is like a cash-accounting insurance company is that it is not in a position to understand *and act upon* knowledge of its aggregate position.

While progress has been made in bringing attention to the accrual position of major entitlement and benefit programs, the major players in allocating federal resources—the Office of Management and Budget (OMB), the key Congressional committees, and the Congressional leadership—do not *consciously* act on the basis of accrual positions as either an objective or a constraint.

Maybe a very thin silver lining to the prescription drug benefit is that it was such a clear actuarial and accrual giveaway that Congress is less likely to sign up for such a whopper again any time soon. But I am probably being too optimistic. Let me come back to cash and accrual accounting in a moment.

There is an important way in which the Federal Government is *not* like an insurance company—namely in the apparent lack of market discipline. An insurance company incapable of pricing risk or acting upon knowledge of its net exposures would be punished by the capital markets and eventually find it prohibitively expensive to borrow or to raise capital. The Federal Government, however, does not seem to be subject to this form of market discipline for its recent or its future deficits.

That is right. It is not, and we should not expect it to be.

As we swung from annual surplus to annual deficits in the early years of the Bush administration, interest rates magically fell. I remember doing one of those White House lawn interviews: squinting into the camera, I heard the interviewer in my ear ask me if I was having trouble borrowing all that money now that we had plunged into deficits again. With interest rates approaching historic lows, I decided to take on something easier, and to the interviewer's surprise, switched the subject to accounting for corporate stock options.

If we want useful information about the sustainable path of federal liabilities, I do not think we are going to find it in the bond market. This is because the term structure of yields on the least risky asset is principally determined by the expected path of monetary policy. That is why bond yields were falling as the deficits expanded earlier in this decade, and that is why Japanese interest rates are still near historic lows, even as the Japanese government runs a ratio of deficit to gross domestic product (GDP) that is roughly twice (as bad as) ours.

I say this *not* to suggest that we need not worry about the sustainable path of federal liabilities but rather to suggest that we need to worry *even more*. The bond market vigilantes are not going to help us, because they are not focused on our problem; they are focused on the Fed. If anyone wants to sit around and wait for the bond market to exert fiscal discipline *without any assistance from monetary policy,* then I really would recommend a field trip to Japan.

In short, I have more confidence in academia to address this problem than I do in the bond markets.

So, what is to be done? First, improve the process. I have three suggestions.

1. Do not focus on one number or set of numbers; get more information.

A zero-sum debate between cash and accrual accounting is not helpful. The answer is both. I would like to see more emphasis on accrual accounting, but I would not hide or do away with the cash budget. The scope of the

Federal Government's future contingent liabilities has reached the point where we need some constraints placed on accrued liabilities. While we may not be ready for an accrual budget, we need more accrual-based information for decision makers.

At BlackRock, our portfolio managers have a mind-boggling array of risk measures and credit information when making a decision to buy or sell a single bond or stock. Maybe we could get Congress to consider more than one set of numbers when they allocate national resources.

2. Require "accrual accounting impact statements."

Today, we have the cash budget and ten-year cash projections. I would like to see an additional requirement that prior to Congressional votes, there be an accrual accounting impact statement of any proposed legislation, scored by the Congressional Budget Office (CBO) but consistent with the methodologies used in the Treasury's Annual Financial Report.

Thirty years ago, environmental impact statements were in their infancy. They are subject to political interference and are imperfect. But we have learned a great deal over the last thirty years, and I think we are better off for having them. Looking back over the last three decades, I am confident that our nation's finances would be better off if Congress had had to confront the accrual implications of their actions before they voted rather than after.

At the Treasury, we worked hard to get the Annual Financial Report completed in time to be released in December rather than March. We hoped that some day, Congress might take notice of the accrual positions before the start of the legislation season in January rather than when the horses were already out of the barn a few months later. It would be even better if individual bills had to be scored on their accrual implications.

Better enforced budget rules and pay-go disciplines are important. However, inside any budget, there is more than enough latitude for a misallocation of resources. It is my experience that there is no substitute for killing bad ideas one at a time—if you can.

3. We need more program-specific risk and exposure information.

When the Airline Transportation Stabilization Board was set up, the net of the statutory and regulatory guidance we got was this: lend money where private markets fear to tread, but do not take unreasonable risks with the taxpayers' money. Clearer guidance from Congress would have been helpful.

Eventually, we found our way, each board member using their own method. Options-pricing methodologies helped us enormously. For my part, I reconciled our mandate with the thought that private bankers would demand a 90 to 95 percent probability of repayment. I decided to draw the line at fifty-fifty: I needed to believe that the taxpayer had a better than fifty-fifty chance of getting repaid. I thought this was pretty generous for the Treasury. But I was still thrown out of one senator's office by the senator himself—red in the face and screaming at me for all in the corridors to hear—for my lack of generosity.

Risk is deviation from objective. It matters whether the objective is to ensure the survival of the equity holders of all major airlines or only the survival of sufficient air transport capacity to meet likely demand. It matters whether the goal is to make student loans even more affordable for all who want them or to make college education available for those who could not otherwise afford it at all. However you may feel about these different policy objectives, risk measures need to be designed with precision around specific program goals.

Congress wants to make murky compromises that placate as many members as possible. When they create unworkable administrative complexity or take on absurd risks and exposures, the agency head can be paraded in front of the relevant committee and blamed for the entirely predictable problems. It would be funny if it were not costing us so much money and lowering the esteem in which the Federal Government is held by the American people.

The work that the academic community is doing to devise and improve upon the risk and exposure measures that can be applied to specific programs and contingent liabilities is of vital importance. These tools are simply not going to come from anywhere else.

But this not just about process, it is about substance. This is a vicious fight over the allocation of resources. Bringing greater fiscal discipline is about changing the outcomes. It is about shifting the allocation of resources away from some things and toward other things.

Let me offer one example.

Our system of direct and indirect federal intervention in the housing market, by providing guarantees of mortgage payments, does little or nothing in my view to make homeownership more affordable. On the contrary, I think it makes homeownership less affordable for the new home buyer.

If you lower the interest rate that is applied in financing an asset, then the value of the asset goes up. If you raise the interest rate, the value goes down.

I have never been that interested in measuring the value of the subsidy provided by Fannie Mae and Freddie Mac, because I do not think that any of it flows to the net-new home buyer. I think it flows to the asset holder—the home seller. We are pumping up house prices, and it is hard to see how that makes it easier on first-time home buyers.

Our subsidy to mortgage finance simply means that we consume more housing than we otherwise would; more housing and less transportation; more housing and less energy efficiency; more housing and less education.

Rising levels of home ownership over the last fifty years are more likely to be the consequence of productivity and rising standards of living than our interventions in mortgage finance. You may not agree me with about this. You may be able to persuade me that I do not see this correctly. But in the terms I have laid this out, we could actually have a financially literate debate—and one with significant implications for the allocation of resources in our society.

In conclusion, let me say again, thank *you* for bringing your intellects to bear on the problem of measuring and managing federal financial risk.

I always told the staff at the Treasury that they were expected to be the "straight men" of the Federal Government. In defending the federal fisc, they had to play Stan Laurel while everyone else in Washington got to play Oliver Hardy.

Playing the straight man is hard work, and you need good material. Thank you for creating the material to be used by future under secretaries and future Treasury staff in trying to bring a little more financial literacy to Washington.

2

Measuring and Managing Federal Financial Risk
A View from the Hill

Donald B. Marron

This timely conference began with an unusual but important question: what do Social Security, terrorist attacks, farm programs, Hurricane Katrina, private pensions, student loans, and environmental risks have in common?

The answer, as the following chapters demonstrate, is federal financial risk. The Federal Government has established itself as perhaps the world's largest provider of financial services, including property and casualty insurance, pensions, student loans, health insurance, mortgage insurance, and loan guarantees. In so doing, the government has taken on a correspondingly broad range of financial risks.

However, it is unclear whether policymakers and the general public fully appreciate the magnitude of these risks. Thus, the goal of the conference was to explore ways in which measurement, management, and understanding of these risks might be improved.

My particular charge was to provide a view from Capitol Hill. In some ways, that is an impossible order—no one could possibly summarize the views of our 535 elected representatives on Social Security, terrorism insurance, farm programs, and so forth. What I can offer, however, is perspective on how the policy process works and how information about budget impacts, in general, and financial risk, in particular, gets analyzed, communicated, and used. That perspective offers three particular insights.

First, the most useful techniques for measuring federal financial risk will

Donald B. Marron is a visiting professor at the Georgetown Public Policy Institute and president of Marron Economics, LLC.

This chapter is based on a presentation at the February 6, 2007 conference; at the time, the author served as Deputy Director of the Congressional Budget Office (CBO). The views expressed here are his own and should not be attributed to the CBO.

be those that fit well within the realities of the budget process. Transparency and ease of use, not just technical accuracy, are crucial considerations.

Legislators often design or change programs under tight budgets and tight deadlines. Tight budgets mean that policy development is often an iterative process, with legislators making repeated changes to ensure that a proposal neither goes above budgeted amounts (which could kill it) nor leaves money on the table. Tight deadlines place a premium on the scoring agencies providing scores quickly at each iteration. In that environment, simple, quick, and robust models often have more practical use than complex models (which may take hours to run) or fragile models (which may analyze a particular program structure extremely well but be difficult to adjust when legislators tweak the program's design).

Similar considerations apply at the agency level. The agencies of the executive branch take the lead in implementing federal financial policies and in reporting their costs in the budget. Agencies do not always have access to the same level of financial and economic sophistication that exist at, say, the Congressional Budget Office (CBO). For that reason, the potential benefits of sophisticated approaches to financial measurement and management must sometimes be balanced against the need for implementable approaches.

A similar balance must also be struck between technical sophistication and transparency. Understandably, legislators and their staffs are often hesitant to rely on the results of purely "black-box" models. Policymakers value being able to understand the rationale behind those models and their implications for budget scores. Transparent, explainable modeling approaches are thus particularly useful, so policymakers can understand how legislative changes translate into scoring changes.

Second, measures of financial risk can be useful, even if they are not incorporated in official budget measures. Official budget measures carry great weight because of their role in the legislative process, but they are not the only source of budget information. The CBO, for example, often provides supplementary information in response to questions from interested legislators. Such information usually takes the form of additional detail about the assumptions underlying a particular budget score. In cases where financial risk is an issue, however, the additional information may also take the form of alternative measures of the budget impact of particular policy changes.

During the 2005 debate over pension legislation, for example, the CBO prepared official budget estimates that reflected the somewhat arcane cash budgeting used for the Pension Benefit Guarantee Corporation (PBGC).[1] However, that budgeting does not fully capture the financial impacts of the

---

1. See, for example, Congressional Budget Office, Cost Estimate, *H. R. 2830, Pension Protection Act of 2005,* December 2, 2005. Available at: http://www.cbo.gov/ftpdocs/69xx/doc6935/hr2830.pdf.

PBGC on the federal budget. In particular, it excludes the present value of some benefit payments that fall outside the budget window, ignores the costs of financial risk, and omits some impacts that are treated as nonbudgetary. To address these omissions, the CBO had earlier been asked to develop techniques for analyzing the full financial impact of the PBGC.[2] In response to Congressional queries, the CBO was able to use those techniques to provide supplementary information about how proposed legislation would change those alternative financial measures.[3]

The financial statements of the United States are another source of financial information about the Federal Government.[4] Those statements, which have received increasing attention in recent years, present the government's financial position using the principles of accrual accounting; the budget, in contrast, relies almost exclusively on cash accounting. The key difference between the two approaches is timing. Cash accounting records budget impacts when cash comes into or out of the Federal Treasury. Accrual accounting, on the other hand, records transactions when an economic event occurs (e.g., when a commitment to spend money in the future is made), even if the resulting cash flows happen in a different year. The difference between these accounting approaches can be significant, particularly for certain activities—for example, pensions for federal employees, claims against government insurance, and large capital investments—in which cash flows may be separated by many years from the moment at which key economic events occur.[5] In recent years, the financial statements have suggested that the fiscal situation of the Federal Government has been weaker than portrayed by standard budget measures, primarily because the government has been accruing future pension obligations to employees and veterans that are not reflected in the current cash budget.

Third, it is useful to distinguish between different elements of measuring and managing financial risk: uncertainty about outcomes, the spread of budget impacts over multiple years, the time value of money, and the

2. Congressional Budget Office, *The Risk Exposure of the Pension Benefit Guaranty Corporation,* September 2005. Available at: http://www.cbo.gov/ftpdocs/66xx/doc6646/09-15-PBGC.pdf.

3. See, for example, Congressional Budget Office, letter to the Honorable Carolyn McCarthy on the net economic costs of the Pension Benefit Guarantee Corporation, December 29, 2005. Available at: http://www.cbo.gov/ftpdocs/70xx/doc7002/12-29-PBGC.pdf.

4. The most recent statements are by the Department of the Treasury Financial Management Service, 2007 *Financial Report of the United States Government.* Available at: http://fms.treas.gov/fr/07frusg/07frusg.pdf.

5. For a detailed comparison of the two approaches to federal accounting, see Congressional Budget Office, *Comparing Budget and Accounting Measures of the Federal Government's Fiscal Condition,* December 2006. Available at: http://www.cbo.gov/ftpdocs/77xx/doc7701/12-07-FiscalMeasures.pdf. For a brief overview of how the two measures complement each other, see Donald B. Marron, *The ABCs of Long-Term Budget Challenges,* opening remarks at the Congressional Budget Office Director's conference on Budgeting and Accounting for Long-Term Obligations, December 8, 2006. Available at: http://www.cbo.gov/ftpdocs/77xx/doc7703/12-08-OpeningRemarks.pdf.

cost of risk bearing. Full-blown measurement of financial risk requires appropriate treatment of all four of these elements. However, each of those elements poses challenges within traditional budgeting techniques. Improvements at each level may enhance the budget process, even if all four are not fully addressed.

The first step in addressing risk, of course, is recognizing that a range of future outcomes is possible. Program outlays may depend on the outcome of future events such as the magnitude of disasters, the frequency of loan defaults, or the level of commodity prices. Over time, the scoring agencies have made substantial progress in ensuring that such uncertainty is reflected in baseline projections and budget scores of policy changes. In projecting potential outlays under farm support programs, for example, the agencies do not rely on a single projection of future crop prices. Instead, they use a probabilistic approach that reflects the potential distribution of future crop prices and the resulting distribution of farm support payments. That distribution can then be used to calculate the expected value of future payments.[6]

The second step in addressing risk is accounting for the fact that future budget impacts may be spread over multiple years. The use of ten-year budget windows in the Congressional process means that the budget impacts of some programs are captured fully in the budget process. However, many programs have impacts that go beyond ten years. That is particularly common for financial programs. A loan guarantee, for example, would typically be in place for the full life of the insured loan, which may extend for twenty or thirty years. This timing mismatch used to put direct loans at a substantial disadvantage relative to loan guarantees. A ten-year budget window would typically capture all of the outlays of providing a direct loan but only some of the repayments; repayments outside the window would not be scored. Conversely, all the inflows (from fees) from a loan guarantee would appear inside the window, while many outflows (due to future defaults) would be ignored, because they occur outside the budget window. This imbalance between the length of obligations and the length of the budget windows was one of the driving forces behind the Federal Credit Reform Act of 1990 (FCRA). Under the FCRA, many financial obligations are analyzed based on their entire lifetime of expected cash flows. This framework allows a more balanced comparison of different financial structures.[7]

The third step in reflecting financial risk is accounting for the time value

6. Congressional Budget Office, *Estimating the Costs of One-Sided Bets: How CBO Analyzes Proposals with Asymmetric Uncertainties,* October 1999. Available at: http://www.cbo.gov/ftpdocs/15xx/doc1589/onesided.pdf.

7. For a discussion of the FCRA and its impacts, see Congressional Budget Office, *Estimating the Value of Subsidies for Federal Loans and Loan Guarantees,* August 2004. Available at: http://www.cbo.gov/ftpdocs/57xx/doc5751/08-19-CreditSubsidies.pdf.

of money for programs that stretch across multiple years. This is an area of weakness for standard budgeting techniques. In most cases, programs are evaluated based on their direct budget impacts over periods such as five or ten years. By convention, those impacts are simply summed across years without any accounting of the time value of money. As a result, a proposal that would move $1 billion in spending from ten years in the future to today would be scored as having no direct budget impact over a ten-year window, despite the real increase in overall spending.

That problem could be addressed in two ways. One approach would be to express budget impacts in terms of net present value. Scoring agencies would project the year-by-year budget impacts of policy proposals, just as they do today, but instead of simply adding up the nominal budget impacts across all the years in the scoring window, the agencies would use a discount rate (or a year-by-year series of discount rates) to determine the net present value of the budget impacts. Treasury interest rates would be the natural discount rates to use in such calculations.

That approach would incorporate the time value of money in a manner that is familiar to economists and financial analysts but would represent a significant break from a long-standing tradition of focusing solely on year-by-year streams of nominal budget impacts. If budget policymakers wish to maintain that tradition, they could turn to a second approach that imputes the future interest costs (or savings) that would result from particular budget policies. In that alternative, the scoring agencies would project the direct year-by-year budget impacts of policy proposals, just as they do today, and then, in addition, would add a projection of the future change in government interest payments that would result from the proposals. A proposal to increase spending, for example, would be scored not only as increasing federal outlays directly, but also as increasing the federal debt, resulting in higher interest payments through the end of the budget window; an increase in taxes would similarly be credited with reducing interest payments through the end of the budget window.[8]

It is easy to show that this approach, imputing interest costs, results in budget scores that are equal to the *future value* of program spending as measured in the last year of the budget window. In other words, this approach is functionally equivalent to the present value approach, except that budget

8. This approach is already used when scoring agencies analyze the budget as a whole. The innovation here is suggesting that this approach could also be used for analyzing individual budget proposals. Doing so would yield budget projections that are perfectly consistent with analyses of the overall budget. When adding together the individual budget proposals, the imputed interest costs resulting from proposals to increase spending or reduce revenues would get netted against any interest savings that would result from proposals to reduce spending or increase revenues. Thus, the net change in interest payments imputed to the individual budget proposals would add up to match the change in interest payments estimated for the budget as a whole.

scores are expressed in terms of the budget impact in a future year (the end of the budget window) rather than the current year.[9]

These approaches would add some additional complexity to the budget process. Policymakers would have to become comfortable with the use of discounting or would have to accept the idea of adding interest costs on top of direct budget impacts. In either case, the benefit would be that budgeting would reflect the time value of money. At the moment, however, budget calculations reflect the time value of money only for a limited set of government programs—most notably, those that are subject to the FCRA. Under the FCRA, the future cash flows of a loan, loan guarantee, and so on are measured as a net present value, calculated using Treasury interest rates of appropriate maturity.

The final stage of incorporating financial risk—which has been addressed in very few instances—is to reflect the cost of risk bearing. As noted in other chapters, this cost is usually excluded from federal budgeting. The sole exceptions occur in instances where doing otherwise would obviously lead to perverse outcomes. Thus, the federal budget records neither gains nor losses when the government changes the way it finances itself (e.g., by changing the maturity of the debt). Nor does it record gains or losses when the Railroad Retirement Fund takes inflows and invests them in assets (e.g., corporate bonds) that have higher expected returns than Treasuries. When Congress created the Troubled Asset Relief Program (TARP), finally, it required that risk be considered when valuing the securities that the government would purchase under the program.

The logic underlying those budget accounting decisions is very simple: the government should not record a gain or loss when it trades one asset for another of equal value. If the government issues $1 billion in Treasuries and uses the proceeds to purchase $1 billion in corporate bonds, for example, the immediate effect on the budget should be zero. The net worth of the government is unchanged, since the value of the new asset exactly offsets the value of the new liability. (The corporate bonds may generate profits over time, of course; the point is that they do not create those gains immediately.)

This example highlights a problem with the way that the FCRA measures the cost of federal financial programs. If the FCRA were applied to the purchase of corporate bonds, it would show an immediate gain to the federal budget. Why? Because the expected return on corporate bonds is higher than the interest rate on Treasuries of comparable maturity. As a

9. To illustrate, consider a simple example in which budgeting is done over a three-year window, a proposal would increase spending by $100 in the first year of the budget window, and the Treasury interest rate is 10 percent. In that case, the budget score would be $100 in the first year (the spending), $10 in the second year (interest on the $100 the government had to borrow in the prior year to pay for the new spending), and $11 in the third year (interest on the original spending and on the prior year's interest payments; in other words, the interest is compounding). Adding those together, the total budget score over the window would be $121, which is equal to the future value of the original spending ($100 × 1.1 × 1.1) in the third year.

result, the net present value of the expected returns on the corporate bond (calculated using Treasury rates) would be greater than the initial cost of purchasing the bonds.

That perverse result occurs because of a mismatch between the discount rate used in the FCRA and the discount rate that financial markets actually use to value corporate bonds. The FCRA would use Treasury rates, regardless of the riskiness of the bond, but financial markets use discount rates that reflect the bond's financial risk.

This example is important, not because the FCRA is used to value federal investments in corporate bonds (it is not), but because it is used to value other risky assets such as loans and loan guarantees. Like corporate bonds, loans and loan guarantees are risky; as a result, financial markets value their expected cash flows using discount rates that incorporate a risk premium. Discounting their expected cash flows using risk-free Treasury interest rates is thus likely to be misleading. The FCRA likely overstates the value of the loans and loan guarantees that the Federal Government offers and thus understates the budgetary cost of providing that financing.[10] That understatement could be corrected, however, if the FCRA instead used risk-adjusted discount rates—that is, rates that reflect the cost of bearing financial risk.[11]

Conclusion

There is clearly room for improvement in the measurement and management of the federal budget, generally, and in the management and reporting of financial risk, in particular. Improvements have been made over the years both through statute (e.g., the FCRA) and innovations by the scoring agencies (e.g., use of expected values), but more remains to be done. Some improvements may require the use of modern financial techniques—for example, greater use of risk-adjusted discount rates—but significant gains may also come from simpler changes (e.g., greater recognition of the time value of money).

10. Federal loans and loan guarantees usually have a positive "beta" and therefore should be valued using a positive risk premium. Of course, there may be instances in which loans or loan guarantees have a negative "beta"; in those cases, the FCRA approach would understate the value of the loan or loan guarantee and thus overstate the cost to the Federal Government.

11. One prominent use of risk adjustment has been in the CBO's analysis of proposals to add individual accounts to Social Security. Focusing solely on the expected returns of such accounts would potentially be misleading, since it would not reflect the costs of risk bearing. For that reason, the CBO has often used risk-adjusted returns, equal to Treasury interest rates, when modeling such proposals. See, for example, Congressional Budget Office, letter to the Honorable Max Baucus, analysis of H.R. 3304, Growing Real Ownership for Workers Act of 2005, September 13, 2005. Available at: http://www.cbo.gov/ftpdocs/66xx/doc6645/09-13 -BaucusLetter.pdf.

The Cost of Risk to the Government and Its Implications for Federal Budgeting

Deborah Lucas and Marvin Phaup

3.1 Introduction

The idea of "state prices"—that the value today of a dollar in future purchasing power depends on the future state of nature—dates back to the classic work of Arrow and Debreu (1954) and Debreu (1959) and is the basis for most neoclassical theories of asset valuation used today. It offers an explanation for why some securities, such as common stocks and risky loans, earn an expected return in excess of the risk-free rate: these securities tend to have high payoffs when the economy is strong and low payoffs when the economy is weak. Since dollars received in good times are worth less in utility terms than in bad times (a result of decreasing marginal utility of wealth), the price of a risky security is less than its expected payoff discounted at the risk-free rate. Equivalently, its expected return is higher than the risk-free rate; there is a market risk premium.

While it is widely accepted that investors require a market risk premium, it is less established that market risk should be treated as a cost to the Federal Government. In practice, the price of risk is almost entirely absent from federal budgeting. This omission makes federal credit and some insurance programs appear to cost less than their market value, thereby favoring such assistance over alternatives that are accounted for at market prices. It also gives federal investments in risky securities financed

Deborah Lucas is the former Donald C. Clark HSBC Professor of Consumer Finance at the Kellogg School of Management, Northwestern University, and is currently a research associate of the National Bureau of Economic Research. Marvin Phaup is professorial lecturer at the Trachtenberg School of Public Policy and Public Administration at George Washington University.

We are grateful to Andy Abel, Bob Dennis, Peter Diamond, Douglas Hamilton, Henning Bohn, and David Wilcox for helpful comments.

with Treasury debt the appearance of generating free money for the government.

In this chapter, we revisit the question of the cost of risk to the Federal Government and its implications, both conceptual and practical, for federal budgeting. We begin in section 3.2 with a brief review of the academic literature that speaks directly to the cost. We then review the economic case for treating market risk as a legitimate cost and consider how this conclusion is affected by considerations such as the government's ability to increase risk pooling, to transfer resources across generations, and in general, to reduce credit market imperfections.

In section 3.3, after briefly describing the current budget treatment of credit, insurance, and investments in private securities, we present the "budgetary case" for including the cost of market risk in budget estimates. This requires an understanding of what budget estimates are used for and also of their limitations. In the debate over whether the cost of risk should be incorporated into budget estimates, an important but often overlooked observation is that the budget records only costs, not benefits. The question of whether it is socially optimal for the government to make a particular investment is distinct from the question of whether including the market cost of risk in budget estimates improves their usefulness to policymakers. Certainly, budget cost is an input into cost-benefit analyses of policies, but assessing benefits requires nonbudget information as well. To the extent that budget estimates have an allocative effect, it is because of aggregate spending limits, and because they are used to make comparisons between different types of expenditures that satisfy a given policy objective. To make such constraints and comparisons meaningful, budget accounting aims to price alternative expenditures in consistent units of cost. Since the government generally procures other goods and services at market prices, considerations of consistency and transparency favor using market values in budgeting for financial obligations as well. Alternatives for measuring and accounting for market risk in government transactions—and some of the practical difficulties involved—are also discussed.

Even if, in principle, market risk should be included in budget estimates, whether it is worthwhile to modify budgeting practice depends on whether the potential improvements are material. A number of academic studies—including several in this volume and a series of academic papers and studies by the Congressional Budget Office (CBO)—provide some evidence on the magnitudes involved. Those findings, reviewed in section 3.4, show that the distortions from neglecting the price of risk in some cases have been considerable and suggest that investing in the capacity to provide this information to lawmakers through the budget process is likely to be worthwhile.

3.2   Cost of Risk to the Government

3.2.1   The Early Debate

The question of the cost of risk to the government received considerable attention in the mid- to late 1960s and early 1970s, but much less has been written on the topic since then.[1] Academic interest during that period arose naturally from recent advances in general equilibrium theory—particularly the contributions of Arrow and Debreu (1954) and Debreu (1959). Those developments allowed more general welfare analyses of policy, underscored both the benefits of risk sharing and the aggregate limit on risk sharing, and clarified the role of market prices in aggregating the risk preferences of society.

In this vein, Diamond (1967) analyzed an economy with technology risk and a stock market. His conclusions regarding government investment can be paraphrased by saying that if markets are sufficiently complete for stock prices to reflect the social cost of risk, then those prices are also relevant to the government in evaluating its investment policy. In other words, the private cost of risk is a reasonable proxy for the social cost of risk and the right metric for evaluating government investment decisions. Hirshleifer (1964, 1966) reached similar conclusions and argued forcefully for the use of market prices.

A distinctly different view of the cost of risk to the government was put forth by other leading economists of the time. In Jorgenson et al. (1964), Samuelson and Vickrey argue that because of the large and diversified portfolio held by the government, the marginal return from public investment overall is virtually risk free and hence should be evaluated at the risk-free rate rather than the higher market rate demanded by less diversified individuals. In a very influential paper, Arrow and Lind (1970) formalize this argument. Specifically, they study a model with complete contingent claims (i.e., complete insurance markets) and no aggregate uncertainty. They conclude that in this setting, the social and private discount rate is equated at the risk-free rate. They further show that even when markets are incomplete, the cost of risk bearing to taxpayers goes to zero as the number of taxpayers becomes large and the share of risk borne by each diminishes.

Arrow and Lind acknowledge that these conclusions depend on the assumption that government investment entails no aggregate risk: "The results . . . depend on returns from a given public investment being independent of other components of national income" (1970, p. 373). They defend this assumption as plausible, asserting that correlated risk is likely to be

---

1. A notable exception is Bazelon and Smetters (1999), which also surveys some of the earlier literature and addresses many of the same issues as this chapter.

insignificant for many government investments. This is also noted by Sandmo (1972, p. 287), who writes that the Hirshleifer view can be reconciled with Arrow and Lind's conclusions only by recognizing that

the two sets of arguments are based on entirely different assumptions concerning the relationship between private and public investment with respect to risk. Arrow and Lind assume that the returns on private and public investment are uncorrelated; indeed this assumption is crucial for their main result. The Hirshleifer view, however, is clearly based on the assumption that for each type of public investment it is possible to find a private industry such that the returns are highly correlated.

Sandmo goes on to suggest that for the modern economies of Europe and the United States, Hirshleifer's view is likely the more plausible one. Interestingly, he observes that the contributions of Sharpe (1964), Lintner (1965), and Modigliani and Miller (1958)—a body of work that provides the underpinning of modern financial economics—are highly relevant to this debate but rarely cited in the context of public investment.

A lively discussion of the closely related question of whether there is a well-defined social (risk-free) discount rate and whether it can be gleaned from market prices was also occurring at that time (see Sandmo and Dreze [1971] and references therein). The rate of time preference reflected in capital market prices—that is, Treasury rates—can lead to suboptimal government investment decisions when markets are incomplete. Analyses of these issues led to the broad conclusion that in the presence of distorting taxes and various other sources of market incompleteness, there is not a unique rate of time preference appropriate for evaluating all pubic investments. As in the debate about market risk, a critical question that was left unresolved is whether it is possible to determine a better general rule than relying on market prices for choosing a discount rate.

3.2.2   The Economic Case

In this section, we briefly revisit the arguments for and against using market prices to evaluate risky government investment opportunities and review some more recent evidence from the finance literature that bears on the question of whether, as Arrow and Lind posited, diversifiable risk is priced.

To explain the expected returns on risky assets, financial economists often abstract from the general notion of state prices and describe risk as falling into two broad categories: nondiversifiable or market risk, and diversifiable or idiosyncratic risk. Market risk arises from fluctuations in aggregate output, which logically is inclusive of the effects of government actions on the aggregate economy, including stabilization policy. Idiosyncratic risks, on the other hand, can in principle be avoided through insurance and other contractual risk-sharing arrangements and by portfolio diversification. When markets are complete, individual optimization eliminates idiosyncratic risk, and in equilibrium, only market risk is priced.

In terms of this decomposition of risk and return, evidence that idiosyncratic risk is not priced in financial markets supports Hirshleifer's position that markets are sufficiently complete for the government to rely on market prices. Conversely, evidence that idiosyncratic risk is priced supports Arrow and Lind's argument. Specifically, Arrow and Lind conjecture that the reason for the high rates of return on risky securities relative to the risk-free rate—the market risk premium—is mainly compensation for these diversifiable risks rather than for aggregate or market risk. If government investment more effectively diversifies risk than does the private sector, using a market discount rate that includes compensation for diversifiable risk would result in systematic undervaluation of government investments.

Since the 1970s, numerous empirical studies have examined whether diversifiable risk is priced in financial markets. Most cross-sectional evidence on asset returns suggests that this risk is not priced. In particular, tests of the Sharpe and Lintner Capital Asset Pricing Model (CAPM), which decomposes asset returns into market and idiosyncratic components, show that idiosyncratic risk has little or no explanatory power for the cross-section of stock returns. The CAPM, which equates market risk with the volatility of Standard and Poor's (S&P) 500 returns, has been criticized for its low explanatory power. However, tests of better performing multifactor alternatives to the CAPM[2] also provide little support for the idea that differences in idiosyncratic risk explain the cross-section of returns (e.g., Fama and French 1992). These empirical findings are consistent with the observation that even small investors can diversify financial risk quite inexpensively—for instance, through mutual funds—and that most large investors hold fairly diversified positions. This evidence weighs against the argument of Arrow and Lind that market prices overstate the cost of risk to the government because investors put excessive weight on diversifiable risk.

Some observers have also interpreted the equity premium puzzle—the inability of parameterized versions of standard neoclassical general equilibrium models to account for the historically high average spreads between risky securities and short-term Treasury rates—as evidence of capital market imperfections. Attempts to explain the equity premium puzzle by appealing to individual risk exposure, however, have been largely unsuccessful (e.g., Heaton and Lucas 1996). In fact, the robust predictions of economic theory put very few quantitative restrictions on price levels or returns, suggesting that the observed equity premium is difficult to interpret as evidence for or

2. Testing for whether only aggregate risk is priced is complicated by the difficulty of finding an adequate empirical proxy. As famously noted by Roll (1977), the CAPM may appear to be rejected in tests, not because it is wrong, but because the proxies for the market return are not close enough to the true market portfolio.

against the efficiency of financial markets in sharing risk. Hence, we view this literature as silent on the question of whether market prices deviate from social values.

Some (mostly nonacademic) observers have further suggested that market risk is not costly to the government, because the government can borrow at a risk-free Treasury rate. The problem with this reasoning is that the cost of debt financing is only one component of the government's cost of capital. When the government finances risky investments by selling safe Treasury securities, investment risk is shifted onto current and future taxpayers and other federal stake holders, who effectively become equity holders in a leveraged investment.

Imagine, for instance, that the government finances an investment in common stock through the sale of Treasury securities. This is an exchange of financial assets between the public and private sector that as a first approximation should have no effect on aggregate real investment or output. To be concrete, assume that the government borrows $100 to buy $100 in stock and will liquidate the entire position in one year. The Treasury securities promise 5 percent risk free, whereas the stock will return–2 percent in a recession and 20 percent in a boom. Assuming an equal probability of a boom or a bust, the expected return on the stock is 9 percent, a 4 percent premium over the Treasury rate. At the end of the year, taxpayers are liable for repayment of the Treasury debt, regardless of whether the stock gains or loses value. In a recession, the government will be short $7—money that must be obtained from the public through expenditure cuts, higher taxes, or increased debt liabilities. In a boom, it will be ahead by $15, which again will be passed through to the public through changes in expenditures, taxes, or government debt. This shows that the stock is not really entirely financed by the Treasury debt. The public serves as the residual claimant of the return on the stock minus the Treasury rate; it is as if the public is a highly leveraged equity holder in the stock investment.

A taxpayer accepting the same risk in a private financial transaction would expect compensation equal to the levered market risk premium to participate. In fact, the same transaction is readily available to the public without government intervention. An individual can sell $100 of Treasury securities and use the proceeds to invest $100 in the common stock. The 4 percent increase in expected return is compensation for taking on the higher risk of the new portfolio, not an arbitrage gain.

The argument that the government cannot create value by exchanging safe for risky claims is an application to public finance of the well-known Modigliani-Miller theorem (Modigliani and Miller 1958). They show that in the absence of market imperfections, the cost of risk associated with an asset depends only on its own characteristics, not on the combination of financial securities used to finance it. In our example, the value of the stock purchased by the government is independent of the combination of Treasury securities and contingent public obligations used to fund the purchase.

3.2.3 Implications of Incomplete Markets

Notwithstanding the preceding arguments for the relevance of market prices, market incompleteness can complicate the evaluation of social costs and benefits for risky government investments.[3] In this section, we discuss several ways in which incomplete markets complicate valuation, but we emphasize the strong case for using market prices to measure costs, even in the presence of incomplete markets.

A classic example of market incompleteness arises in credit markets, where informational asymmetries combined with weak enforcement mechanisms can cause markets to break down. For instance, Stiglitz and Weiss (1981) consider a credit market with borrowers of mixed quality, where lenders cannot distinguish between borrower types. If lenders attempt to increase interest rates to make up for expected losses on bad credits, good borrowers leave the market, driving up the expected loss rate. In the extreme, no interest rate clears the market at a nonnegative profit to lenders. Private credit is rationed at a suboptimally low level relative to a "first-best" allocation.

When credit rationing occurs, it may be welfare improving for the government to intervene by making credit available.[4] The federal student loan program, which provides credit for students who have little or no credit history and might not be able to obtain loans on their own, is an example of a government intervention thought to reduce such credit rationing. Of course, such interventions may not always improve welfare: credit subsidies will induce some people to borrow more than is socially desirable and can impose considerable costs on taxpayers. Since the marginal utilities of constrained borrowers are unobservable and likely to vary across individuals, it seems that evaluating the benefits from government credit programs will always include a subjective element.

Market incompleteness also complicates the evaluation of the cost of federal credit assistance. When private credit markets fail or when government credit crowds out private credit provision, an appropriate market price may not be readily identifiable. In such cases, using the standard methods in financial valuation discussed next, the cost—in terms of what markets (and presumably taxpayers) would demand for receiving the same state-contingent payoffs from borrowers—can be found by projecting those payoffs on securities that are trading in financial markets. This projection approach identifies the amount of market risk embedded in the transaction

3. Bohn (2004), for instance, examines the welfare effects of alternative fiscal policies when market incompleteness is generated by imperfect risk sharing across generations.
4. Gale (1991) observes that when government credit simply substitutes for credit that would have otherwise been privately extended and hence has little effect on real resource allocations, government provision has little effect on social welfare.

and incorporates the price of market risk into the estimated cost to the government. For instance, one can infer the value of government student loans from market prices for unsecured consumer credit, and government credit guarantees to small businesses can be valued using information on similar, nonguaranteed bank loans to small firms. These examples illustrate that the absence of a market price does not preclude the existence of a similar private credit arrangement that can be used to infer market value. Further, the absence of an analogous private contract does not imply that a government program will be exceptionally expensive or risky; rather, it reflects the absence of a profitable private lending opportunity.

Future generations are not directly represented in current market transactions, and some economists believe that this source of incompleteness causes too little weight to be placed on the welfare of future generations when future costs and benefits are discounted at market rates. That is, the social cost of long-term federal liabilities and the social value of long-term public investments are both understated using market discount rates. This point of view, for example, was forcefully presented in Stern (2007). Others argue the opposite: because of investments made today and the fruits of technological progress, future generations will likely be better off, and hence it is optimal to incur liabilities that they will be at least partially responsible for.

How the competing interests of current and future generations should be weighed in public policy decisions is an important and difficult problem but one that may be largely separable from the question of whether the market price of risk should be incorporated into federal budget estimates. Kaplow (2006) develops a framework that formalizes the idea that the question of efficiency and of how much weight should be placed on different generations can be separated. In his analysis, increasing efficiency is to the benefit of all generations, and efficiency is properly assessed using market prices. To the extent that the purpose of the federal budget is to assist the government in making efficient trade-offs at a point in time, the implication of his analysis is that market prices are appropriate for federal budgeting, even when generational welfare is assessed at a below- or above-market rate.

It is important to note that if generational equity or other externalities cause one to seriously question the appropriateness of market prices for guiding government allocation decisions, these objections apply equally to the leading alternative for discounting government obligations: Treasury yields. Like the yields on risky securities, Treasury yields are determined by supply and demand in financial markets and hence fail to capture any nonmarket notion of the correct social discount rate.

In general, market incompleteness can drive a wedge between market prices and social costs and benefits. This is true for noncredit as well as credit programs and in itself does not justify selectively deviating from market prices in the case of budgeting for credit. Whether it is possible to improve upon market prices clearly will depend on the source and consequences of the market imperfection under consideration. We return to the issue of whether introducing risk adjustment in federal budgeting is likely to improve the allocative efficiency of the budget process in a second-best world in section 3.3.2.

3.3 The Cost of Risk and the Federal Budget

To evaluate the pros and cons of including the cost of risk in federal budget estimates, it is first necessary to understand the basic principles that govern budgetary accounting, and specifically the rules related to credit, insurance, and investments in private securities.[5] It is also important to consider how Congress uses these estimates in making resource allocation decisions.

3.3.1 Federal Budget Accounting

The federal budget primarily relies on cash accounting to depict the cost of federal activities. This basis of accounting records federal costs in terms of net cash outlays in the year in which it occurs rather than when it accrues. The budget also includes projected outlays over a period of up to ten years. The out-year projections of cost receive less attention, however, because they do not affect the current budget deficit or surplus.

For certain long-lived contractual obligations such as capital leases, interest on Treasury securities, and federal credit assistance, the budget has moved gradually away from pure cash accounting in favor of up-front or capitalized accrual accounting. That treatment recognizes all projected payments associated with the obligation, even if some cash flows will occur outside the budget period. It also introduces discounting into budget calculations, which raises the question of whether and how risk should be accounted for.

The fact that the budget is primarily on a cash rather than accrual basis can distort resource allocation decisions—for instance, by making rental appear less costly than capital investment, even when in present value terms, the capital investment is cheaper and the facility will be used indefinitely. Accruals, however, require more assumptions about uncertain future cash flows, making them easier to manipulate. Assessing the pros and cons of cash versus accrual budgeting is beyond the scope of this analysis; we take the cash treatment of most expenditures as given. The main conclusions about risk adjustment, however, would appear to become even more important were accruals more widely used in the budget.

5. Much of the discussion in this section is based on Lucas and Phaup (2008), which also includes a more detailed description of current and historical accounting practices.

Loans and Loan Guarantees

Before 1990, the budget cost for federal credit activity was similar to that for most other programs—the net cash outflows for the program in the fiscal year. The mix of cash flows included in the budget account made net outlays an inaccurate measure of cost. For existing programs, an increase in net outlays could result from increases in new lending, higher defaults on outstanding guarantees, legislated increases in debt forgiveness, or other factors. For new direct loan programs, the cost reported was not comprehensive and hence was also hard to evaluate. Cost included net outlays in the budget period but no offset for expected repayments outside the budget window and no adjustment for time value. New guarantee programs were scored with few, if any, cash outflows in the year the program began, because outlays for defaults usually occur a year or more after the loan is disbursed. In fact, new guarantees often had a negative cost because of the inflow of guarantee fees early on. This accounting favored new guarantee programs over almost all alternatives intended to achieve the same policy objectives, including new direct loan programs.

The Federal Credit Reform Act of 1990 (FCRA) effectively put credit on an accrual basis, with cost measured as the discounted value (at the maturity-matched Treasury rate) of current- and future-period cash flows from budget-period transactions. Its stated objectives were to: measure the cost of federal credit programs more accurately, place the cost of credit programs on a budgetary basis equivalent to other federal spending, encourage the delivery of benefits in the form most appropriate to the needs of beneficiaries, and improve the allocation of resources among credit programs and between credit and other spending programs.

Although the FCRA was partially successful in meeting its objectives, it fell short of measuring cost in terms completely equivalent to cash spending. The largest discrepancy arises from the mandated use of interest rates on maturity-matched US Treasury securities for discounting rather than a market-based cost of capital that includes the cost of market risk.[6] The understatement of cost is most evident in those programs that report a gain to the government while delivering credit at rates that are below those charged for credit of similar risk in competitive markets. In those cases, the budget creates a bias in favor of federal credit programs compared with noncredit assistance and encourages expansion of federal credit services that can crowd out private provision of credit. Section 3.4 provides information on the likely size of the distortion for several federal credit programs.

6. The treatment of administrative costs, floating rate loans, and reestimates is also problematic (CBO 2006b), but those issues are beyond the scope of this chapter.

Insurance

Insurance programs generally are budgeted for on a cash basis. For property casualty coverage such as federal flood or crop insurance, this approach is consistent with the annual coverage period that is standard in private contracts. For such insurance programs, market risk is unlikely to represent a major cost. Programs such as deposit and pension insurance, however, also can be viewed as credit guarantees, although they are not covered by the FCRA. Deposit and pension insurance are distinguished from the types of transactions covered by the FCRA by their lack of a fixed maturity date. The market risk associated with these programs is not treated as a budget cost.

Investments in Private Securities

Despite their similarity to federal loans, federal investments in private securities (e.g., stocks, corporate bonds, mortgages, foreign securities) are not covered by the FCRA. Rather, such investments are generally accounted for under the Office of Management and Budget (OMB) Circular A-11, which directs agencies to account for investments in private equities on a cash basis. That is, such investments are reported as outlays when made, despite the offsetting receipt of a security of equal value.

As for direct lending before the FCRA, scoring financial investments as outlays tends to discourage such activity, and until recently, federal investments in private securities have been quite limited. The possibility of booking a profit, however, has influenced several proposals to increase federal investments in private securities, usually in the context of Social Security reform. The passage of the 2001 amendments to the Railroad Retirement Act was a notable step in this direction.

The railroad retirement system, which predates Social Security, provides two tiers of benefits to retired railroad workers and their dependents. The first approximates benefits payable under Social Security. The second is specified in the Railroad Retirement Act and is based on years of railroad employment. Both tiers are financed by payroll taxes levied on employees and the railroads. The 2001 amendments authorized a newly created National Railroad Retirement Investment Trust (NRRIT) to invest in a diversified portfolio of risky securities. Further, the legislation specified that the purchase and sale of private securities by the Trust be treated in the budget as having no effect on budget outlays or the deficit. Only capital gains and losses were to be treated as affecting outlays.

The Railroad Retirement Act posed new challenges to the CBO and the OMB. There was general agreement that booking the market risk premium as expected profit, an offset to program expenses, should be avoided. Otherwise, the appearance of an arbitrage opportunity from selling Treasury securities and buying risky securities would reward increased risk-taking and perhaps encourage increased spending from illusory resources. Consistent with the legislation, it was agreed that the outlay of cash for securities would be treated as an equal value exchange. Gains and losses would be recognized in budget net outlays (gains as negatives) only as incurred. Notably, Treasury rates of return were adopted for projecting budget baseline income for the railroad retirement system. This effectively adjusts those returns for risk and avoids the appearance of a free lunch in budget projections.[7]

3.3.2   Risk as a Budgetary Cost

The federal budget serves multiple purposes: it is a record of and a partial check on total federal spending, and it allows trade-offs to be made among competing uses of resources. For the Congress, the budget resolution limits the budget costs that authorizing and appropriations committees can incur during a fiscal year. Those constraints create an incentive for the committees to choose policies that provide the greatest benefit from the limited budget resources available. To make comparisons between policy alternatives meaningful and to avoid accounting arbitrage opportunities, it is important that cost be recorded on a consistent basis.

The principle of consistency suggests the use of market prices in budgeting for federal financial commitments. The reason is that almost all non-credit transactions—including grants, purchases of goods, and the direct provision of services—appear in the budget at market prices. The largest category of expenditures is transfers. People get money, from Social Security benefits, food stamps, and so on. Cash is accounted for at its market price by definition—the real value of a dollar is what you can get by spending it on a consumption bundle. Then, there are government purchases from the private sector: military hardware, the labor of the federal workforce, buildings, computers, electricity, and so forth—all expenditures that occur at market prices, since goods, services, and capital are mostly purchased from private suppliers.

There are other categories of transactions where administrative prices appear to play a role, but ultimately, expenditures reflect market values. For instance, administrative prices set limits on Medicare payments, but no doctor is conscripted to participate in the program, and many choose not to when they can make more money elsewhere. Presumably, the economic value delivered to Medicare patients is in some ways tailored to make the administrative payment fair to the service provider, and it therefore is fundamentally still a market price (albeit a possibly distorted one).

It is useful to revisit the implications of incomplete markets for federal

---

7. This budget treatment did not prevent Congress from committing to spend these illusory gains. In assessing the sustainability of promised benefits, the legislation treated the equity premium as creating real resources. Under the act, benefits can be increased with higher-than-expected investment returns, but beneficiaries are partially protected from investment losses.

budgeting and to consider whether in a second-best world, risk adjustment is likely to move decisions closer to or further away from the social optimum. Although it is impossible to answer this definitively, we believe that the evidence on how budget numbers are used in practice strongly supports the contention that risk adjustment would improve allocative efficiency and transparency.

The conclusion that risk adjustment would be beneficial depends in part on the observation that the budget process affects resource allocation primarily by allowing policymakers to weigh the costs of alternative means of satisfying fairly specific goals—such as increasing access to higher education or encouraging investment in alternative energy sources. For these types of decisions, it is easy to find examples (several are described next) where risk adjustment reduces distortions in cost comparisons. It is much more difficult to imagine cases where risk adjustment would distort such comparisons. Broader trade-offs, where the question of the social discount rate is more important—such as whether to raise taxes or leave more debt to future generations—are decided primarily through the political process, not the budget process.

Several examples from legislation recently before Congress illustrate the problems that arise when market risk is not priced in the budget (see also in section 3.4). In the debate over reauthorization of the Higher Education Act, one point of contention was over whether to increase aid to low-income students by increasing Pell grants or by lowering the interest rate on subsidized loans.[8] Since there is no risk charge on the loans, increasing their supply involves a lower budget cost than increasing outright grants of equal market value. Cost considerations favor loans over more-targeted Pell grants, even though the latter are generally thought to be the more efficient policy.[9]

A second example, which illustrates how ignoring risk adjustment can circumvent budget discipline and reduce transparency, is a provision (Title XVII) in the Energy Policy Act of 2005. That provision provides qualifying developers of innovative fuel technologies with federal loan guarantees. The legislation is structured so that the guarantees have zero budget cost, regardless of the size of the guarantee program. The zero budget cost is achieved by requiring the developers, most of which are subsidiaries of large utilities with ample access to capital markets, to pay an up-front fee that covers the estimated government cost of the credit guarantee. The value of the subsidy is the difference between the market value of the credit guarantee and value calculated without risk adjustment. In fact, even though no budget cost would be recorded, budget analysts use market value estimates to determine whether the subsidies are sufficient to make the projects viable. Growing

8. S. 1642 and H.R. 2669 (passed in July 2007).

9. Research suggests that grants are more effective than loans in inducing low-income students to pursue a college education. Further, there is growing concern that high levels of student loan debt create financial risk for students and for the government.

awareness of this legislative mechanism has resulted in increasing numbers of proposals designed to exploit it.

Another concern arising from considerations of the second best is that the very limited use of discounting in the budget may favor using low discount rates when discounting does occur. Recall that the budget records most expenditures on a cash basis, with undiscounted numbers projected over a ten-year window, but that credit is on an accrual basis. The conjecture is that by discounting the cash flows associated with credit transactions but not discounting alternative expenditures, comparisons are distorted. While there is no doubt that cash-basis accounting can impede meaningful comparisons across alternatives with different expenditure patterns and time horizons, the limited use of discounting for credit and some other long-lived contractual obligations tends to mitigate, not worsen, distortions due to timing differences.[10] Returning to the example of higher education, consider the choice between instituting a grant program or new student loan program, both of which will run for ten years. The grant program authorizes $100 million each year for new grants. In terms of resources committed to students in a given year, the equivalent student loan program would authorize lending each year in an amount such that the incremental annual subsidy is $100 million. The comparable cost for each year is exactly what is recorded when credit is accounted for correctly on a net present value basis.[11]

In considering alternative approaches to incorporating market prices into budgeting for credit, an important conceptual question is how broadly to define cost. A broad view of opportunity cost suggests using a comprehensive measure of private production costs, including not only the market risk premium but also taxes, liquidity, marketing expenses, and so forth. That is, the cost is what it would cost to contract for the same service in the private market.[12] The alternative is to focus on government production costs, including a risk charge. Private-sector costs can exceed government production costs because of the liquidity advantage of the Treasury market,[13] the exemption of Treasury debt from state and local taxes, and the fact that the

10. Federal agencies address this limitation in part by undertaking capital budgeting exercises outside of the budget process to evaluate program alternatives.

11. One might still object to the mixing of accruals with cash and prefer that the budget serve entirely as a statement of cash flows.

12. The Monetary Control Act governing the charge the Fed assesses on priced services to depository institutions is a precedent for using a broad definition of opportunity cost in evaluating the cost of government services. The act mandates the Fed "to recover, over the long run, all direct and indirect costs actually incurred as well as imputed costs that would have been incurred, including financing costs, taxes, and certain other expenses, and the return on equity (profit) that would have been earned, if a private business firm provided the services" (Federal Reserve System, Docket No. OP-1229).

13. To the extent that the greater liquidity of the Treasury market is due to taxpayers bearing a firmer obligation to repay than available through private contracts, the savings to the government comes at a cost to taxpayers.

government often avoids the higher marketing and service costs typically incurred by private providers.[14]

The question of whether to use private-sector or government production costs in estimating market values is not resolved by the principle of consistency—the budget generally records narrowly measured production costs for services the government produces, but it also records the full price of privately produced goods and services it purchases. In practice, it is difficult to separate out the various components of the market price of financial transactions. Hence, estimates based on comparable market prices are likely to reflect a fairly broad measure of opportunity cost, even when adjustments are made for identifiable differences, such as in administrative cost.

3.3.3 Alternative Valuation Methods

Three basic approaches can be used to incorporate market risk in the pricing of federal financial transactions: comparable market prices, risk-adjusted discount rates, and options or derivative pricing. Although all methods should provide similar answers if correctly implemented,[15] the most logical approach will vary with the transaction under consideration.

Comparable Market Prices

The most straightforward estimate of market cost is obtained in those instances when comparable products are offered by competitive private financial institutions. Clearly, government purchases of publicly traded stocks, bonds, and other financial securities fall into this category. Several federal credit offerings also have direct market counterparts, although favorable government terms can crowd out private provision. Federal Housing Administration (FHA) and Veterans Affairs (VA) mortgages, for instance, are similar in terms of size and borrower credit risk to some segments of the private market, where prices are readily observable. Still, adjustments must be made to account for differences in borrower and product characteristics.

Risk-Adjusted Spreads

For direct loan programs and sometimes for loan guarantees, risk adjusting the discount rate is often the most straightforward approach to estimating

14. The higher private-sector administrative costs generally reflect higher service levels and hence a different product than would be offered by the government. Adjusting for such differences is consistent with reporting program costs, not benefits.

15. It is well established in financial theory that for options such as loan guarantees, there is generally no single discount rate that can be applied to projected cash flows to obtain a correct answer. This complication is avoided using an options pricing approach, which implicitly incorporates the appropriate, potentially time-varying discount rate. Standard options pricing methods often produce cost estimates that are lower than those based on risk-adjusted rates. Nevertheless, all of the approaches yield estimates closer to market value than the current practice of omitting all risk adjustment.

market value. Risk-adjusted discount rates are higher than comparable maturity Treasury rates, because they include a premium or spread that compensates investors for risk bearing and other costs of extending credit. An advantage of this method is that for direct loans, it allows budget analysts to follow procedures similar to those currently used under the FCRA, where projected future cash flows are discounted to present values using rates on Treasury securities of the same maturity. The method of risk-adjusted discount rates also involves projecting future cash flows and discounting them to the present at a maturity-matched rate, but the rate is risk adjusted.

The risk-adjusted spread often can be inferred from comparable market rates. For loans to rated corporations, loan maturity and credit rating provide guidance in identifying the expected return. For unrated companies, such as the small businesses served by the Small Business Administration (SBA), bank rates on small business loans serve as useful starting points. Estimated spreads can be further refined by taking into account attributes such as whether the loan is collateralized and other debt obligations of the borrower. For consumer credit such as student loans and mortgage insurance, the private market provides useful reference rates that can be further refined with information such as credit scores or collateral value. Even for loans that do not have a close market analog, it is possible to glean information from market rates. For instance, a loan to a young company developing new energy technologies could be valued with reference to spreads on high-yield bonds or yields on venture capital investments in energy.

A number of caveats apply to the estimation and application of risk-adjusted rates. Rarely can market spreads be applied directly, and the required adjustments can be subtle. First, consistency must be maintained between cash flows and discount rates. The approach under the FCRA of estimating expected cash flows already adjusts for expected losses in the numerator of present value calculations. To avoid double counting by using too high a discount rate, expected losses must be subtracted from the reference market spread. For example, if the reference spread were based on BB bond yields, the spread could be adjusted by subtracting average realized loss rates on BB bonds of similar maturity.

Identifying the cost of risk from primary market spreads—those based on loan terms at origination—generally requires further adjustments for administrative costs included in the rate spread. Secondary market prices, when available, largely avoid this complication. However, secondary market prices may be affected by subordination structures and other mechanisms to redistribute risk that also must be recognized and adjusted for.

Finally, adjustments must be made for the value of prepayment options embedded in many federal loans and guarantees and for prepayment options affecting market spreads.

Once market spreads are adjusted down for expected losses, administrative costs, and prepayment options, the remaining spread represents compensation not only for market risk but also for liquidity and tax differentials. From a broad opportunity cost perspective, liquidity and tax differentials can also be considered legitimate elements of government expense. Under a narrower interpretation of cost, the size of tax and liquidity effects must be estimated and subtracted to isolate the cost of market risk.

Additional care is required in using risk-adjusted spreads to value loan guarantees. On a direct loan, the spread over Treasury rates results in a lower present value of loan payments: the loan is worth less because of market risk. For a loan guarantee, risk adjusting discount rates increases guarantee value, because the guarantor assumes the market risk. That is, calculating the present value of guarantee payments effectively requires using a discount rate that is lower than the risk-free rate. This follows logically from the identity that the value of a loan with credit risk plus the value of a 100 percent credit guarantee equals the value of a risk-free loan. The risky loan is worth less than if cash flows were discounted at a risk-free rate, and the guarantee is worth more. This relation suggests that loan guarantees can be valued by taking the difference between the value of a risk-free loan with equivalent cash flows and the estimated market value of the underlying risky loan. However, complications arise in applying this approach for guarantees that cover less than 100 percent of loan value, as is often the case. The value of a guarantee can interact with other loan features such as the prepayment option, also complicating the analysis. For some loan guarantees, a conceptually and operationally more appealing approach is to rely on derivative pricing methods.

Derivative Pricing

A loan guarantee is equivalent to a put option, a derivative security that can be valued using well-established methods employed by private financial institutions. The equivalence arises because the lender has the option to put the loan to the guarantor—the writer of the put option—at a strike price equal to the face value of the loan. In the event of default, it is optimal for the lender to exercise the option, leaving the guarantor with a loss equal to the difference between the loan's face value and the amount collected in default.

Derivative pricing methods are often the preferred method for valuing loan guarantees to commercial enterprises. They are also relatively straightforward to apply in valuing insurance products that entail significant market risk, such as pension and deposit insurance. The method is rarely applied to credit extended to individuals, however, because critical model inputs, such as the underlying asset value or the conditions triggering default, are difficult to identify. In such cases, risk-adjusted rates are likely to be a more reliable starting point for estimation. The choice of valuation methods used in the examples described in section 3.4 are consistent with these considerations.

3.3.4   Additional Considerations

The costs of modifying budget practice—including drafting and passing new legislation, retraining analysts, and revamping methods and models—are a serious obstacle to the adoption of risk-adjusted pricing for federal budgeting. The added complexity could also make it harder to explain budget estimates to nonspecialists. An approach that would partially mitigate some of these problems would be to concentrate analytical efforts on developing standard models and relatively simple guidelines for valuation at the CBO and OMB. The results could then be disseminated to the relevant credit agencies, as was done by the OMB following the passage of the FCRA. The task of developing standard tools is made more feasible by the fact that only a few programs provide most of the assisted credit (see table 3.1).

3.4   Evidence

Whether it is worthwhile to incur the costs of budget reform depends on how serious the distortions are from ignoring the price of risk. A series of recent studies quantifies those effects in a variety of contexts. They also illustrate the potential and challenges of estimating the cost of risk for federal financial transactions.

3.4.1   Loans and Loan Guarantees

Strikingly, some of the government's largest credit programs—including mortgage insurance, small business 7(a) loan guarantees, rural utilities loans, and some student loan programs—appear to cost nothing or to make money for the government (see table 3.2). Extending the budget measure of subsidy cost to include the market cost of risk and other excluded factors seems likely to raise estimated subsidy costs and eliminate most zero and negative subsidies. This is because opportunities to extend credit on terms that more than cover cost tend to be taken by private lenders without taxpayer assistance. A growing body of evidence is consistent with this expectation.

Corporate Debt Guarantees

The CBO (2004a) uses a derivatives pricing approach to valuing loan guarantees and compares the results with and without the inclusion of a market risk premium. The study looks at two similarly structured loan guarantees to distressed corporations: $1.5 billion to Chrysler in 1980, and $380 million to America West Airlines (AWA) in 2002. In exchange, the government received guarantee fees and ten-year warrants granting the right to purchase shares at a fixed strike price.

For both Chrysler and AWA ex ante, the net cost to the government is the cost of the guarantee less the value of warrants and guarantee fees. Uncertainty about default, prepayment, and future asset and stock values affects

Table 3.1   **New federal direct loans and guarantees by program, 2005 (billions of dollars and percent of total)**

Direct Loans		
Stafford and PLUS student loans[a]	$12.9	52.4%
Rural electric and telecommunications	4.8	19.5
Rural community facilities	1.7	6.9
Rural Housing Insurance Fund	1.3	5.3
SBA disaster loans	1.3	5.3
Other	2.6	10.6
Total direct loans	$24.6	
Guaranteed loans		
Stafford and PLUS student loans[a]	$43.3	22.6
FHA Mutual Mortgage Insurance	58.0	30.3
FHA general and special risk	19.7	10.3
VA housing	22.5	11.8
SBA general business	19.9	10.4
Other	27.9	14.6
Total guaranteed loans	$191.3	

Source: OMB, *Analytical Perspectives,* FY 2007, pp. 89–90.
[a]Excludes consolidation loans.

Table 3.2   **Selected loan and loan guarantee subsidy rates**

	Subsidy rate (%)
Direct loans obligations	
Rural Housing Insurance Fund	14.70
SBA disaster loans	12.86
Agricultural Credit Insurance Fund	7.38
Rural community advancement	6.81
Student loans	3.32
Rural electric and telecommunications	–0.96
Guaranteed loan commitments	
Student loans	11.09
Commodity Credit Corporation export	5.07
Export-Import Bank	1.09
Agricultural Credit Insurance Fund	3.27
SBA 7(a)	0.0
FHA, MMI	–1.80
FHA, general and special risk	–0.85
VA housing	–0.32

Source: OMB, *Analytical Perspectives,* FY 2007, pp. 89–90.

each cost component. Following a standard binomial modeling approach (see CBO [2004b] for technical details), the stochastic evolution of asset value is modeled based on expected returns and historical volatility of assets, estimated from historical stock return and industry data. Default is triggered when asset value falls below the value of maturing debt and current liabilities.

Similarly, prepayment is triggered when assets exceed liabilities, since recovery would likely allow a switch to lower-fee, nongovernment financing. The distribution of cash flows to the government fans out over time, with large gains in states of the world where the firm recovers and the warrants become valuable and with large losses in states where the firm defaults and the warrants are worthless.[16]

The same statistical models for estimating the distribution of future cash flows are used for both the FCRA-style and market value estimates, ensuring that the underlying cash flows are the same for both. Only the discount rates differ. The FCRA estimates are discounted using a contemporaneous Treasury rate, whereas the market value estimates incorporate the price of risk implicitly through the binomial options pricing approach.

The inclusion of the price of market risk has a large effect on the value of guarantees to high-risk borrowers. For AWA, the price of risk changes the net value from a gain to the government of 9.8 percent of loan value to a loss of 11.5 percent. For Chrysler, the net loss increases from 7.2 percent to 15.9 percent of the amount loaned. Table 3.3 shows the results for each firm, broken down into guarantee, fee, and warrant components. Risk adjustment increases the value of loan guarantees, because defaults tend to occur in bad aggregate states. Conversely, it decreases the value of warrants, which tend to be most valuable in good aggregate states. Two offsetting effects on fee value make the net effect of risk adjustment small: prepayments reduce fees in good times, but defaults reduce fees in bad times.

FHA Mortgage Guarantees

The FHA operates the Mutual Mortgage Insurance program (MMI), which provides access to homeownership to individuals who lack the savings, credit history, or income to qualify for a conventional mortgage. Under this program, the FHA provides credit guarantees on fifteen- and thirty-year fixed and adjustable rate, amortizing mortgages. The FHA charges borrowers both an up-front and annual fee for this service. To target the program to low- and moderate-income borrowers, the FHA sets limits on the dollar value insured.

Conveniently for valuation, the MMI program has a close counterpart in the private sector, and market prices are readily available. In fact, the FHA share of the mortgage guarantee business has declined sharply in the mid-2000s, as private competitors attracted an increasing portion of relatively low-risk borrowers by selectively pricing below the FHA.

In a recent analysis of proposed changes in the MMI program, the CBO (2006a) includes a calculation of the effect of market risk on program cost. Although comparable market prices are available, adjustments had to be made for differences in loan-to-value ratios, the government's lower market-

---

16. Both firms recovered, yielding the government large gains ex post.

Table 3.3   **Comparing subsidy rates, credit reform versus market values (percentages)**

	AWA		Chrysler	
	Credit reform	Market value	Credit reform	Market value
Warrants	(21.2)	(13.2)	(7.9)	(5.4)
Guarantee fees paid	(13.8)	(14.9)	(1.93)	(1.86)
Loan guarantee	25.2	39.6	17.0	23.2
Net government subsidy	(9.8)	11.5	7.2	15.9

ing costs, and differences in the distribution of credit scores for FHA-insured versus privately insured borrowers.

The effect of market risk on estimated subsidy cost is once again considerable. After adjusting for the loan differences the CBO estimates that the FHA's subsidy cost for the MMI program is 56 basis points per year versus a 33 basis point cost without risk adjustment. With new annual guarantee volume of about $40 billion, the 23 basis point difference indicates a cost of risk of $90 million per cohort.

Student Loans

Two of the largest federal credit programs are the Federal Family Education Loan (FFEL) program and the Federal Direct Student Loan (FDSL) program. The FFEL guaranteed loans are originated and serviced by private lenders but are guaranteed against credit risk by the Federal Government. Private lenders are also assured of a gross return that is a spread over the commercial paper rate through payments from the Federal Government that make up the difference between the student loan rate and the guaranteed rate. The direct loan program provides funds directly from the Federal Government to students, without the use of a private financial intermediary. The terms on guaranteed and direct loans are approximately the same for students and are generally more favorable than those available to consumers on nonfederal unsecured loans.

As is the case with federal mortgage insurance, a private market has developed in parallel with the federal student loan program, mostly to provide funds to students who have reached the federal borrowing limit. Using a combination of data from private and federal lenders, Lucas and Moore (see chapter 7 in this volume) have estimated that market risk adds 1 to 2 percentage points per year to the rate charged on private student loans. Using this estimate to calculate the cost of federal student loans adds about 8 percentage points to the subsidy rate for both guaranteed and direct loans.

SBA 7(a) Loans

To promote access to loan capital for small businesses, the SBA offers loan guarantees covering 50 percent to 85 percent of principal. In fiscal year

2005, new guarantees issued by the agency totaled about $14 billion. The interest rate paid by borrowers on those loans is negotiated with the lender and appears to be about 5 percent over short-term Treasury rates (a premium that is hard to reconcile with historically low default rates and the substantial credit guarantee). Borrowers also pay guarantee fees to the SBA.

By applying an options pricing model to the SBA's cash flow data, the CBO has estimated that taking account of market risk and recent default experience doubles the cost of 7(a) guarantees from 1.1 percent of the loan amount to 2.2 percent (CBO, 2007).

3.4.2   Insurance Programs

Unlike federal credit, insurance is budgeted for on a cash rather than accrual basis. Nevertheless, multiyear analyses suggest that the cost of risk is significant for some of these programs.

Pension Benefit Guaranty Corporation (PBGC) Insurance

The cost of federal insurance for defined benefit pension plans provided by the PBGC has two main drivers: it increases with the frequency of insolvency of plan sponsors and with the shortfall between plan assets and plan liabilities. Both of these factors contribute to higher payouts by the PBGC in bad aggregate states: insolvency rates increase in downturns, and the value of plan assets, which are heavily invested in equities, falls relative to the more stable value of plan liabilities. Consequently, the cost of market risk is a large component of the market price of this insurance.

The CBO (2005) evaluates the market value cost of insurance using an options pricing framework and compares it to an estimate based on identical cash flows but risk-free discounting.[17] The market value of federal pension insurance net of premiums for single-employer plans over the next ten years is estimated to be $86.7 billion. That sum includes $23.3 billion for plans that have already been terminated and $63.4 billion for insured claims projected to be put to the PBGC during the period. For the forward-looking component of cost, discounting new projected PBGC claims at Treasury rates implies a present value cost estimate of $32.4 billion, or just over half the market value of $63.4 when the cost of market risk is included.

Deposit Insurance

Recent estimates of the cost of federal deposit insurance also indicate a significant contribution from market risk. For example, Falkenheim and Pennacchi (2003) and Pennacchi (2006) develop an options pricing model

---

17. The compound nature of the option is accommodated using a risk-neutral Monte Carlo simulation approach. The model is used to evaluate the joint probability distribution of insolvency and the shortfall in plan assets for each covered firm. The total discounted cost is then a sum over all covered firms for which data is available. Pennacchi and Lewis (1999) examine a related pricing model.

for deposit insurance to banks and thrifts. To differentiate the market cost of deposit insurance from the expected cost discounted at risk-free rates, they report and compare the risk-adjusted or "risk-neutral" cumulative ten-year probabilities of bank insolvency with the cumulative actual or "physical" probabilities of insolvency. Their results show markedly higher cumulative risk-neutral probabilities of default than actual probabilities. For example, the average cumulative ten-year probability of insolvency for a large sample of private banks was 11.19 percent (risk neutral) and 4.5 percent (actual). For the publicly traded sample, the respective probabilities were 12.13 percent (risk neutral) and 4.98 percent (actual).[18]

3.4.3   Investments in Private Securities

If investments in private securities were treated analogously to credit under the FCRA, an apparent arbitrage opportunity would arise (CBO, 2003).[19] Imagine issuing $100 billion in Treasury bonds yielding 5 percent and investing the money in private equities. Clearly, in market value terms, this is a neutral transaction for the government—equal value is paid and received. When the cash flows from the equity investment are projected into the future, those cash flows include an equity premium, conservatively, 4 percent more than the risk-free rate. At the end of ten years, the accumulated value of the equity is then expected to be $100(1.09)^{10} = $237 billion. Discounting at the Treasury rate of 5 percent, the present value of the equity investment is $145 billion. Under FCRA-type accounting, the transaction appears to make $45 billion for the government (the $145 equity value less the $100 in Treasury securities issued).

Failing to take into account market risk can also distort the perception of the magnitude of liabilities, as discussed in Geanakoplos and Zeldes (see chapter 8 in this volume) in the context of Social Security. Further, an even larger discrepancy between market value and estimated cost can arise for benefit guarantees, such as those contemplated in some proposals to supplement Social Security with investments in private securities (Lachance and Mitchell 2002; CBO 2006b; Biggs, Burdick, and Smetters 2009). Such guarantees provide a floor on benefits to protect against poor investment returns. Like credit guarantees, benefit guarantees are a type of put option that confers the right to sell an asset for a predetermined price should it lose value. Benefit guarantees are particularly susceptible to market risk, however, because of the leveraged exposure to stock market risk.

Many observers inside and outside the government have emphasized the importance of avoiding the temptation to treat the risk premium as an

18. The difference between actual and risk-neutral probabilities over this horizon does not map directly into a cost differential, because it neglects time value, but nevertheless, it is indicative of the relative magnitude of costs with and without risk adjustment.

19. At present, private investments are accounted for as cash outlays in the budget under the OMB Circular A-11.

arbitrage opportunity in the budget. For instance, in describing the budget treatment of the private investments in the railroad retirement fund discussed previously, the OMB writes,[20]

> Equities and private bonds earn a higher return on average than the Treasury rate, but that return is subject to greater uncertainty. Sound budgeting principles require that estimates of future [railroad retirement] trust fund balances reflect both the average return and the cost of risk associated with the uncertainty of that return. . . . [T]he difference between the expected return of a risky liquid asset and the Treasury rate is equal to the cost of the asset's additional risk as priced by the market. Following through on this insight, the best way to project the rate of return on the Fund's balances is to use a Treasury rate. This will mean that assets with equal economic value as measured by market prices will be treated equivalently, avoiding the appearance that the budget could benefit if the government bought private sector assets.

The 1999 Social Security Technical Advisory Panel[21] similarly warns against presentations "that tend to show that 'financial arbitrage'—borrowing to purchase equities with a higher expected rate of return—creates some sort of free lunch" (p. 7). Nevertheless, agreement has yet to be reached on how the risk premium should be treated in the budget or in other types of government financial reports.

Opposition to booking an arbitrage profit from government risk-taking should not be interpreted as an argument against incorporating private investments into the Social Security system. As suggested by Diamond and Geanakoplos (1999), there may be legitimate reasons to reallocate risk via the retirement system—for instance, if some people are constrained from participating privately in financial markets by borrowing constraints. These considerations are important for evaluating the relative merits of alternative policy proposals. Here, however, the emphasis is on accounting for cost, which, for the reasons discussed earlier, seems best accomplished using market prices.

References

Arrow, K., and G. Debreu. 1954. Existence of an equilibrium for a competitive economy. *Econometrica* 22 (3): 265–90.
Arrow, K., and R. Lind. 1970. Uncertainty and the evaluation of public investment decisions. *American Economic Review* 60 (3): 364–78.

---

20. "The Budget System and Concepts," chapter 26, *Analytical Perspectives,* FY 2007. Budget of the US Government, p. 392. Available at: http://www.budget.gov/budget.
21. 1999 Technical Panel on Assumptions and Methods, *Report to the Social Security Advisory Board.* Available at: http://www.ssab.gov/publications/financing/tech99.pdf.

Bazelon, C., and K. Smetters. 1999. Discounting inside the Washington, D.C. Beltway. *Journal of Economic Perspectives* 13 (4): 213–28.

Biggs, A., C. A. Burdick, and K. Smetters. 2009. Pricing personal account benefit guarantees: A simplified approach. In *Social security policy in a changing environment,* ed. J. R. Brown, J. B. Liebman, and D. A. Wise, 229–55. Chicago: University of Chicago Press.

Bohn, H. 2004. Intergenerational risk sharing and fiscal policy. Meeting Paper no. 22. University of Connecticut, Society for Economic Dynamics.

Congressional Budget Office (CBO). 2003. *Evaluating and accounting for federal investment in corporate stocks and other private securities.* Washington, DC: CBO.

———. 2004a. *Estimating the value of subsidies for federal loans and loan guarantees.* Washington, DC: CBO.

———. 2004b. *Technical notes on valuing federal loans and loan guarantees using options pricing methods.* Washington, DC: CBO.

———. 2005. *The risk exposure of the Pension Benefit Guaranty Corporation.* Washington, DC: CBO.

———. 2006a. Assessing the government's costs for mortgage insurance provided by the Federal Housing Administration. Attachment to letter to Congressman Jeb Hensarling. Available at: http://www.cbo.gov/doc.cfm?index=7412&zzz=33862.

———. 2006b. *Evaluating benefit guarantees in social security.* Washington, DC: CBO.

———. 2007. Federal financial guarantees under the Small Business Administration's 7(a) program. Washington, DC: CBO.

Debreu, G. 1959. *Theory of value: An axiomatic analysis of economic equilibrium.* New Haven: Yale University Press.

Diamond, P. 1967. The role of the stock market in a general equilibrium model with technological uncertainty. *American Economic Review* 57 (3): 759–76.

Diamond, P., and J. Geanakoplos. 1999. Social security investment in equities I: Linear case. NBER Working Paper no. 7103. Cambridge, MA: National Bureau of Economic Research, April.

Falkenheim, M., and G. Pennacchi. 2003. The cost of deposit insurance for privately held banks: A market comparable approach. *Journal of Financial Services Research* 24 (2–3): 121–48.

Fama, E. F., and K. R. French. 1992. The cross-section of expected stock returns. *Journal of Finance* 47 (2): 427–65.

Gale, W. 1991. Economic effects of federal credit programs. *American Economic Review* 81 (1): 133–52.

Heaton, J., and D. Lucas. 1996. Evaluating the effects of incomplete markets on risk sharing and asset pricing. *Journal of Political Economy* 104 (3): 443–88.

Hirshliefer, J. 1964. Efficient allocation of capital in an uncertain world. *American Economic Review* 54:72–85.

———. 1966. Investment decisions under uncertainty: Applications of the state preference approach. *Quarterly Journal of Economics* 80:252–77.

Jorgenson, D. W., W. Vickrey, T. C. Koopmans, and P. A. Samuelson. 1964. Discussion. *American Economic Review* 54:93–96.

Kaplow, L. 2006. Discounting dollars, discounting lives: Intergenerational distributive justice and efficiency. NBER Working Paper no. 12239. Cambridge, MA: National Bureau of Economic Research, May.

Lachance, E. M., and O. Mitchell. 2002. Understanding individual account guarantees. NBER Working Paper no. 9195. Cambridge, MA: National Bureau of Economic Research, September.

Lintner, J. 1965. The valuation of risk assets and the selection of risky investments in stock portfolios and capital budgets. *Review of Economics and Statistics* 47 (1): 13–37.

Lucas, D., and M. Phaup. 2008. Reforming credit reform. *Public Budgeting and Finance* 28 (4): 90–110.
Modigliani, F., and M. H. Miller. 1958. The cost of capital, corporation finance, and the theory of investment. *American Economic Review* 48 (3): 261–97.
Pennacchi, G. 2006. Deposit insurance, bank regulation, and financial system risks. *Journal of Monetary Economics* 53 (1): 1–30.
Pennacchi, G., and C. Lewis. 1999. Valuing insurance for defined-benefit pension plans. In *Advances in futures and options research,* vol. 10, ed. P. Boyle, G. Pennacchi, and P. Ritchken, 135–69. Greenwich, CT: JAI Press.
Roll, R. 1977. A critique of the asset pricing theory's tests. *Journal of Financial Economics* 4:129–76.
Sandmo, A. 1972. Discount rates for public investment under uncertainty. *International Economic Review* 13 (2): 287–302.
Sandmo, A., and J. Dreze. 1971. Discount rates for public investment in closed and open economies. *Economica* 38 (152): 395–412.
Sharpe, W. F. 1964. Capital asset prices: A theory of market equilibrium under conditions of risk. *Journal of Finance* 19 (3): 425–42.
Stern, N. 2007. *The Economics of Climate Change: The Stern Review.* Cambridge, UK: Cambridge University Press.
Stiglitz, J., and A. Weiss. 1981. Credit rationing in markets with imperfect information. *American Economic Review* 71 (3): 393–410.

Comment   Henning Bohn

Debbie Lucas and Marvin Phaup present an excellent overview of how economists and policymakers should think about risk-taking in the public sector. The first part reviews the economic theory of risk sharing and of how risks are priced. The second part applies the principles of state-contingent claims pricing to practical questions of budget accounting. I agree wholeheartedly with the two main points: taking a systematic risk has a cost to the government, and the market value of such risks should be reflected in the budget.

The theoretical part reviews state-contingent claims pricing—the standard technical framework for pricing risks in finance—in a way that should be readable in policy circles. The key insights are that taking systematic risks is costly and that options are valuable. Lucas and Phaup also discuss how finance theory can be adapted to deal with realistically incomplete markets. The main lessons are that public policy can improve risk sharing and that well-designed risk-sharing policies can improve social welfare.

The applied part applies state-contingent claims pricing to questions of budget accounting. The key points are that assets and liabilities should be valued at market, that cost-benefit calculations should be based on economic opportunity cost, that costs should be recognized when they are accrued and

Henning Bohn is professor of economics at the University of California, Santa Barbara.

not when the cash outlays occur, and that costs and benefits to the government should be distinguished from broader social cost and benefits. In a series of insightful applications, Lucas and Phaup demonstrate how these principles apply to the accounting for government activities that involve economic uncertainty—notably to loans and loan guarantees.

Because the chapter well summarizes the state of the art, I have no substantive disagreements. Hence, my comments dwell mostly on issues where the state of the art is unsatisfactory and on issues that may complement Lucas and Phaup's exposition.

Incomplete Markets: A Challenge for Economic Theory

In the theory section, the least satisfactory topic is the pricing of risks when markets are incomplete. When market prices are readily available, the economics profession's message for policymakers is clear and simple: use the market prices, and follow the market in distinguishing systematic from idiosyncratic (diversifiable) risks. When markets are incomplete, however, economists' theoretical answers, as reviewed in the chapter, seem to be more a list of special cases, each requiring special considerations, than a set of general principles.

To evaluate a policy intervention in an incomplete markets environment, two questions are helpful to identify the economic issue at hand and to organize the list of special cases:

1. What is the source of the market incompleteness?
2. Does the government have a comparative advantage over the private sector in addressing this source of market incompleteness?

At a microeconomic level, the sources of the market incompleteness are mostly problems of asymmetric information—moral hazard and adverse selection. At the macroeconomic level, the source of market incompleteness is often the inability of future generations to participate in financial and insurance markets.

The question about comparative advantage helps clarify what is assumed about the government's ability to address the problem—an important issue that is often not addressed explicitly in policy debates. If government intervention faces the same information problems as the private sector, there is a strong case for using market prices, even when markets are incomplete. This may mean placing a zero value on a "security" with no private market.

A case for "adjustments" to market prices is much stronger if the government has an identifiable comparative advantage. For example, the government has enforcement powers through tax authorities, threats of criminal punishment, and a multitude of investigative and regulatory agencies. In some instances, this may give the government a comparative advantage in collecting information and in suppressing moral hazard. In such cases, the government's production cost—the cost of producing superior information—is arguably the relevant marginal cost, contrary to Lucas and Phaup's principle of using private cost as benchmark.

Macroeconomic Risks: Key Issues That Deserve More Attention

In the applied section, my main concern is that Lucas and Phaup devote most attention to microeconomic issues—the accounting for loans and credit guarantees—without sufficiently alerting readers to huge macroeconomic risks for which the accounting is arguably much worse. The "elephants in the room" here are the public debt, the government's commitments to Social Security and Medicare, and public employee pensions.

Public debt is commonly issued in the form of safe (default-free) debt securities, which are safe for bondholders but hugely risky for the taxpayers who are liable for the debt service. The welfare implications are discussed in Bohn (2005, 2009). Briefly, my analysis suggests that unless old people are intrinsically much more risk averse than younger cohorts, efficient inter-generational risk sharing calls for contingent debt—for obligations offering returns that are sensitive to macroeconomic and demographic variables.

Lucas and Phaup argue in this context that "considerations of generational equity" may justify the use of below-market risk-free interest rates. This argument blurs the distinction between budget accounting and social optimality—a distinction the authors correctly emphasize elsewhere—and it needlessly undermines the principle of market pricing. Generational considerations do not invalidate standard principles: budget accounting should use market prices for both safe and risky claims, and welfare involves more than accounting. Regarding the latter, a straightforward application of Bohn (2005, 2009) implies that certain aggregate risks have social cost below their market prices—namely, risks to which future generations are less exposed than current market participants. Thus, if below-market risk-free rates were accepted for "equity" reasons, the same argument would justify below-market risk premiums—but neither makes sense.

Turning to Social Security and Medicare, the accounting is much disputed. With cash flows approaching a trillion dollars and disputed obligations in the tens of trillions, these programs are so huge that the choice between trust fund accounting, unified budget accounting, or accrual accounting swamps all other government accounting questions. Keeping two or more inconsistent sets of books is considered fraudulent in most areas of accounting. Yet, the US government is telling Social Security participants that their benefits are held in trust—appealing to trust fund accounting—while using unified budget accounting for most fiscal decision making; and in the unified budget, Social Security revenues are used to cover other expenditures.

Either accounting system would be internally consistent and therefore more acceptable than the current mishmash. But both systems are inferior to accrual accounting, because they ignore other government assets and liabilities. The US government is actually publishing accrual-based financial statements, namely in the annual *Financial Report of the U.S. Government,* a publication that has received remarkably little attention in the policy debate. United States government financial statements are also in Bohn (1992)—consistently for 1947 to 1989, a period long enough to identify trends and to make intertemporal comparisons.

Pension promises to the government's own civilian employees and to military veterans should be less controversial than Social Security, because the government is acting as employer in this context. Hence, the same accounting principles as for private pension plans should apply. (One might quibble that military service is special, but unlike Social Security recipients, veterans have served the government.) Available estimates suggest that accrued employee and veterans pensions amount to 4 to 5 trillion dollars, or about as much as the public debt. Pension liabilities are ignored, however, in almost all accounts of government indebtedness. The notable exception is—again—the *Financial Report of the U.S. Government.*

There are two broad arguments for accrual accounting in the public sector. First, public accounting is centrally about accountability to the public. Economists and the accounting profession should therefore insist that the government follows generally accepted accounting principles (GAAP) to the maximum extent possible. A host of mundane government accounting questions can be resolved straightforwardly by reference to how private companies account for similar activities. Accountability derives from the fact that the government cannot change the rules without changing the rules for everyone, which would be visible, costly, and time consuming. Secondly, accrual-based debt and deficit measures are more insightful for economic analysis than cash numbers. As explained in Bohn (1992), this applies especially in economies where citizens have property rights (so accruals matter) and governments must use distortionary taxes to extract resources from their residents.

The only area that may require an extension of private-sector accounting principles is the accounting for contributory pay-as-you-go transfer systems. Because promised transfers are backed by future taxes—an exercise of sovereign power—they do not have a private-sector counterpart to which one could appeal for GAAP. Yet, the legalistic position that Social Security and Medicare are not liabilities because Congress could abolish them instantly defies economic reality. In this area, the ideal accounting standard is debatable (see Bohn [2007] for my preferred rules), but getting away from the current multiplicity of accounting systems is probably more important than the details.

A relevant distinction here is between official government reporting and the analysis by outside economists. This is analogous to the relationship between corporate accounting and the financial analysts community. Whereas outside analysts may apply discretion and judgment for the interpretation, official financial reporting requires strict rules and consistent principles to ensure accountability in the government no less than in the corporate sector.

Three Examples

Three examples should help clarify the general accounting issues.

First, consider government holdings of marketable securities—say, corporate stocks in the railroad retirement fund. Marketable securities are straightforward from a microeconomic perspective, because government production is not an issue and market prices are observed. There is no asymmetric information. The main questions are normative and macroeconomic: what is the optimal policy? Should the government take systematic risk in security markets? These are standard questions of optimal asset liability management. One challenge is perhaps the intergenerational aspect: if government policy improves intergenerational risk sharing, a clever politician may argue that the risk reduction should be recognized ex ante as a cost reduction. This argument would, however, confuse accounting and welfare. Even if a government's portfolio shift improves welfare, there is no reason not to value the portfolio at market prices.

Second, consider student loans. Student loans are a prime example of a government activity that poses microeconomic problems of adverse selection and moral hazard. Market prices reflect private lenders' cost of collecting debts. The key economic question here is if the government has a comparative advantage. Because tax authorities can withhold future tax refunds and threaten audits, one may suspect that the Internal Revenue Service (IRS) is more effective in collecting debts than private debt collectors. If so, the accounting question reduces to when and how the government's lower cost of producing information is recognized; and there is a good case for using the government's "production cost" (probabilities of suffering defaults) to value student loans. Otherwise efficient government lending would be discouraged. At market discount rates, negative subsidy rates are not implausible. They would simply reflect the government comparative advantage—monopoly power over enforcement tools.

Third, consider flood insurance. Flood insurance faces adverse selection problems like student loans but without government production. The main issues are therefore how to compute the subsidy and how to hold policymakers accountable in a timely manner when new subsidies are granted. In this example, Lucas and Phaup's arguments for accrual accounting and for using market prices are impeccable and worth endorsing strongly. The reason I mention flood insurance is because this type of example is probably much more common than the securities and student loan examples (which I selected to raise objections). That is, for most applications, Lucas and Phaup are right on target.

What Is a Risk Premium?

The term "risk premium" is widely used but should be clarified to avoid confusion between true risk premiums and mere spreads between safe and risky interest rates. Consider a promised future payment X—say, on a student loan. Let the actual payment x be distributed on $[0, X]$ with expected value $E[x]$. The percentage difference between X and $E[x]$ is known as the expected default rate, $E[x] = (1 - \text{default rate})^* X$. If r is the safe interest rate, the market value V of the promised payment can be expressed in terms of a "risk spread" over the safe interest rate as

$$V = X/(1 + r + \text{risk spread}).$$

Alternatively, the same value V can be written in terms of a risk premium as

$$V = E[x]/(1 + r + \text{risk premium}).$$

For diversifiable risks, asset pricing theory predicts a zero risk premium. Then, V equals the expected payment discounted at the safe rate. The risk spread is nonetheless positive whenever the expected default rate is nonzero.

For systematic risks, asset pricing theory specifies that market values are obtained as expectation over state-contingent payments weighted by an appropriate pricing kernel: $V = E[u^*x]$, where u denotes the pricing kernel, and $E[u] = 1/(1 + r)$ is the safe discount factor. The value V can be expressed equivalently in terms of the covariance of payoffs and pricing kernel, $V = E[x]/(1 + r) + \text{cov}(u,x)$. Compared to the formula $V = E[x]/(1 + r + \text{risk premium})$, one finds that a positive or negative covariance implies a positive or negative risk premium. Again, the risk premium differs from the risk spread whenever the default rate is nonzero.

For Lucas and Phaup's examples, which are mostly in the area of government credit, I suspect that the systematic risks are quantitatively small compared to the uncertainty surrounding the respective default probabilities. In the Chrysler bailout case, for example, the main issue is not how correlated Chrysler's value is with aggregate US consumption or other risk factors but how likely it was ex ante that the various contingent claims would pay off. The central problem for practical budgeting is therefore to estimate default risks reliably and in a manipulation-proof fashion. True risk premium would be more important for valuing macroeconomic risks (e.g., the risks implied by alternative pension or debt-management policies).

Conclusions

My discussant quibbles should not distract from the main message: Lucas and Phaup provide an excellent survey and convincing prescriptions for government budgeting that should be considered authoritative, especially in the areas of government credit and insurance. My main concerns are about the treatment of macroeconomic risks and about the lack of public accountability due to the US government's parallel use of multiple and mutually inconsistent accounting systems.

References

Bohn, H. 1992. Budget deficits and government accounting. *Carnegie-Rochester Conference Series on Public Policy* 37:1–84.

———. 2005. Who bears what risk? An intergenerational perspective. In *Restructuring retirement risks,* ed. D. Blitzstein, O. S. Mitchell, and S. P. Utkus, 10–36. Oxford: Oxford University Press.

———. 2007. Comments on "Accounting for social security, revised." Available at: http://www.fasab.gov/pdffiles/si16_bohn.pdf.

———. 2009. Intergenerational risk sharing and fiscal policy. *Journal of Monetary Economics* 56 (6):805–16.

Federal Financial Exposure to Natural Catastrophe Risk

J. David Cummins, Michael Suher, and George Zanjani

4.1 Introduction

In the aftermath of the terrorist attacks of September 11, 2001, Congress passed supplemental appropriations of over $26 billion for redevelopment, clean up, and aid to attack victims and their families. By the standards of the time, the nature and extent of the expenditures were unprecedented. However, the new standard would be broken only a few years later, when Congress appropriated emergency funds for over $80 billion in disaster assistance in the aftermath of Hurricane Katrina and three other hurricanes, which all occurred in one four-month period.

Viewed in the context of federal disaster policy over the last century, the responses to September 11 and Hurricane Katrina fit well with a long-term trend of a continuously increasing federal role in disaster assistance (e.g., Moss 1999, 2002). Over twenty years ago, Kunreuther and Miller (1985) observed:

The role of the federal government with respect to hazards has been changing . . . there has also been a realization that government has been

J. David Cummins is the Joseph E. Boettner Professor of Risk Management, Insurance, and Financial Institutions at the Fox School of Business, Temple University. Michael Suher is a graduate student in economics at Brown University. George Zanjani is associate professor of Risk Management and Insurance at Georgia State University.

The views expressed in this chapter are those of the authors and do not necessarily represent the positions of Temple University, the Federal Reserve Bank of New York, the Federal Reserve System, Brown University, or Georgia State University. We would like to thank Karen Clark, Gary Kerney, Robert Klein, Deborah Lucas, Greg Niehaus, two anonymous reviewers, and participants at the NBER/Kellogg conference on Measuring and Managing Federal Financial Risk and the American Risk and Insurance Association (ARIA) 2007 annual meeting for their insightful comments.

viewed as the protector of risks in ways that would have been unthinkable 50 years ago. Even 30 years ago there was a reluctance by local communities to rely on federal relief for recovery purposes.

Reactions to more recent disasters have revealed a telling shift in political sentiments at the state and local level. The response of Missouri Governor Mel Carnahan to calls for fiscal restraint in the aftermath of the Mississippi River flooding in 1993[1] ("This is not the time for debating the fine points of long-term policy!") seems more representative of local opinion today. Moreover, development has been steadily increasing in catastrophe-prone areas, so the property at risk is far greater now than at any time in the past.[2] Indeed, the subsidization of high-risk areas embedded in federal disaster policy has almost certainly encouraged development in those areas, thereby increasing federal exposure.[3]

The combination of rising standards for federal assistance and the growing private exposure suggests that the "stealth entitlement" of federal disaster assistance has grown large enough to merit a deeper assessment. Following Governor Carnahan's exhortation, we make no attempt in this chapter to dissect the "finer points" of public disaster policy. Instead, we set ourselves the more concrete objective of assessing the federal exposure. In other words, if we take as given the current generosity of federal disaster policy and the current state of development in catastrophe-prone areas, what is the taxpayer's expected annual bill for disaster-related expenditures? And what could the bill be in a bad year?

The numbers we estimate in answering the foregoing questions are significant. Based on the historical relationship between catastrophe damages and federal expenditures, together with prospective assessments of future catastrophe damages from (a) a leading catastrophe modeling firm, Applied Insurance Research (AIR), and (b) the projection of historical catastrophe loss data from Property Claims Services (PCS), we estimate the average expected bill for disaster assistance related to hurricanes, earthquakes, thunderstorms, and winter storms to be about $20 billion a year. In a bad year, corresponding to a catastrophic event of severity expected only once every century, the bill could exceed $100 billion. Conservative methods guide both estimates, so more liberal assumptions (e.g., extrapolating recent growth in federal generosity to the future instead of assuming no change) would yield considerably higher estimates.

To get a sense of the significance of these figures in relation to other, more familiar obligations of the Federal Government, we take the expected

---

1. Cited by Moss (1999, 259).

2. For example, the amount of property exposed to hurricane losses in Florida grew by 27 percent to $2.5 trillion between 2004 and 2007. See Hartwig (2008).

3. This is an important moral hazard issue that is beyond the scope of the present chapter. It would be useful to explore the link between federal disaster policy and development in future research.

annual expense over the next seventy-five years and compute a net present value (NPV) of this "unfunded liability." Doing so yields a figure between $1.2 and $7.1 trillion, depending on assumptions of growth and discount rates. For comparison, the trustees of Social Security project a shortfall with an NPV of $4.9 trillion over this same horizon.

Even the conservative estimate of $20 billion a year is far higher than the Federal Emergency Management Agency (FEMA) regular budget for disaster relief. Regular appropriations for the Disaster Relief Fund (DRF; the main vehicle for federal relief) averaged about $1 billion over the fiscal years from 2001 to 2005, while supplemental appropriations to the Disaster Relief Fund averaged $16.5 billion over the same period (GAO 2007). Our estimate of future relief spending is accurate enough to allow budgeting for disasters in the regular appropriation process.

The rest of this chapter is organized as follows. Section 4.2 offers background, including details on federal disaster policy. Section 4.3 discusses the methodology used for (a) assessing the relationship between federal disaster relief and catastrophe damages and (b) estimating the prospective distribution of aggregate catastrophe losses for the United States. Section 4.4 discusses the results, including the effects of modifying assumptions. Finally, section 4.5 concludes with a discussion of the policy implications of our findings.

4.2   Background

The Federal Government's financial exposure to catastrophic risk stems mainly from ad hoc disaster relief distributed to individuals, business, and communities; direct exposure of government facilities and service provision operations to disasters; and government insurance programs such as the National Flood Insurance Program (NFIP) and the Terrorism Risk Insurance Program (TRIP). We discuss each of these sources next.

4.2.1   Disaster Relief

Historically, disaster relief expenditures have been the most significant component of federal catastrophe exposure. One consequence of the seemingly ad hoc nature of the relief is that only a small portion of anticipated relief expenditures is contained in the budget. However, although the full extent of the federal obligation to assist may not be explicitly enumerated by legislation, history suggests that federal action is inevitable after major disasters; indeed, assistance seems discretionary in name only. In the words of Moss (1999, 334):

> Disaster spending has become a political sacred cow. . . . Again and again in the aftermath of disasters, representatives from the affected states have insisted that their constituents deserve no less than what other victims

received and that the particular nature of their disaster might justify even more. Federal catastrophe coverage has thus been subject to a ratcheting-up process.

The Stafford Emergency Assistance and Disaster Relief Act of 1988 and its antecedents, beginning with the Disaster Relief Act of 1950, guide the process for federal relief in the aftermath of catastrophes. The act formally requires the Federal Government to offer aid when state and local resources are overwhelmed by a major catastrophe. The Stafford Act designates FEMA to give declaration recommendations to the president after a disaster, and the Homeland Security Presidential Directive (HSPD)-5 makes the secretary of homeland security "responsible for coordinating Federal resources within the United States to prepare for, respond to, and recover from terrorist attacks, major disasters, and other emergencies" (DHS 2006b).

If the president makes a declaration, then FEMA is charged with overseeing the response, both directly and by administering funds to other federal agencies. The money comes from the DRF, a "no-year" account (i.e., any dollars appropriated remain available until expended) that receives annual appropriations though is largely reliant on supplemental appropriations from Congress in the event of major catastrophes.

The other sources of significant federal spending on disasters are the Small Business Administration (SBA), which makes subsidized disaster loans to households and businesses, and the US Department of Agriculture (USDA), which dispenses disaster loss funds to farmers. Most funding for the SBA is provided through its annual appropriations from Congress. The president may make a major disaster declaration or an emergency declaration. The latter is less significant and aims for federal costs not to exceed $5 million. If the president makes a more substantial major disaster declaration, some types of available federal aid actually have Stafford Act mandated *floors* on the federal share of expenditures. These mandated floors include 75 percent of eligible costs for "essential assistance" and "debris removal" and 100 percent of "housing assistance" (Bea 2006).

4.2.2   Exposures to Federal Facilities and Operations

Federal Government property, such as military bases or Veterans Affairs (VA) hospitals, can be susceptible to direct physical damage from catastrophes. The Federal Government is also bound to provide certain everyday public services, including providing Social Security and Medicare benefits and running federal law and order institutions. The prompt resumption of these services postdisaster can entail significantly higher-than-normal operational costs (DHS 2006a).

4.2.3   Insurance Programs

The US Federal Government plays significant roles in disaster insurance markets. In particular, it essentially acts as the major underwriter of residential flood insurance (through the NFIP, administered by FEMA); it also effectively acts as the country's largest reinsurer of terrorism risk through the TRIP.

The maximum government exposure under the TRIP is laid out by statute. For 2009 to 2014, the Federal Government is technically liable for up to $61.625 billion of terrorism losses, of which some fraction may be recouped from the industry.[4] To date, no losses have been paid under the TRIP. Of course, it is likely that the government's exposure to terrorism losses is significantly larger than the limits laid out in the TRIP. The government paid out approximately $16 billion through the September 11 Victims' Compensation Fund of 2001,[5] and pressures for ad hoc payments are likely to develop if a terrorist event larger than the $100 billion maximum under the TRIP were to occur.

The NFIP boasts about $1.1 trillion in exposures nationally.[6] Although it is described as a "self-financing" program, the NFIP has borrowing rights at the Treasury when losses exceed its resources. This borrowing authority was increased dramatically to $20.8 billion to cover claims following Hurricane Katrina. In reality, the NFIP is not self-supporting and has been criticized for leaving a high proportion of flood-exposed properties uninsured and not operating on sound actuarial principles (Cummins 2006; Jenkins 2006). Hence, in its present form, the NFIP creates more financial exposure for the Federal Treasury than was envisioned when the program was established.

Other federal insurance programs are also exposed to catastrophe losses. Notably, the US Department of Agriculture insured $50 billion of crop value in 2006 through the Federal Crop Insurance Corporation (Federal Crop Insurance Corporation 2007).

4.2.4   Additional Sources of Exposure

The aftermath of a major catastrophe will entail significant economic disruption for the affected region and potentially for entire national industries. Lost jobs, reduced wages, and lower output will all result in a lower tax base. This means less federal revenue at a time of increased federal spending. Government postdisaster aid will contribute to rebuilding the tax base and thus over the long run will lessen the size of indirect exposure created by lost tax revenues.

Next, we describe our collection and analysis of data on federal disaster expenditures and catastrophe losses.

4. The figure of $61.625 billion is obtained by multiplying the federal coinsurance share for 2007 to 2014 (85 percent) by $72.5 billion (calculated as the maximum insured loss amount of $100 billion less the aggregate industry retention of $27.5 billion). See Dunham and Dembeck (2008).

5. Victims' compensation is not explicitly part of the TRIP, which primarily provides reinsurance for property-casualty insurance coverages. Data on September 11 victims' compensation are from the following website: http://www.usdoj.gov/archive/victimcompensation/payments _deceased.html.

6. See: http://www.fema.gov/business/nfip/statistics/cy2007cov.shtm.

4.3   Data and Methodology

As noted previously, ad hoc disaster assistance has historically been the most important source of direct federal financial exposure to catastrophes. Hence, the remainder of the chapter focuses on that component of exposure. We use data on disaster damages and disaster assistance to project the distribution of expected federal disaster relief expenditures.

There are three basic steps to this analysis. The first step is to document the relationship between catastrophe damages and federal relief expenditures over the period from 1989 to 2008 to estimate the amount of federal relief expenditures likely to be "produced" by catastrophe losses. The second step is to develop a prospective annual catastrophe loss distribution for the United States. The third and final step, performed in the results section, is to apply the estimated ratio of federal relief expenditures to catastrophe damages (obtained in the first step) to the estimated catastrophe damage distribution (obtained in the second step) to produce an estimated annual federal disaster expenditure distribution for the United States. In this step, we also calculate the net present value of the implicit government liability arising from catastrophe losses.

4.3.1   Data on the Relationship between Catastrophe Loss and Federal Disaster Relief

We combine loss estimates for recent catastrophes with figures for emergency supplemental appropriations to assess the generosity of postdisaster federal aid.

We restrict our attention to catastrophes with at least $1 billion in total damages (in nominal terms) between 1989 and 2008. The main source for total damage estimates is data from the National Oceanic and Atmospheric Administration's (NOAA) National Climactic Data Center (NCDC) and Munich Re (2008, 2009). For each catastrophe, we also identify insured losses using the Insurance Services Office's (ISO) Property Claims Services estimates of privately insured losses and the National Flood Insurance Program payouts for flood losses under the NFIP. Our selection criterion yields sixty-five events, with the majority being hurricanes and tropical storms. Also included are the Loma Prieta, Northridge, and Nisqually earthquakes;[7] the Oklahoma City and September 11 terrorist attacks;[8] and various significant floods, storms, and wildfires.[9] As the NOAA relates, unlike with private

7. Total losses for the Loma Prieta and Northridge earthquakes, described as overall losses in the entire affected region, come from Munich Re (2005). Total losses for the Nisqually earthquake come from Meszaros and Fiegener (2002).

8. Oklahoma City bombing total damage figure comes from "Governor, Finance Director Release Bomb Damage Estimates," press release from the Office of Governor Frank Keating. Available at: http://www.state.ok.us/osfdocs/nr5-18.html. September 11 total damage figure comes from Bram, Orr, and Rapaport (2002).

9. The NOAA damage estimates are used for all events except the three earthquakes, the Oklahoma City bombing, and the September 11 terrorist attacks.

and NFIP insured losses, where every dollar paid out in claims is recorded, there is no federal agency tasked with keeping track of total losses resulting from catastrophes in the United States.

The NOAA bases its estimates on compilations of statistics from Storm Data (NCDC publication), the National Weather Service, the Federal Emergency Management Agency, other U.S. government agencies, individual state emergency management agencies, state and regional climate centers, and insurance industry estimates.[10] The figures from the NOAA and the others we use for total damages always encompass insured and uninsured property damages. For longer duration events, like the 1993 Mississippi Flood, droughts, and the earthquakes in our sample, our total loss figures include additional economic costs, such as reduced agricultural output. In the case of September 11, our total loss figure explicitly includes economic costs associated with labor losses. The catastrophes, with the associated estimates of total and insured losses, are summarized in figures 4.1 and 4.2, where figure 4.1 presents nominal losses and figure 4.2 presents exposure and price-adjusted losses.

The gap between insured and total losses is, of course, significant. In the case of earthquakes, this can be attributed partly to low rates of earthquake insurance purchase; similarly, in the case of hurricanes and tropical storms, significant amounts of damage can result from flood—and many households are either uninsured or only partially insured against flood. Deductibles, coinsurance, and uninsured damages (e.g., certain "economic costs" just described) further contribute to insured losses being substantially below our estimate of total losses. For the entire sample of sixty-five events, the ratio of insured to total loss averages less than 50 percent.

For federal expenditures, we only use figures for emergency supplemental appropriations for disaster assistance. This is legislation outside of the regular annual budgeting process. By our estimates, it accounts for about 80 percent of all federal disaster spending over the period, as we discuss next. The money can go to any agency involved in relief, but the majority is provided through FEMA's Disaster Relief Fund. The appropriations include funds for disaster relief, repair of federal facilities, and hazard mitigation activities directed towards reducing the effects of future disasters. Not included are funds for "counterterrorism, law enforcement, and national security" (Murray 2006, p. 2).

It should be noted that the narrow focus on supplemental appropriations ignores some elements of federal financial exposure to disasters. We do not include the budgeted portion of federal disaster spending, which covers annual appropriations to FEMA's Disaster Relief Fund, much of the

---

10. The National Oceanic and Atmospheric Administration describes their estimates of total costs as "the costs in terms of dollars and lives that would not have been incurred had the event not taken place. Insured and uninsured losses are included in damage estimates. . . . Economic costs are included for wide-scale, long-lasting events such as drought" (Lott and Ross 2006, p. 1).

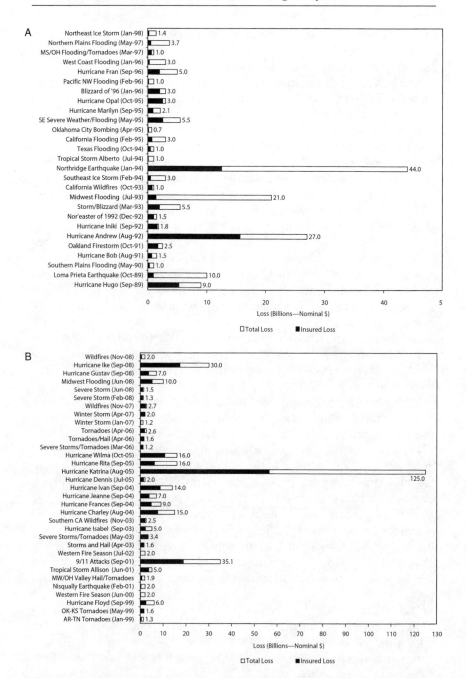

Fig. 4.1   Sample of major disasters, nominal losses: *A*, 1989–1998; *B*, 1999–2008

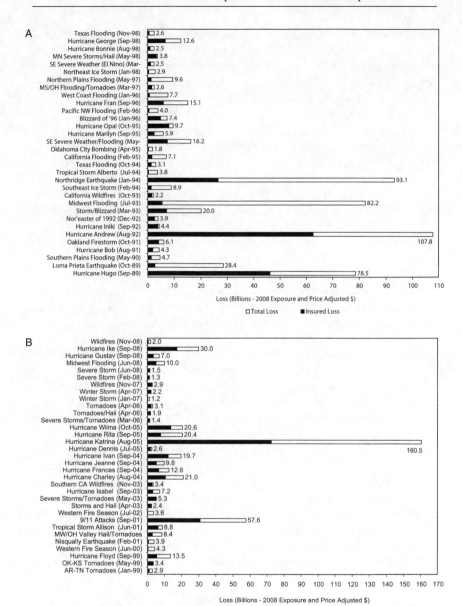

Fig. 4.2   Sample of major disasters, exposure and price adjusted losses: A**, 1989–1998;** B**, 1999–2008**

Note: Insured and total loss figures are adjusted at the state level by our 2008 exposure index. This index captures both price-level changes and changes in the size of the housing stock. The intent is to estimate the losses a past disaster would cause if it occurred today.

Small Business Administration's subsidized disaster loans program, and reconstruction projects that take place long after the fact. Also not included are farm and economic supplemental appropriations through the USDA for specifically agricultural disasters, like droughts. Total USDA spending on farm disaster aid totaled $54.4 billion over this time horizon.[11] We also treat NFIP losses as insurance payments and thus exclude them from the expenditure data. Of course, a case could be made for including them: while the program was close to being self-financing through 2004 (at which point the NFIP had aggregated only a $200 million deficit), the picture looked far different after record flood losses of the 2005 hurricane season, when the cumulative deficit of losses over premiums was $4.9 billion. Although the deficit was reduced to $556 million by 2007, the program is unlikely to be self-supporting in the long run and is badly in need of reform.[12]

Other special items are also excluded: for example, in the case of the 2001 terrorist attacks, we have not included the billions in indemnification distributed through the Victims' Compensation Fund. In summary, our figures for total federal disaster expenditures capture a significant portion, but not all, of the nonbudgeted federal exposure to disaster risk; furthermore, we do not attempt to capture exposures that are already reflected in the budget.

We draw on the Congressional Research Service analysis of appropriations, the text of the aid legislation, and the date of catastrophe occurrence to assign aid to catastrophes.[13] The appropriation legislation for disasters is usually part of larger bills, and often money is earmarked for multiple recent disasters. This fact, combined with the large number of hurricanes in the sample, make drawing inferences by catastrophe type difficult. Instead, we focus on all the events together.

Figure 4.3 shows the ratio of federal expenditures to total losses. The ratio of aid to total losses has a mean of 33 percent and a median of 30 percent, and the ratio of aid to uninsured losses has a mean of 101 percent and a median of 64 percent. In aggregate, the sixty-five events, in values adjusted to 2008 exposure and price levels, comprise about $1.1 trillion in total losses, $450 billion in insured losses, and $375 billion in emergency spending. These aggregated figures are summarized in table 4.1 (panel B).

While there is significant volatility in the aid ratios across the sample,

11. Chite (2006). See also Murray and Lindsay (2008).
12. Data are from the FEMA website (http://www.fema.gov/business/nfip/statistics/statscal .shtm) and represent cumulative premiums minus cumulative losses from 1978 to 2007. Statements about FEMA being self-supporting are usually based on a comparison of premiums and loss payments. However, this comparison is misleading, because it ignores program expenses. Hence, even during periods when premiums exceed loss payments, it is not necessarily the case that the program is truly self-supporting.
13. Appropriation legislation is sometimes explicit in assigning particular dollars to a particular catastrophe or set of catastrophes, in which case the allocation is straightforward. In other cases, legislation appropriates funds for unspecified catastrophes in the future, in which case the date of occurrence is relevant for assignment.

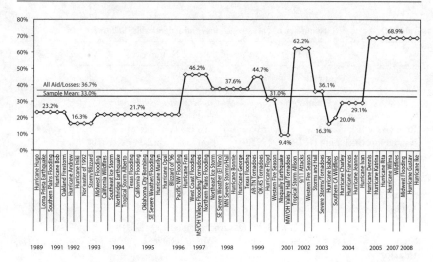

Fig. 4.3   Federal aid ratios: 1989 to 2008

Note: Each data point represents a specific disaster in our sample, with labels for the most significant disasters. The "all aid/losses" ratio is computed after adjusting loss and aid figures by our 2008 exposure index. This index captures both price-level changes and changes in the size of the housing stock. This yields a ratio that is not overweighted by recent disasters.

there is some evidence of an increase in generosity over time: emergency federal aid/total losses for 9/11 and surrounding natural disasters was 62 percent, even though federal aid did not breach 50 percent of total loss for any of the previous events in the sample. Beginning in the 2005 hurricane season and continuing through 2008, federal aid averaged 69 percent of total losses.[14]

To obtain a more comprehensive picture of Federal Government spending on disaster aid, we tabulate annual total federal disaster spending and compare it to annual catastrophe losses for fiscal years from 1989 to 2008. The data are presented in table 4.1 and figure 4.4. In addition to the emergency supplemental appropriations previously discussed, we include regular annual appropriations to FEMA's Disaster Relief Fund, USDA emergency funding for agriculture disasters,[15] and the subsidization cost of SBA disaster loans.[16] Annual catastrophe losses are comprised of NOAA's billion-dollar weather events; the Loma Prieta, Northridge, and Nisqually earthquakes; and the Oklahoma City and September 11 terrorist attacks. Over this span, in values adjusted to 2008 exposure and price levels, we observe $512 billion

14. It is difficult to distinguish the level of funding for the specific events during this period, because the Congressional acts authorizing the payments tended to lump together funding for several events rather than distinguishing specific funding per event.

15. Funding for "market loss payments to compensate for low farm commodity prices" is excluded.

16. Emergency supplemental figures are adjusted to avoid double counting for some SBA disaster loan subsidies and DRF original appropriations.

Table 4.1   **Summary of catastrophe loss and federal aid: 1989 to 2008**

Panel A–Values in billions: Nominal $

Aggregate		Mean	Median
Emergency supplemental appropriations by event			
Number of events	65	Aid to total loss	33.0%	30.1%
Total loss	510.0	Insured loss to total	45.7%	44.6%
Insured loss (including NFIP)	235.9	Aid to uninsured loss	101.4%	63.8%
NFIP	27.2		
Federal aid	240.6		
Aid to total loss	47.2%		
Insured loss to total	46.3%		
Aid to uninsured loss	87.8%		
Total federal disaster spending by year			
Number of years	20	Aid to total loss	62.0%	55.7%
Total loss	542.1		
NFIP	32.9		
Federal aid	285.7		
Aid to total loss	52.7%		

Panel B–Values in billions: 2008 exposure and price adjusted $

Aggregate		Mean	Median
Emergency supplemental appropriations by event			
Number of events	65	Aid to total loss	33.0%	30.1%
Total loss	1,021.9	Insured loss to total	45.7%	44.6%
Insured loss (including NFIP)	449.9	Aid to uninsured loss	101.4%	63.8%
NFIP	44.2		
Federal aid	374.7		
Aid to total loss	36.7%		
Insured loss to total	44.0%		
Aid to uninsured loss	65.5%		
Total federal disaster spending by year			
Number of years	20	Aid to total loss	62.0%	55.7%
Total loss	1,136.6		
NFIP	59.8		
Federal aid	511.8		
Aid to total loss	45.0%		

Note: In panel B, loss figures are adjusted at the state level by our 2008 exposure index. This index captures both price-level changes and changes in the size of the housing stock. The intent is to estimate the losses a past disaster would cause if it occurred today. Federal disaster spending is also adjusted using the same index, which yields an aggregate aid ratio that is not overweighted by recent disasters.

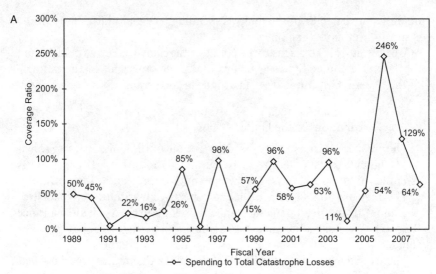

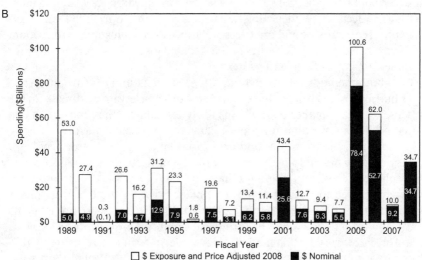

Fig. 4.4   Total federal disaster spending: FY1989 to FY2008

Note: In panel B, values are adjusted at the state level by our 2008 exposure index. This index captures both price-level changes and changes in the size of the housing stock. The intent is to estimate the spending that would have resulted if a past disaster occurred today.

in total disaster spending and $1.1 trillion in catastrophe losses,[17] for a coverage ratio of 45 percent. It should be noted that the annual coverage ratios in

17. The main distinction between the catastrophe losses used in this calculation relative to those used previously relates to the inclusion of drought losses. This augmentation is necessary due to the inclusion of the USDA expenditures.

figure 4.4 are partially misleading, as spending on a major disaster typically is spread over more than one year.

We now proceed to discuss projections of the catastrophe loss distribution for the entire United States, which will form the other half of the estimate of the Federal Government's catastrophe loss exposure.

4.3.2   Data on the Aggregate Catastrophe Loss Distribution for the United States

The prospective catastrophe loss distribution for the United States is obviously difficult to estimate precisely, but a rough sense of its character is essential for our exercise. We use two methods to project the distribution.

The first method starts with the prospective distribution of catastrophe losses from a leading catastrophe modeling firm, Applied Insurance Research. We make adjustments to AIR's distribution to account for uninsured losses (e.g., such as flood losses incurred in hurricanes).

The second method starts with ISO's Property Claims Services database, which contains data on insured losses from US catastrophes spanning more than five decades. We then adjust the historical figures to account for changes in property exposure and price levels. We also make adjustments to account for insurance penetration rates and uninsured losses. The methodology for these adjustments is described next.

In both methods, we restrict our attention to natural catastrophes, such as hurricanes and earthquakes. This leads to a conservative estimate (in the sense of being smaller than what is likely) of catastrophe exposure in two respects. First, we omit man-made catastrophes such as terrorist attacks, oil spills, oil platform fires and explosions, and nuclear power accidents. Second, our methodology almost certainly neglects to fully reflect catastrophe exposure from flooding, since our data sources are focused on privately insured losses. While we have made adjustments to events in the data to reflect the presence of uninsured flood losses, these adjustments are applied only to events that produced significant insured losses (such as a tropical storm). Such a methodology understates flood exposure by failing to account for events with significant flooding but insignificant wind involvement.

4.3.3   Aggregate Catastrophe Loss Distribution Based on the AIR Model

Catastrophe modeling is recognized globally as the standard technique for risk assessment and management. It is utilized by insurers and other firms exposed to catastrophic risk in pricing, risk selection and underwriting, loss mitigation, reinsurance decision making, and overall portfolio management. Applied Insurance Research Worldwide, which provided the catastrophic loss estimates discussed here, is one of the three global leaders in catastrophe modeling. Although catastrophe modeling began in the 1980s, the development of the technology accelerated following Hurricane Andrew in 1992 and the Northridge earthquake in 1994.

The AIR model is a stochastic simulation model that incorporates mathematical representations of the natural occurrence patterns and characteristics of hurricanes, earthquakes, and other catastrophes.[18] The model incorporates meteorological and seismological data, actuarial loss data, and information on property values, construction types, and occupancy classes (classifications that indicate what the structure is being used for, such as residential, retail, etc.). In most major geographical areas, the AIR model maps insurer exposure to catastrophic losses to the level of the individual building structure. Incorporated in the model are property characteristics and insurance coverage parameters. Thus, the model provides simulated loss distributions for individual insurers in finely divided geographical areas.

The structure of the AIR model is shown in figure 4.5. The simulations begin with event generation, which entails random generation of events in terms of their location, frequency of occurrence, and severity. The simulations incorporate probability distributions based on historical data for each variable that defines the events. By sampling from these distributions, a large stochastic catalogue of simulated event scenarios is generated. This process is represented schematically in figure 4.6 for the simulation of hurricanes.

To estimate the damage potential of natural hazards, the model estimates their physical parameters, not only at the source but also at the sites of the affected building inventory. The local intensity part of the model's hazard module is designed to capture how intensity changes as the simulated catastrophe propagates or travels over the affected area. Detailed scientific and geophysical data and algorithms are employed to model the local effects of each simulated event.

The damage estimation or vulnerability component of the model superimposes the local intensities of each simulated event onto a database of exposed properties and estimates the expected level of damage to buildings and their contents. Loss estimates are based on region-specific damage functions for many different construction types and occupancies. Total damage estimates can be generated for the entire insurance industry, for individual insurer policy portfolios, or for individual buildings.

In the final component of the model, insured losses are calculated by applying specific insurance policy conditions to the total damage estimates. Policy conditions include deductibles by coverage, coverage limits and sublimits, coinsurance, and other policy conditions. The output of the model is an estimated loss distribution for a specific insurance portfolio and location, often presented as an exceedance probability curve that plots the probability of exceeding various loss amounts.

For purposes of the present study, AIR provided expected average losses

---

18. The discussion of the AIR model is based on Clark (2004).

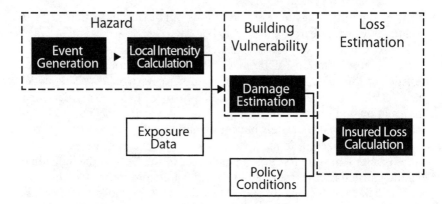

Fig. 4.5 The structure of the AIR simulation model

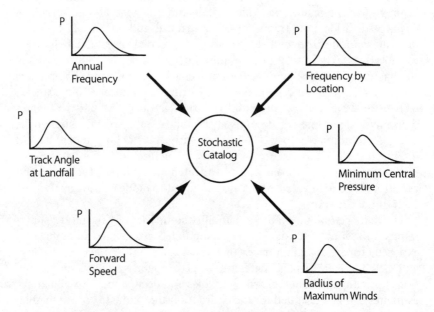

Fig. 4.6 Simulating a stochastic catalogue of storm events

and the higher percentiles, in aggregate and by occurrence, for hurricane, earthquake, winter storm, and severe thunderstorm. For all perils except earthquake, the estimates project insured losses, while the earthquake projection addresses insurable losses. As a result, AIR estimates of insured losses for perils other than earthquake will differ from total losses because of deductibles, policy limits, and uninsured losses. Accordingly, we adjust losses for the hurricane, thunderstorm, and winter storm perils upward to account for the historical relation between insured losses and total property losses observed in our sample of catastrophes. The intention is, to the extent possible, to adjust the AIR output to a basis consistent with the total loss estimates used in the previous section. However, we do not attempt to adjust the earthquake losses to reflect uninsured economic costs absent from the AIR calculations. As a result, the loss estimates should be lower than those that would be fully consistent with the "total losses" used in the previous section. Hence, our ultimate projections of total loss exposure from the AIR model will be conservative in the sense of yielding estimates of federal exposure that are probably on the low side.

Table 4.2 summarizes the average annual aggregate and occurrence losses produced by adjusting the AIR losses as described. In addition, we list the ninety-ninth percentile for all cases—the amount of loss corresponding to that expected with a frequency of once per century.[19] The estimates show an annual aggregate expected average total loss of 35 to 43 billion dollars. The higher figure uses a shorter historical time series of hurricanes to account for the recent trend of more frequent and severe hurricanes. For all perils, there is a 1 percent chance of an annual loss of at least 273 to 282 billion dollars (without attempting the adjustment to hurricane and thunderstorm losses described previously).[20]

4.3.4 Aggregate Catastrophe Loss Distribution Based on PCS Data

In this section, we discuss the estimation of catastrophe loss distributions using the PCS data on insured catastrophe losses. The PCS reports losses at the state level, beginning in 1949, for various types of catastrophes. We adjust the data for changing exposure levels, as explained next, to provide estimates of the losses that would have resulted from the historical catastrophes recorded by the PCS if today's property values had existed at the time of the events. Maximum likelihood estimation is used to fit the adjusted losses to underlying parametric loss distributions. In this fashion, we can project expected losses and various percentiles to compare with the figures provided by AIR.

4.3.5 Data Considerations

Property Claims Services, a division of the Insurance Services Office, compiles data on insured losses from catastrophes. Currently, the PCS defines a catastrophe as an event that causes $25 million or more in damages and

19. Note that the figures for the percentiles for the all perils category do not contain adjustments for the historical relationship between insured losses and total property losses, as we do not have detailed information on the composition of the all perils distribution. The average, however, does reflect the adjustment.

20. This figure represents the ninety-ninth percentile of the distribution of the sum of insured losses for all perils except earthquake and insurable losses for earthquake. Since we do not have the composition of the all perils distribution, we cannot make the referenced adjustments without making further assumptions. In the case of the average, however, the adjustments yielded an increase of about 50 percent; a similar impact on the ninety-ninth percentile would suggest a figure above $400 billion.

Table 4.2   AIR based projections of US catastrophe loss exposure

	Aggregate	Occurrence
All perils (standard hurricane model)		
Expected average loss	35.2	21.6
99th percentile	272.6	234.6
All perils (Near-term hurricane sensitivity)[a]		
Expected average loss	43.1	27.7
99th percentile	281.6	240.3
Hurricane (standard model)		
Expected average loss	19.9	16.8
99th percentile	109.0	97.4
Hurricane (near-term sensitivity)		
Expected average loss	27.8	22.9
99th percentile	138.7	122.0
Earthquake		
Expected average loss	16.3	14.7
99th percentile	238.2	213.8
Winter storm		
Expected average loss	4.1	2.0
99th percentile	8.8	5.5
Severe thunderstorm		
Expected average loss	11.2	2.8
99th percentile	19.7	10.3

Note: Perils include hurricane, earthquake, winter storm, severe thunderstorm, and implicitly, flood. Hurricane expected average loss scaled by 47.7 percent insured-to-total-loss ratio. Severe thunderstorm expected average loss scaled by 74.3 percent insured-to-total-loss ratio. Winter storm expected average loss scaled by 55.6 percent insured-to-total-loss ratio. Amounts in billions of dollars. An occurrence loss is the largest loss from a single simulated event in a given year, and the aggregate loss is the sum of losses from all simulated events in a given year.

[a]Near-term hurricane sensitivity uses a shorter historical time series of hurricanes to account for the recent trend of more frequent and severe hurricanes.

affects a significant number of policy holders.[21] The PCS loss estimates are for personal and commercial property along with vehicle losses covered by comprehensive coverage.[22] The data are collected by canvassing the insurance industry following major loss events and conducting supplemental field research in some instances.[23] The PCS maintains data from 1949 through the present, broken down by state and by type of event. The PCS analysis in this chapter focuses on the period from 1950 through 2006.

In this study, we develop models based on fitting probability distributions

21. The monetary threshold used by the PCS to define a catastrophe has been adjusted over time. From 1949 to 1981, the dollar threshold was $1 million; from 1982 to 1996, the threshold was $5 million; and since 1997, the threshold has been $25 million.

22. Auto losses generally represent 10 percent or less of total losses from catastrophes (e-mail from Gary Kerney of the PCS).

23. The PCS generally combines two methods to develop the best estimate of insured catastrophe losses. First, the PCS conducts confidential surveys of insurers, agents, adjusters, public officials, and others to gather data on claim volumes and amounts. The PCS analyzes the data and combines it with trend factors to determine a loss estimate. The PCS also maintains a database containing information on the number and types of structures for every US state.

to the PCS data. We then estimate the loss quantiles to measure exposure to loss from various perils.

Prior to fitting probability distributions, it is important to adjust the PCS loss data for changes in the value of property exposed to loss. The reason for this adjustment is that the value of property exposed to loss in the United States expanded dramatically during the period from 1949 through 2006, both from growth in the housing stock and price appreciation. Consequently, events from prior decades would be likely to cause much greater damages if they occurred today. To adjust the data for changes in property values, we created an exposure index for each state using the US Census Bureau's decennial Census data on housing values.[24] Values for years between the decades are calculated based on logarithmic interpolation; values for 2001 to 2006 are calculated based on the annual growth rate that prevailed from 1990 to 2000. This series gives the aggregate value of owner-occupied homes for each state in nominal dollars, so an increase in these figures over time represents both more houses being built and increases in the price level. The index is computed simply as the ratio of the 2006 value in a given state to the value in a past year:

$$\mathrm{ExposureIndex}_{\mathrm{state}}^{\mathrm{year}} = \frac{\mathrm{AggregateHomeValue}_{\mathrm{state}}^{2006}}{\mathrm{AggregateHomeValue}_{\mathrm{state}}^{\mathrm{year}}}.$$

Then, the nominal loss value reported by the PCS for a given catastrophe in a given year and state is multiplied by the value of the exposure index for that year and state. This is an estimate of the losses a past catastrophe would cause if it occurred today, considering present price levels and the size of exposed infrastructure.[25]

Because the PCS focuses on insured losses from catastrophic events, we also adjust the PCS data to estimate the total (insured and uninsured) losses from each event. These adjustments differ by peril, because the proportion

---

Using that information, the PCS can estimate the number of insurable risks in a specific geographic area. Combined with survey information, the structure data forms the basis for the PCS damage estimates. For large or unusual events, the PCS resurveys the affected insurers to obtain updated information. The PCS estimation methodology is described in more detail in Property Claims Services (2006).

24. The series used is: H024, AGGREGATE VALUE. Universe: specified owner-occupied housing units, defined by the Census Bureau as the "total number of owner occupied housing units described as either a one family home detached from any other house or a one family house attached to one or more houses on less than 10 acres with no business on the property. The data for 'specified' units exclude mobile homes, houses with a business or medical office, houses on 10 or more acres, and housing units in multi-unit buildings."

25. The use of a housing value index implicitly assumes that the value of commercial property and automobiles exposed to loss has expanded at the same rate as the value of residential property. Because population growth in a geographical region is likely to be accompanied by corresponding growth in commercial activity and the number of automobiles, this is likely to be a reasonable assumption. The use of housing values implicitly assumes that the value of land as a proportion of total housing value remains more or less constant over time. This assumption is potentially important, because storm damages are to structures and other property rather than to land, whereas the value of land is incorporated in the value of the housing stock.

of property covered by insurance varies significantly by peril. For example, earthquake insurance take-up rates in California are substantially smaller than homeowners insurance take-up rates in the Southeast. These adjustments are described in detail next.

For hurricane/tropical storm, thunderstorm, and winter storm losses, we scale up the losses by a constant factor—the inverse of the ratio of insured to total loss for the corresponding peril in our federal expenditure sample (with NFIP losses not included in the insured figure).

Similarly for earthquakes, we use known take-up rates for earthquake insurance since 1996 for California (available from the California Department of Insurance) and project earlier take-up rates based on the relationship between annual California earthquake premium data (also from the California Department of Insurance), California aggregate housing value, and the known take-up rates since 1996.[26] We apply the inverse of these known and estimated take-up rates to the PCS insured earthquake loss for the year it occurs to get a total loss figure.

4.3.6   Statistical Methodology

To estimate an aggregate annual claims distribution, we use a Fast Fourier Transform (FFT) inversion method. The approach requires separate estimates of the severity of loss and annual frequency of occurrence distributions for each specific peril. We then compound these estimates to produce distributions of aggregate annual claims by peril and for all catastrophes.

Thus, the estimation has five phases:[27]

1. Estimate the severity of loss and annual frequency distributions separately for each of the major catastrophe perils using maximum likelihood estimation.

2. Discretize the severity distribution by dividing the full range of possible loss into equal segments and placing all the probability within a segment at its midpoint.

3. Apply the FFT to the discretized severity distribution to obtain its characteristic function.

4. Transform this characteristic function using the estimated frequency

---

26. Take-up rates since 1996 are from the California Department of Insurance (http://www.insurance.ca.gov/0250-insurers/0600-data-reports/0100-earthquake-cov-exp/). Annual earthquake premium data were obtained by fax from Richard Roth Jr. at the California Department of Insurance.

27. The reason for applying the Fast Fourier Transform approach is that the total claims distribution cannot be computed by convoluting the severity random variables and then compounding the convolutions with the frequency distribution for most realistic frequency and severity distributions. However, the total claims distribution can be recovered by computing and then inverting the characteristic function. The FFT approach is discussed in Klugman, Panjer, and Willmot (2004). The severity distributions are discretized using the rounding method on 4,096 segments of $100 million of loss. Any further tail probability, corresponding to losses exceeding $409.6 billion (number of segments • loss per segment), is placed on the last point of the discretized severity probability density function.

distribution, yielding the characteristic function of the aggregate annual claims distribution.

5. Apply an inverse FFT to recover the aggregate annual claims distribution functions.[28]

For fitting the severity of loss data, three different distributions are used, which have been shown to provide good models of loss distributions in prior research (e.g., Cummins et al. 1990; Cummins, Lewis, and Phillips 1999). The distributions—the lognormal, the Pareto, and the Burr 12—are specified as follows.

The lognormal:

$$f(x) = \frac{1}{x\sigma\sqrt{2\pi}} \, e^{-(1/2)\{[\ln(x) - \mu]/\sigma\}^2}, x > 0.$$

The Pareto:

$$f(x) = \alpha\lambda^\alpha(\lambda + x)^{-\alpha-1}, x > 0.$$

The Burr 12:

$$f(x) = |a| \, q \, x^{a-1} \, b^{-a}[1 + (\frac{x}{b})^a]^{-q-1}.$$

We use the Poisson distribution, specified as follows, to fit the annual occurrences of a given peril over our sample period, 1950 to 2005.

The Poisson:

$$f(x) = e^{-\lambda} \frac{\lambda^x}{x!}, x = 0, 1, 2 \ldots$$

4.3.7   Results

Summary statistics on catastrophe losses are presented in table 4.3, which have been adjusted for changes in housing exposures, both from growth in the housing stock and price level increases (but not to account for differences between insured losses and total losses). All data are from the PCS. Hurricanes have the highest average and median loss severity at $8.8 billion and $1.2 billion, respectively. Hurricanes also have the highest standard deviation of loss. As expected, the observed losses are highly skewed for all perils.

The trends in the total number of catastrophic events and the total insured losses are shown in figure 4.7. The loss amounts have been adjusted to 2006 property values, and catastrophes that would not have caused at least $25 million in losses at 2006 property value levels have been deleted for purposes of preparing this figure. Even though Hurricane Katrina was the largest loss event recorded during the sample period in nominal dollars, based on

---

28. This implicitly assumes that losses from catastrophe perils such as hurricanes, tornadoes, and earthquakes are statistically independent. The calculation utilizes the result that the characteristic function of the sum of independent random variables is the product of the characteristic functions of the individual random variables in the sum.

Table 4.3   Summary statistics: Exposure adjusted insured loss values (Billions of 2006 exposure and price adjusted $)

Catastrophe type	N	Mean	Median	Standard deviation	Variation coefficient	Skewness	Minimum	Maximum	P75	P90	P95	P99
Wind and thunderstorm event	1,150	664	163	6,806	1,025.41	32.40	2	227,673	370	923	1,845	5,534
Winter storm	128	1,382	312	2,908	210.44	3.92	17	18,619	1,147	3,437	6,180	16,383
Hurricane	85	8,830	1,220	22,158	250.93	4.23	11	132,032	5,435	29,601	44,357	132,032
Fire: other	47	1,390	146	4,401	316.54	4.73	12	26,197	429	2,202	7,863	26,197
Wildland fire	18	572	254	822	143.64	3.06	35	3,534	681	1,227	3,534	3,534
Earthquake	15	1,785	79	5,748	322.06	3.81	16	22,450	504	2,317	22,450	22,450
Tropical storm	15	808	178	1,705	211.06	2.70	58	6,011	290	3,719	6,011	6,011
Riot	11	2,952	1,044	6,574	222.69	3.20	6	22,581	1,613	3,074	22,581	22,581
Utility service disruption	1	221	221				221	221	221	221	221	221
Volcanic eruption	1	260	260				260	260	260	260	260	260
Water damage	1	971	971				971	971	971	971	971	971

Source: PCS data: 1950 to 2006

Note: Figures are in billions of dollars and are adjusted at the state level by our 2006 exposure index. This index captures both price-level changes and changes in the size of the housing stock. The intent is to estimate the losses a past disaster would cause if it occurred today. PX indicates the Xth percentile.

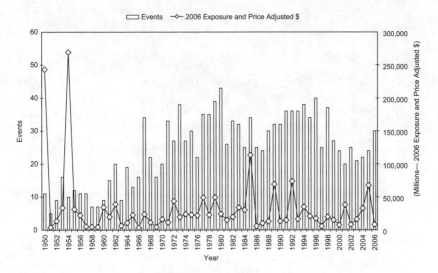

Fig. 4.7   PCS aggregate insured loss: Threshold of \$25 million by event

Note: Figures are adjusted at the state level by our 2006 exposure index. This index captures both price-level changes and changes in the size of the housing stock. The intent is to estimate the losses a past disaster would cause if it occurred today.

the housing value-adjusted loss data, there were five previous events of approximately equal or greater magnitude. In 1950, a major wind and thunderstorm event caused substantial property losses from Maryland to Maine. If a similar event occurred at present, the estimated losses would be greater than \$227 billion. In 1954, Hurricane Carol caused major damage ranging from New Jersey to Maine, with particularly large losses in Massachusetts and New York. The same year, Hurricane Hazel caused devastating losses ranging from South Carolina to New York. If those storms occurred today, it is estimated that Carol and Hazel would cause losses of \$132 billion and \$125 billion, respectively. A storm of the magnitude of Hurricane Gloria, which struck several northeastern states in 1985, would cause estimated losses of \$65 billion if it occurred today. By contrast, insured losses from Hurricane Katrina were "only" \$44 billion.

Parameter estimates for the various distributions and perils are shown in table 4.4, along with log-likelihood function values. Estimates are shown both for insured and total losses. The last column of the table shows the best-fitting distribution based on an approximate likelihood ratio test.[29] The Pareto provides the best fit for all perils except earthquake.

29. The likelihood ratio test results are only approximate, because the distributions estimated are not nested in the sense that they can be obtained by imposing parameter restrictions on the distribution with the largest number of parameters. The significance tests are based on a chi-square distribution with 1 degree of freedom. The likelihood test statistic is $2 \cdot [\log(L:\text{distribution } 1) - \log(L: \text{distribution } 2)]$ for pairwise tests of the distributions.

Table 4.4   **Maximum likelihood parameter estimates and log-likelihood function values: PCS loss data**

Severity

Catastrophe type	Loss type	N	Lognormal			Pareto			Burr 12			
			Mu	Sigma	Log(L)	Alpha	Lambda	Log(L)	a	b	q	Log(L)
Hurricane/tropical storm	Insured	100	6.870	2.112	-903.657	0.577	322.117	-905.820	1.526	1.40E+02	0.300	-905.113
	Total		7.610	2.112	-977.681	0.577	675.294	-979.844	1.526	293.922	0.300	-979.136
Earthquake	Insured	15	4.869	1.988	-104.620	0.645	51.028	-103.840	2.088	20.390	0.236	-102.292
	Total		7.354	1.749	-139.977	0.741	768.985	-139.416	0.763	4,095.999	1.713	-141.08
Wind and thunderstorm	Insured	1,150	5.150	1.337	-7,888.080	1.696	335.761	-7,909.861	1.554	1.16E+02	0.710	-7,868.334
	Total		5.447	1.337	-8229.698	1.696	451.900	-8251.479	1.554	1.56E+02	0.710	-8209.952
Winter storm	Insured	128	5.983	1.535	-1,002.358	1.104	424.458	-1,005.737	1.738	1.35E+02	0.418	-1,001.830
	Total		6.570	1.535	-1,077.492	1.104	763.414	-1,080.871	1.738	2.43E+02	0.418	-1076.965

Catastrophe type	Loss type	N	Frequency Poisson		Max-log(L)	Likelihood ratio tests				
			Lambda	Log(L)		LN-Pareto	Burr-LN	Burr-Pareto	Chi-square(5%,1)	Best fit
Hurricane/tropical storm	Insured	100	1.768	-96.925	905.820	4.326	-2.912	1.414	3.84	Pareto
	Total				979.844	4.326	-2.910	1.416	3.84	Pareto
Earthquake	Insured	15	0.268	-36.146	104.620	-1.560	4.656	3.096	3.84	LN
	Total				141.080	-1.122	-2.206	-3.328	3.84	Burr 12
Wind and thunderstorm	Insured	1,150	20.089	-257.147	7,909.861	43.562	39.492	83.054	3.84	Pareto[a]
	Total				8,251.479	43.562	39.492	83.054	3.84	Pareto[a]
Winter storm	Insured	128	2.214	-135.893	1,005.737	6.758	1.056	7.814	3.84	Pareto[a]
	Total				1,080.871	6.758	1.054	7.812	3.84	Pareto[a]

Note: LN = lognormal.

[a]Indicates the distribution provides a significantly better fit than the other distributions based on an approximate chi-square likelihood ratio test.

As an example of one of the estimated distributions, the severity distribution of total losses from hurricanes and tropical storms is shown in figure 4.8. The likelihood ratio results show that the Pareto provides the best fit to this set of data but not at a high level of statistical significance. The graph bears this out but suggests that all three distributions fit the data reasonably well, with the Pareto and Burr 12 perhaps overestimating the probability in the tail of the distribution. In figure 4.9, we present the annual aggregate claims distribution of total losses for all perils. These distributions are not directly estimated from the data. They are derived by compounding the separately estimated severity and frequency distributions for each individual peril through the FFT method described previously. Due to computational limitations, all three distributions are capped at $409.6 billion, leading to underestimation of probability in the tail of the distribution.

Table 4.5 presents the means and upper percentiles of the estimated severity of loss distributions for the models whose parameters are shown in table 4.4. The percentiles shown are the 50th, the 75th, the 90th, the 95th, the 99th, and the 99.9th. The latter three percentiles would correspond to event "return periods" of twenty, one hundred, and one thousand years, respectively.

In table 4.6, we present annual aggregate losses by peril and for all perils (hurricanes, earthquakes, wind and thunderstorms, and winter storms) combined. For all perils, we project an expected annual insured loss range of 24 to 35 billion dollars and a total loss range of 39 to 48 billion dollars. The ninety-ninth percentiles of the insured and total loss distributions are 181 to 310 billion dollars and 272 to 337 billion dollars, respectively. These estimates suggest very large exposure to catastrophic losses for both the government and the insurance industry.

4.4   Estimated Annual Losses and Projected Liabilities

The AIR model projects expected annual catastrophe total losses of 35 to 43 billion dollars; this is roughly comparable to the projections from the PCS data, which indicate annual average losses of 39 to 48 billion dollars. For the ninety-ninth percentile, the AIR model indicates insurable loss of 273 to 282 billion dollars, which is again comparable to the total loss figures from the PCS methods—which indicate a range from 272 to 337 billion dollars, depending on the distribution chosen.

Reasonable estimates of the recent relation between federal aid and losses, based on the analysis presented, range from 30 percent to 50 percent—with figures at the higher end of the range supported by generosity observed in recent events such as the 2005 hurricanes and by the aggregated ratios of aid to losses over the period. It is true that the aggregates are skewed to some degree by the larger events that have happened in recent years, but even a straight average, by event, of the ratio of aid to loss yields a figure in excess of 30 percent.

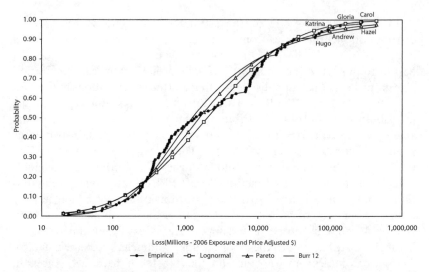

Fig. 4.8   Hurricane/tropical storm occurrence severity: Total loss

Note: The data used in this estimation were adjusted at the state level by our 2006 exposure index. This index captures both price-level changes and changes in the size of the housing stock. The intent is to estimate the losses a past disaster would cause if it occurred today.

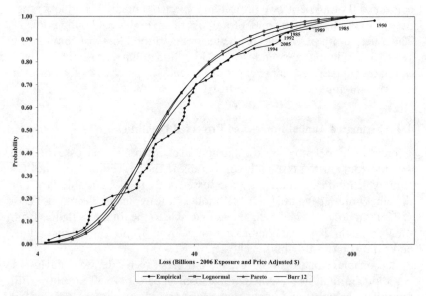

Fig. 4.9   All perils annual aggregate claims: Total loss

Note: The data used in this estimation were adjusted at the state level by our 2006 exposure index. This index captures both price-level changes and changes in the size of the housing stock. The intent is to estimate the losses a past disaster would cause if it occurred today.

Table 4.5 Expected loss and upper percentiles of PCS severity distributions (values in billions of dollars)

Catastrophe type	Loss type	Mean	Percentiles						Best fit
			50.0	75.0	90.0	95.0	99.0	99.9	
			Lognormal distribution						
Hurricane/tropical storm	Insured	9.0	1.0	4.0	14.4	31.1	131.0	657.8	Pareto
	Total	18.8	2.0	8.4	30.2	65.1	274.6	1,378.6	Pareto
Earthquake	Insured	0.9	0.1	0.5	1.7	3.4	13.3	60.6	LN
	Total	7.2	1.6	5.1	14.7	27.7	91.4	347.6	Burr 12
Wind and thunderstorm	Insured	0.4	0.2	0.4	1.0	1.6	3.9	10.7	Pareto[b]
	Total	0.6	0.2	0.6	1.3	2.1	5.2	14.5	Pareto[b]
Winter storm	Insured	1.3	0.4	1.1	2.8	5.0	14.1	45.5	Pareto[b]
	Total	2.3	0.7	2.0	5.1	8.9	25.4	81.9	Pareto[b]
			Pareto distribution						
Hurricane/tropical storm	Insured	54.0[a]	0.7	3.2	17.1	57.6	942.0	50,970.4	Pareto
	Total	113.2[a]	1.6	6.8	35.9	120.8	1,974.9	106,855.5	Pareto
Earthquake	Insured	2.5[a]	0.1	0.4	1.8	5.3	64.3	2,285.4	LN
	Total	10.0[a]	1.2	4.2	16.4	43.1	383.8	8,599.3	Burr 12
Wind and thunderstorm	Insured	0.5	0.2	0.4	1.0	1.6	4.7	19.4	Pareto[b]
	Total	0.6	0.2	0.6	1.3	2.2	6.4	26.1	Pareto[b]
Winter storm	Insured	4.1	0.4	1.1	3.0	6.0	27.1	221.0	Pareto[b]
	Total	7.3	0.7	1.9	5.4	10.8	48.7	397.5	Pareto[b]
			Burr 12 distribution						
Hurricane/tropical storm	Insured	510.9[a]	0.6	2.9	21.4	97.4	3,277.2	501,031.6	Pareto
	Total	1,070.9[a]	1.2	6.0	44.9	204.2	6,869.9	1,050,296.8	Pareto
Earthquake	Insured	25.7[a]	0.1	0.3	2.2	8.9	233.4	24,973.2	LN
	Total	11.6	1.6	5.5	16.1	31.5	126.6	789.7	Burr 12
Wind and thunderstorm	Insured	1.2	0.2	0.4	0.9	1.7	7.5	60.7	Pareto[b]
	Total	1.6	0.2	0.5	1.2	2.3	10.1	81.6	Pareto[b]
Winter storm	Insured	2.2[a]	0.3	0.9	3.2	8.4	76.6	1,823.4	Pareto[b]
	Total	3.8[a]	0.6	1.6	5.8	15.0	137.8	3,279.4	Pareto[b]

Note: LN = lognormal.

[a]Indicates true means do not exist due to skewness of distribution; these are simulated means computed as the mean from 0 to the 99.9 percentile + loss(0.999) • 0.001.

[b]Indicates the distribution provides a significantly better fit than the other distributions based on an approximate chi-square likelihood ratio test.

Table 4.6   Expected loss and upper percentiles of aggregate annual claims distributions (values in billions of dollars)

			Percentiles					
Catastrophe type	Loss type	Mean	50.0	75.0	90.0	95.0	99.0	99.9
		Lognormal						
Hurricane	Insured	12.5	2.0	9.3	29.6	56.7	175.8	391.5
	Total	22.2	4.3	19.2	58.8	108.1	275.2	409.4
Earthquake	Insured	0.2	0.0	0.0	0.1	0.7	4.5	26.7
	Total	1.8	0.0	0.0	2.5	7.4	36.1	165.6
Wind and thunderstorm	Insured	8.4	7.4	10.2	13.7	16.4	24.0	41.1
	Total	11.4	10.0	13.8	18.5	22.2	32.4	55.4
Winter storm	Insured	2.8	1.1	3.1	6.7	10.5	24.7	67.8
	Total	5.1	2.0	5.6	12.2	19.0	44.4	120.6
All perils	Insured	23.6	14.4	23.7	43.9	70.0	180.6	355.8
	Total	39.4	23.5	41.7	81.7	128.4	271.8	388.4
		Pareto						
Hurricane	Insured	16.7	1.5	7.7	34.1	84.4	324.3	409.4
	Total	24.5	3.1	15.1	60.9	134.4	383.7	409.4
Earthquake	Insured	0.8	0.0	0.0	0.1	0.5	8.1	246.1
	Total	3.0	0.0	0.0	1.9	6.5	60.2	409.4
Wind and thunderstorm	Insured	9.5	7.6	10.9	15.7	20.3	39.1	117.6
	Total	12.8	10.3	14.7	21.2	27.4	52.5	152.4
Winter storm	Insured	4.2	1.0	3.1	7.8	14.4	54.5	249.0
	Total	7.0	1.9	5.6	14.0	25.6	91.5	316.9
All perils	Insured	28.3	14.4	25.4	55.5	101.7	268.6	390.1
	Total	42.2	22.8	42.3	92.3	155.4	315.2	397.9
		Burr 12						
Hurricane	Insured	18.9	1.1	6.9	38.4	104.1	388.9	409.4
	Total	25.8	2.4	13.2	64.4	152.8	409.4	409.4
Earthquake	Insured	1.5	0.0	0.0	0.0	0.5	15.1	409.4
	Total	2.2	0.0	0.0	2.7	8.0	41.6	254.2
Wind and thunderstorm	Insured	13.0	7.8	12.5	22.2	34.9	104.7	306.1
	Total	17.0	10.5	16.9	29.8	46.4	132.2	330.5
Winter storm	Insured	6.5	0.8	2.9	9.8	23.1	125.9	395.8
	Total	9.7	1.6	5.2	17.2	38.8	176.4	409.4
All perils	Insured	34.5	15.3	31.5	78.5	142.1	309.7	397.3
	Total	47.8	24.1	49.6	114.4	187.1	337.1	401.1

Thus, our analysis suggests an expected annual federal exposure in the neighborhood of 10 to 25 billion dollars, with the exposure in a bad year (once in a century) in the neighborhood of 80 billion to about 170 billion dollars.[30] These figures have two significant aspects. First, even the low end of our

30. These ranges are rounded figures computed by multiplying the lower bound of our estimates of expected annual catastrophe losses by the lower bound of observed federal aid ratios, 30 percent, and the higher bound of our estimates by the higher bound of observed federal aid ratios, 50 percent.

expected estimate is substantially higher than current regular appropriations. Second, the projections are accurate enough to be used for determining the size of regular appropriations. As Holtz-Eakins (2005, pp. 18–19) states, "Many analysts believe that current federal budget procedures can lead to inappropriate evaluations of the trade-offs involved in providing assistance and can reduce incentives for mitigation and recovery efforts by state and local governments." He continues that one option, instead of relying so heavily on emergency supplemental appropriations, is to "appropriate money for disaster programs in regular appropriations bills in amounts equal to the expected funding need for each program" (Holtz-Eakins 2005, p. 19). One way of realizing this would be to simply require that the midpoint of our estimate range be budgeted in advance for disaster relief. Then, going forward, projections can be updated fairly easily each year to encompass improvements in catastrophe modeling, revised assumptions about disaster frequency and severity, or changes in expected relief generosity. By aligning policymaker incentives and allowing proper comparison of competing spending priorities, implementing such a system would reduce the substantial future costs of disaster relief.[31]

Assuming our current system of disaster relief is left unreformed, we can compute the net present value of the liability to the Federal Government of disaster spending over a given time horizon (for purposes of comparison with the unfunded liability associated with other social programs). We take the midpoint of our estimate of expected annual spending, $17.5 billion. We assume growth in exposure equal to the long-term trend (1950 to 2006) annual growth rate in the value of the US housing stock index, 9 percent. Currently, about $2 billion is set aside for disaster aid each year, and we assume this grows with nominal gross domestic product (GDP) based on the same 1950 to 2006 span, which is 7.1 percent. Using a 5 percent discount rate, the net present value of the liability over a seventy-five-year horizon is $7.1 trillion. If we assume everything grows at the 5 percent discount rate, the NPV is $1.2 trillion. Over this same horizon, the trustees of Social Security project a shortfall with a NPV of $4.9 trillion.[32]

4.5   Concluding Remarks

The tremendous growth in federal disaster spending observed over the twentieth century has continued in more recent years. The $82 billion in

31. Of course, challenges arise when shifting to explicit recognition of expected disaster relief in the budget. In particular, bureaucratic motivations to overspend on particular disasters would have to be addressed. On the other hand, it is debatable whether an official budgetary acknowledgment of this entitlement, based on current levels of generosity, would encourage or restrain further growth in generosity.

32. "The present value of future tax income minus cost, plus starting trust fund assets, minus the present value of the ending target trust fund amounts to −$4.9 trillion for the OASDI program" (see SSA [2006, p. 57]). Available at: http://www.ssa.gov/OACT/TR/TR06/.

emergency federal spending on Katrina and other proximate hurricanes in 2005 exceeded the fiscal year (FY) 2005 budget of all but five government agencies, as well as the total amount appropriated for the much-maligned Congressional earmarks.[33] Our analysis shows that the expected annual expenditure on disaster assistance—an estimated 10 to 25 billion dollars—is quite significant and could be even higher if more aggressive assumptions that put a greater weight on recent trends are used. While this estimate is obviously not precise, different assumptions or methods seem unlikely to alter the basic inferences about the significance of the annual cost.

The cost is indeed significant: given the current approach to disaster relief funding, we project an "unfunded" liability for disaster assistance over the next seventy-five years comparable to that of Social Security. The current annual budget of FEMA falls far short of expected annual federal disaster assistance, most of which is financed through supplemental appropriations on an "as needed" basis. Over the period from FY1989 to FY2006, FEMA's Disaster Relief Fund received original appropriations for less than $15 billion while experiencing outlays of over $58 billion (Bea 2006).

This budgetary treatment may not be unusual, but the lack of transparency with respect to acknowledging the commitment and accounting for its size is unfortunate in at least two respects. First, the costs and benefits of the disaster assistance program currently cannot be weighed against other national priorities. Second, federal disaster policy itself cannot be optimized without understanding the commitment and the dollars involved. For example, if a scaling back of the federal disaster assistance program is not politically realistic, federal subsidization of state and local mitigation expenditures may be in the taxpayers' interest—at least in the short run. Our projections make explicitly incorporating expected relief spending in the regular budgeting process a real possibility. Doing so would force the informed decision making that will optimize relief, although such incorporation would have to be combined with careful consideration of spending authority and bureaucratic incentives to insure that spending is ultimately restrained.

In designing disaster relief policy, there are many important considerations that we do not attempt to analyze. Notably, many have observed that disaster assistance embodies a "samaritan's dilemma" in the sense of its presence encouraging development in high-risk areas. Implicit in our approach is the notion that prior to probing the deeper implications of the economic incentives embedded in disaster relief policy, it makes sense to

---

33. The agencies were Health and Human Services (HHS; Medicare), Social Security, Defense, Treasury (debt interest), and Agriculture (Winters 2006). The FY2005 earmarks totaled approximately $50 billion (CRS Appropriations Team 2006).

first ask how extensive it is. Thus, we have attempted to measure and document the financial extent of current policy, with the belief that reform and management must be informed by measurement.

We document that disaster assistance is a large and continuous liability to the Federal Government, which increases with the value of infrastructure exposed to catastrophes. Though we are accustomed to think of catastrophes as unpredictable, our analysis demonstrates that it is possible to forecast expected future costs for disaster assistance. Knowing the magnitude of these figures can inform both the budgeting process and, ultimately, the design of disaster relief policy.

References

Bea, K. 2006. Federal Stafford Act disaster assistance: Presidential declarations, eligible activities, and funding. Congressional Research Service (CRS) Report for Congress, Order Code RL33053. Washington, DC: CRS.

Bram, J., J. Orr, and C. Rapaport. 2002. Measuring the effects of the September 11 attack on New York City. *Federal Reserve Bank of New York Economic Policy Review* 8 (2): 5–20.

Chite, R. M. 2006. Emergency funding for agriculture: A brief history of supplemental appropriations, FY1989–FY2006. CRS Report for Congress, Order Code RL31095. Washington, DC: CRS.

Clark, K. M. 2004. Catastrophe modeling: Assessing and managing risk. In *Reinsurance: Fundamentals and new challenges,* 4th ed., ed. R. Gastel. New York: Insurance Information Institute.

Congressional Research Service (CRS) Appropriations Team. 2006. Earmarks in appropriation acts: FY1994, FY1996, FY1998, FY2000, FY2002, FY2004, FY2005. Congressional Research Service Memorandum. Washington, DC: CRS.

Cummins, J. D. 2006. Should the government provide insurance for catastrophes? *Federal Reserve Bank of St. Louis Review* 88 (4): 337–79.

Cummins, J. D., G. Dionne, M. Pritchett, and J. B. McDonald. 1990. Applications of the GB2 family of probability distributions in collective risk theory. *Insurance: Mathematics and economics* 9 (4): 257–72.

Cummins, J. D., C. M. Lewis, and R. D. Phillips. 1999. Pricing excess-of-loss reinsurance contracts against catastrophic loss. In *The financing of catastrophe risk,* ed. K. A. Froot, 93–149. Chicago: University of Chicago Press.

Dunham, W. B. Jr., and J. Dembeck. 2008. U.S. Terrorism Risk Insurance Act extended for seven years. *Real Estate Finance* 24:19–20.

Federal Crop Insurance Corporation. 2007. *Summary of business report for 2004 through 2007.* Available at: http://www.rma.usda.gov/data/sob.html.

Federal Emergency Management Agency (FEMA). 2006. *Watermark: National Flood Insurance Program* 2006 (2). Washington, DC: FEMA.

Hartwig, R. 2008. Financial crisis: Private and public sector impacts. Presentation to the Southeastern Regulators Association Conference. 20 October, Orlando, Florida.

Holtz-Eakins, D. 2005. Macroeconomic and budgetary effects of Hurricanes Katrina and Rita. Congressional Budget Office (CBO) Testimony before the Committee on the Budget, US House of Representatives. Washington, DC: CBO.

Jenkins, W. O. Jr. 2006. Federal Emergency Management Agency: Challenges facing the National Flood Insurance Program. Testimony before the Chairman, Committee on Banking, Housing and Urban Affairs, US Senate, GAO-06-174T. Washington, DC: US General Accounting Office.

Klugman, S. A., H. H. Panjer, and G. E. Willmot. 2004. *Loss models: From data to decisions.* 2nd ed. New York: Wiley-Interscience.

Kunreuther, H., and L. Miller. 1985. Insurance versus disaster relief: An analysis of interactive modelling for disaster policy planning. *Public Administration Review* 45 (special iss.): 147–54.

Lott, N., and T. Ross. 2006. Tracking and evaluating U.S. billion dollar weather disasters, 1980–2005. Paper presented at the 86th annual meeting of the American Meteorological Society. 29 January–2 February, Atlanta, Georgia.

Meszaros, J., and M. Fiegener. 2002. *Effects of the 2001 Nisqually earthquake on small businesses in Washington state.* Washington, DC: US Department of Commerce, Economic Development Administration.

Moss, D. A. 1999. Courting disaster? The transformation of federal disaster policy since 1803. In *The financing of catastrophe risk,* ed. K. A. Froot, 307–63. Chicago: University of Chicago Press.

———. 2002. *When all else fails: Government as the ultimate risk manager.* Cambridge, MA: Harvard University Press.

Munich Re. 2005. *Megacities-megarisks: Trends and challenges for insurance and risk management.* Munich, Germany: Munich Re.

———. 2008. *Topics geo: Natural catastrophes 2007—Analyses, assessments, positions.* Munich, Germany: Munich Re. Available at: http://www.munichre.com/en/publications/default.aspx.

———. 2009. *Topics geo: Natural catastrophes 2008—Analyses, assessments, positions.* Munich, Germany: Munich Re. Available at: http://www.munichre.com/en/publications/default.aspx.

Murray, J. 2006. Emergency supplemental appropriations legislation for disaster assistance: Summary data FY1989 to FY2006. CRS Report for Congress, Order Code RL33226. Washington, DC: CRS.

Murray, J., and B. R. Lindsay. 2008. Emergency supplemental appropriations legislation for disaster assistance: Summary data, updated October 31, 2008. CRS Report for Congress, Order Code RL33226. Washington, DC: CRS.

Property Claims Services (PCS). 2006. *Catastrophe loss estimate procedure description.* Jersey City, NJ: Insurance Services Office.

United States Department of Homeland Security (DHS). 2006a. *Hurricane Katrina: What government is doing.* Washington, DC: DHS.

———. 2006b. *Quick reference guide for the National Response Plan, version 4.0.* Washington, DC: DHS.

United States Government Accountability Office (GAO). 2007. Budget issues: FEMA needs adequate data, plans, and systems to manage resources for day-to-day operations. Report no. 07-139. Washington, DC: GAO.

United States Social Security Administration (SSA). 2006. *2006 Annual Report of the Board of Trustees of the Federal Old-Age and Survivors Insurance and Disability Insurance Trust Funds.* Washington, DC: SSA.

Winters, P. D. 2006. Federal spending by agency and budget function, FY2001–FY2005. CRS Report for Congress, Order Code RL33228. Washington, DC: CRS.

Comment   Greg Niehaus

Introduction

This chapter focuses on an important measurement issue: what is the Federal Government's exposure to catastrophes? In addressing this issue, the authors define "exposure" in two ways, both of which are commonly used by risk managers. One measure of exposure is the expected annual cost. The other measure of exposure captures the cost that might be experienced in a particularly bad year. More precisely, the second measure is the cost level that will be exceeded with a low probability—say, 1 percent—or equivalently, it is the ninety-ninth percentile value of the cost distribution. Given a probability distribution for annual catastrophe costs, calculating the expected annual cost and a specific percentile value is straightforward. The difficult task is estimating the probability distribution for annual catastrophe costs.

Before discussing the empirical methods used in the chapter, it is appropriate to step back and identify why it is important to measure the Federal Government's exposure to catastrophes. Certainly from a budgeting and planning perspective, it is important to estimate both the expected costs and the magnitude of the potential costs. In addition, measuring exposure is the first step in analyzing a number of important economic and public policy issues related to the impact of government disaster assistance, including the impact of this assistance on (a) the incentives to purchase private insurance, (b) the distribution of wealth, and (c) real estate development in catastrophe-prone areas. Thus, this chapter provides an important, initial step in a more comprehensive analysis of public policy related to catastrophes.

In the next section, I summarize and comment on the methodology and the main results of the chapter. In the final section, I briefly discuss some of the implications and possible extensions of the analysis.

The Probability Distribution for Catastrophe-Related Costs?

The Federal Government incurs costs related to natural and man-made catastrophes, and the authors consider costs from both of these categories. The chapter does a nice job of identifying the many different programs that are exposed to catastrophes, including the Federal Emergency Management Agency (FEMA) disaster relief programs, subsidized loans to households and businesses affected by catastrophes, aid to farmers through the US Department of Agriculture, the National Flood Insurance

Greg Niehaus is professor of finance at the Moore School of Business, University of South Carolina.

Program (NFIP), the Terrorist Risk Insurance Program (TRIP), and damage to government property. However, the focus of the chapter is on the largest exposure—disaster assistance. As a result, the estimates understate the actual exposure of the Federal Government.

The procedure for estimating the probability distribution for disaster assistance has three steps. First, the ratio of disaster assistance to catastrophe losses is estimated using historical data from 1989 to 2006: (disaster assistance) / (catastrophe losses). Second, the probability distribution for annual catastrophe losses is estimated: catastrophe loss distribution. Third, the ratio found in step one is combined with the probability distribution from step two to estimate the probability distribution for annual disaster assistance. Given this distribution, the authors calculate expected annual disaster assistance and various percentile values of the disaster assistance distribution.

Step One: Ratio of Disaster Assistance to Catastrophe Losses

The authors use a variety of approaches to estimate the ratio of disaster assistance to catastrophe losses. For the numerator, they either use emergency supplemental appropriations for disaster assistance and thus exclude all budgeted disaster costs, or they use total disaster spending. For the denominator, they use total damage estimates for catastrophe events that caused more than $1 billion in total damages. Most of the catastrophe events are weather related, but the data also include earthquakes and terrorist attacks.

The ratio of disaster assistance to catastrophe losses is calculated using nominal losses and losses that have been adjusted to 2006 prices. In addition, the ratio is calculated in aggregate, by event, and by year. These various approaches yield a ratio of disaster assistance to catastrophe losses that ranges from about 32 percent to 50 percent (see table 4.1).

An interesting result presented in table 4.1 is the ratio of disaster assistance to uninsured losses. The estimates for this ratio range from about 57 percent to 95 percent. Using the maximum value, this implies that 95 percent of losses that are not covered by private insurance are insured for free through disaster assistance. The upper part of this range certainly indicates a coverage ratio that exceeds the coverage ratio commonly available in the private market, in large part because private insurers understand the moral hazard associated with high coverage ratios. Disaster assistance at this level is likely to have an important moral hazard effect on where people decide to locate and the amount of private insurance that they purchase.

Step Two: The Catastrophe Loss Distribution

The authors use two approaches for estimating the probability distribution for catastrophe losses. One approach is essentially a black box approach—they use an estimated distribution for insured losses from a major catastrophe modeling firm, Applied Insurance Research (AIR). Catastrophe models simulate the impact of natural disasters on property damage in specified geographical areas. These models incorporate information about the characteristics of property in terms of its use and construction and are widely used by insurers to assess their property damage exposure. The AIR model indicates that expected total catastrophe losses are in the range of 35 to 43 billion dollars and that the ninety-ninth percentile value is in the range of 273 to 282 billion dollars.

The second approach uses Property Claims Services (PCS) historical data on insured losses from catastrophes. Importantly, these data are adjusted to account for price changes and economic development that have occurred over time. This adjustment, which allows one to estimate the losses that would have occurred today from storms that occurred in the past, leads to several interesting observations:

- Hurricane Katrina in 2005 has the largest nominal loss of $44 billion.
- Adjusted losses from a 1950 wind and thunderstorm event that hit from Maryland to Maine equal $227 billion.
- Adjusted losses from Hurricanes Carol and Hazel in 1954 equal $257 billion.

Using the adjusted catastrophe loss data, the authors estimate the annual frequency and severity distribution for catastrophe losses and then compound these distributions to estimate the total loss distribution. The PCS data indicate that expected losses are in the range of 39 to 48 billion dollars and that the ninety-ninth percentile value is in the range of 272 to 337 billion dollars.

It is important to note that both approaches consider only natural catastrophes (and thus omit man-made catastrophes such as terrorist attacks) and thus understate the actual catastrophe exposure. Also, it is notable that the two approaches lead to similar overall exposure estimates.

Step Three: Federal Government's Exposure to Disaster Assistance

Multiplying the ratio of disaster assistance to catastrophe losses (step one) and the expected annual catastrophe losses (step two) yields an estimate of annual expected disaster assistance between 10 and 25 billion dollars and an estimate for the ninety-ninth percentile value of annual disaster assistance between 80 and 170 billion dollars.

Discussion

According to the authors, the Federal Government currently sets aside about $2 billion for disaster assistance. If one takes the midpoint of the annual expected disaster assistance ($17.5 billion) and subtracts the amount budgeted currently, we are left with the country's liability for disaster assistance—about $15.5 billion annually. Assuming that this liability grows at approximately the same rate as the discount rate over the next thirty-five years, the present value of the liability is over $500 billion. The conclusion is clear: taxpayers bear a significant liability for disaster assistance.

The magnitude of disaster assistance certainly leads one to suspect that there are potentially important moral hazard effects with respect to private insurance coverage and real estate development. Further research on these effects is important for the optimal design of federal disaster assistance policy. Another area of research would be on the distributional effects of disaster assistance. For example, it would be interesting to document the amount of disaster assistance received by people grouped according to income and wealth levels. There also are interesting political economy questions associated with disaster assistance: for example, is the cross-sectional variation in the ratio of disaster assistance to catastrophe loss related to the seniority and/or committee assignments of legislators?

As the authors point out, knowing the magnitude of liability is necessary information for policymakers to develop optimal disaster relief policy. The authors go one step further and suggest that the expected annual cost (between 10 and 25 billion dollars) should be part of the regular budgeting process. Note, however, that there is considerable variability associated with actual costs around the expected value; most years will have far lower costs and a few years will have far higher costs. The politics of government spending raise a concern that budgeting the expected annual cost will lead policy officials to spend the amount budgeted, even in years with relatively low actual catastrophe losses. Under the current regime, politicians must justify assistance beyond the low amount currently budgeted (about $2 billion) to fellow legislators. Granted, this may not be a significant hurdle, but budgeting more money without restricting special appropriations is likely to lead to even higher costs.

In summary, this chapter analyzes an important issue. The analysis is rigorous and carefully executed. Although the estimates of exposure depend on numerous assumptions, the authors justify these assumptions and in each case choose an approach that is likely to lead to a conservative estimate of the Federal Government's exposure to catastrophes. Moreover, the estimates are consistent across the different methods that are used, which lends greater credibility to the estimates. There are a number of interesting results. The main conclusion is that the Federal Government has a significant exposure to catastrophes through its disaster assistance programs. Now, we need additional research on the implications of the effects of this disaster assistance and on the optimal design of public policy for catastrophes.

Housing Policy, Mortgage Policy, and the Federal Housing Administration

Dwight M. Jaffee and John M. Quigley

5.1 Introduction

Federal policy affecting housing is dominated by indirect and off-budget activities directed toward homeowners—tax expenditure policies and federal credit, insurance, and guarantee programs—rather than the direct provision of housing or the payment of housing allowances to deserving renter households. The implicit goal of increasing homeownership was articulated by the secretary of the Department of Housing and Urban Development (HUD) in 2005, and the federal objective of "an ownership society" has been made quite explicit.[1] Since 2005, however, there has been a sea change in the mortgage and credit markets; millions of homeowners, particularly lower-income and first-time homeowners, have been affected. During the fourth quarter of 2008, almost one in ten mortgages in the United States was "in trouble." Delinquencies (i.e., home loans with payments at least thirty days overdue) were 7.9 percent of all outstanding mortgages, and 3.3 percent

Dwight M. Jaffee is the Willis Booth Professor of Banking, Finance, and Real Estate at the University of California, Berkeley. John M. Quigley is the I. Donald Terner Distinguished Professor and professor of economics at the University of California, Berkeley.

Copyright © 2008, by The Regents of the University of California. Reprinted from the *California Management Review,* vol. 51, no. 1. By permission of The Regents.

This chapter was originally presented at the NBER conference on Measuring and Managing Financial Risk, Evanston, Illinois, February 2007. A previous and less complete version of this paper, with a somewhat different emphasis, was also distributed as Jaffee and Quigley (2008). In the light of subsequent events, the chapter has been revised extensively, but we have sought to retain as much of the original material as possible. We are grateful for the comments of Deborah Lucas and Susan Wachter and for the research assistance of Claudia Sitgraves.

1. See, for example, "Statement of the Honorable Alphonso Jackson, Secretary, U.S. Department of Housing and Urban Development," before the United States House of Representatives Committee on Financial Services, April 13, 2005.

of all home mortgages were in foreclosure. (See the National Delinquency Survey of the Mortgage Bankers Association, March 2009.)

This chapter provides a review of the indirect and off-budget activities supporting housing and homeownership, with special emphasis on the mortgage insurance and guarantee programs undertaken by the Federal Housing Administration (FHA). We begin with a brief review of housing subsidy programs, concentrating on the activities of off-budget agencies such as the Federal National Mortgage Association (Fannie Mae), the Federal Home Loan Mortgage Corporation (Freddie Mac), as well as the Veterans Administration (VA) and the FHA. We review the history and operations of these organizations, and we highlight current issues about these institutions and their role in the broader economy. We then concentrate on changes in the role and influence of the FHA, and we consider an expanded role for FHA in a reorganized housing system. We suggest explicit FHA policies designed to protect potential home buyers better from unscrupulous "predatory" lenders, and we suggest that incentives would be improved if many of the activities undertaken by the government sponsored enterprises (GSEs) were assumed by the FHA. This changed emphasis would give a new leadership role to the federal agency that pioneered the long-term self-amortizing mortgage more than a half-century ago.

5.2   Federal Housing Programs: Direct Expenditures

As previously noted, federal housing policy is dominated by off-budget programs supporting homeownership and providing subsidies for middle- and upper-income homeowners and home purchasers. In contrast, direct federal expenditures for housing programs, those that require Congressional appropriations for housing in the annual budget, are concentrated on programs for lower-income households and mostly for rental households.

Direct federal expenditures on housing began with the Public Housing Act of 1937, a federally financed construction program that sought the "elimination of substandard and other inadequate housing." Dwellings built under the program are financed by the Federal Government but are owned and operated by local housing authorities. Importantly, the rental terms for public housing specified by the Federal Government ensure occupancy by low-income households, currently at rents no greater than 30 percent of their incomes.

This program of government construction of dwellings reserved for occupancy by low-income households was supplemented in the 1960s by a variety of programs inviting the participation of limited-dividend and nonprofit corporations. Section 8 of the Housing and Community Development Act of 1974 further increased the participation of private for-profit entities in the provision of housing for the poor. The act provided for federal funds for the "new construction or substantial rehabilitation" of dwellings for occupancy by low-income households. The Federal Government entered into long-term contracts with for-profit housing developers, guaranteeing a stream of payments of "fair market rents" (FMRs) for the dwellings. Low-income households paid 25 (now 30) percent of their incomes on rent, and the difference between tenant payments and the contractual rate was made up by direct federal payments to the owners of the properties.

Crucial modifications to housing assistance policy were introduced in the Section 8 housing program. The restriction that subsidies be paid only to owners of new or rehabilitated dwellings was weakened and ultimately removed, and payments were permitted to landlords on behalf of a specific tenant (rather than by a long-term contract with the landlord). This tenant-based assistance program grew into the more flexible voucher program introduced in 1987. Households in possession of vouchers receive the difference between the "fair market rent" in a locality (that is, the HUD-estimated median rent) and 30 percent of their incomes. Households in possession of a voucher may choose to pay more than the fair market rent for any particular dwelling—up to 40 percent of their incomes—making up the difference themselves. They may also pocket the difference if they can rent a HUD-approved dwelling for less than the FMR.

In 1998, legislation made vouchers and certificates "portable," thereby increasing household choice and facilitating movement among regions in response to employment opportunities. Local authorities were also permitted to vary their payment standards from 90 to 110 percent of the FMR. The 1998 legislation renamed the program the Housing Choice Voucher Program; it currently serves about 1.9 million low-income households.

In addition to these programs providing rental assistance, direct appropriations through the HUD also support a few small programs encouraging homeownership: for example, down payment assistance and sweat-equity grants.

Direct appropriations under all these programs amounted to $40.1 billion in 2009; since 1990, these low-income housing programs have grown hardly at all—by only about 0.5 percent per year in real terms.

5.3   Tax Expenditures

5.3.1   The Federal Tax Code

The most widely distributed and notoriously expensive subsidy to housing is administered by the US Internal Revenue Service (IRS). Under the tax code, investments in owner-occupied housing have always been treated differently from other investments. If taxpayers invest in other assets (such as equity shares), dividends accruing under the investment are taxed as ordinary income, and profits realized on the sale of the asset are taxed as capital gains. At the same time, the costs of acquiring or maintaining the investment are deductible as ordinary business expenses in computing a taxpayer's net tax liability under the Internal Revenue Code.

In contrast, if a taxpayer makes an equivalent investment in owner-occupied housing, the annual dividend (i.e., the value of housing services consumed in any year) is exempt from taxation. In addition, the first $0.5 million (for married taxpayers) of capital gains realized on the sale is exempt from taxation. Two important components of investment costs, mortgage interest payments (up to $1.0 million for married taxpayers) and local property taxes, are considered to be deductible personal expenses. In contrast, depreciation, maintenance, and repair expenses are not deductible.

These benefits have been in effect since the enactment of the Internal Revenue Code. The budgetary costs of the program (i.e., the foregone income tax revenues resulting from these special provisions) are sensitive to monetary policy and tax policy. When interest rates increase, the value of the deduction for interest payments increases. If federal or local tax rates are reduced, the value of the homeowner deduction declines.

The federal tax code also provides two other forms of housing subsidy, both directed to renters rather than homeowners: housing tax credits and tax-exempt bonds.

The Low-Income Housing Tax Credit (LIHTC) Program provides direct subsidies for the construction or acquisition of new or substantially rehabilitated rental housing for occupancy by low-income households. The LIHTC Program permits states to issue federal tax credits that can be used by developers or property owners to offset taxes on other income or that can be sold to outside investors to raise initial development funds for a project. Rents for these dwellings are limited to 30 percent of tenant income, and qualification requires that these units be set aside for occupancy by low-income households for a period of thirty years.

Federal tax credit authority is transmitted to each state, on a per capita basis, for its subsequent distribution to the developers of qualified projects. The credits are provided annually for ten years, so a "dollar" of tax credit authority issued today has a present value of six to eight dollars.

In addition, states have always been permitted to issue debt, and the interest payments made by states (and their local governments) on this debt have been exempt from federal taxation. The Tax Reform Act of 1986 for the first time placed a limit on the volume of bonds that could be issued by states for private purposes. "Private purposes" include the financing of most tax-exempt facilities (e.g., airports), industrial development agencies, student loans, and housing (multifamily construction and homeowner subsidies). The allocation of private-purpose bond authority among these activities is supervised by each state, and the priorities among states may vary substantially.

The subsidy provided by tax-exempt bonds—the net difference between the market interest rate and the rate for tax-exempt paper—varies with changes in federal tax rates and with macroeconomic policy. When interest rates are low and the spread between taxable and tax-exempt interest rates is small, state and local governments may choose not to issue tax-exempt bonds, since the costs of issue (underwriting, bond counsel, etc.) are relatively high.

As indicated previously, the magnitude of tax expenditures for owner-occupied housing is dominated by the large and open-ended subsidies provided to those homeowners who itemize their deductions or who sell their residences in any year. Jaffee and Quigley (2007) provide a discussion of the method applied by the Office of Management and Budget for computing tax expenditures. To understand the method, it is useful first to consider the income taxation of commercial real estate as a baseline, since it receives no important or special tax expenditures. The accrued tax liability for an investment in commercial real estate is the sum of the taxes accrued on the net rental income (NR) generated in any year and the tax on the annual capital gain (CG). At a common tax rate on income and gains, t,

(1) $t(NR + CG) = t(GR - MI - PT - DRM + CG)$,

where the components of net rental income include the gross rents (GR) minus expenses for mortgage interest paid (MI), property taxes paid (PT), and expenditures for depreciation, repairs, and maintenance (DRM).

In contrast, for owner-occupied residential housing, gross rental income (GR) is not taxable, and capital gains (CG) are essentially untaxed. But depreciation, repairs, and maintenance (DRM) are not deductible. This special treatment creates a "tax expenditure" for owner-occupied residential housing of $t(NR + MI + PT + CG)$. From equation (1), it is apparent that

(2) $t(GR - DRM + CG) = t(NR + MI + PT + CG)$.

This means that the tax expenditure for residential housing can equally well be computed as the tax benefit arising from permitting net rental income and capital gains to avoid taxation while allowing the deductibility of mortgage interest and property tax payments. (See Quigley [1998] for a discussion.)

For 2007, it is estimated that the exclusion of capital gains on housing from federal taxation cost the Federal Treasury $34.7 billion in foregone revenue. (US Office of Management and Budget 2008.) This is almost as much as *all* direct Congressional appropriations for low-income housing programs. The deduction for homeowners' mortgage payments represents an additional $100.8 billion in tax expenditures. The property tax exclusion cost an additional $16.6 billion, and the exclusion of imputed net rental income represented another $7.6 billion in foregone tax revenues. In contrast, the Low-Income Housing Tax Credit represented only $5.8 billion in foregone revenues. The issuance of tax-exempt bonds cost about $1.9 billion in federal revenue. Overall, federal tax expenditures for homeowners in 2007 were $182.7 billion, or about five times the tax expenditures for all other housing programs. (See Jaffee and Quigley [2007] for a detailed discussion.)

5.3.2   Mortgage Credit

Federal support for housing credit began in the aftermath of the great depression, with the establishment of the Federal Home Loan Bank (FHLB) System in 1932. FHLBs were chartered by Congress to provide short-term loans to retail mortgage institutions to help stabilize mortgage lending in local credit markets. Interest rates on these advances were determined by the low rates at which this government agency, the FHLB board, could borrow in the credit market. In 1938, the Federal National Mortgage Association (FNMA) was established as a government corporation to facilitate a secondary market for mortgages issued under the newly established FHA mortgage program (described next). The willingness of the FNMA to buy these mortgages encouraged private lenders to make FHA, and later VA, loans.

In 1968, the association was reconstituted as a government sponsored enterprise, Fannie Mae. The change allowed Fannie Mae's financial activity to be excluded from the federal budget. Its existing portfolio of government-insured mortgages was transferred to a wholly owned government corporation, the newly established Ginnie Mae. In contrast, ownership shares in Fannie Mae were sold and publicly traded. Fannie Mae continued the practice of issuing debt to buy and hold mortgages but focused its operations on the purchase of conventional mortgages neither guaranteed nor insured by the Federal Government. Freddie Mac was chartered as a GSE two years later in 1970, but its shares were not publicly traded until 1989. Originally, Freddie Mac chose not to hold purchased mortgages in its portfolio. Instead, mortgages were pooled, and interests in those pools—mortgage-backed securities (MBS)—were sold to investors with the default risk guaranteed by Freddie Mac.

These mortgages, subject to specific balance limits and underwriting guidelines—referred to as "conforming conventional" mortgages—are securitized by Freddie Mac and Fannie Mae. Until the fall of 2008, these MBS were guaranteed against default risk by the GSEs themselves. (They are now guaranteed by the Federal Government.) The two mortgage GSEs, Fannie Mae and Freddie Mac, operate under Congressionally conferred charters, which provide both benefits and obligations. Their federal charters oblige the GSEs to support the secondary market for residential mortgages, to assist mortgage funding for low- and moderate-income families, and to consider the geographic distribution of mortgage funding, including mortgage finance for underserved parts of urban areas. Their foremost benefit is an implicit US government guarantee of their debt and MBS obligations. This guarantee was reinforced when the two GSEs were placed in a conservatorship in September 2008, an event we return to later.

The GSEs carry out this mission through two distinct business lines: (a) they create and guarantee mortgage-backed securities, and (b) they purchase and hold whole mortgages and MBS in their on-balance-sheet retained-mortgage portfolios. The GSEs claim that both business lines are required to meet their charter responsibilities to support the secondary mortgage market and to unify the geographic distribution of mortgage funding. Economists have been quick to point out, however, that the unhedged interest rate risk embedded in the retained-mortgage portfolios creates a large contingent liability for the US Treasury and a systemic risk for US capital markets. Since the GSEs issue MBS, it also seems clear that the retained-mortgage portfolios are not essential for the agencies to carry out their charter obligations.

It is certainly clear that large public subsidies are provided to the GSEs. The more important public subsidy to the GSEs arises from the government's guarantee of all their debt and all their MBS obligations. Other financial institutions would surely be willing to pay a significant fee to receive a comparable guarantee from the Federal Government. This special treatment of the GSEs arose in part because the Federal Government considered the GSEs to be "too big to fail." Alternatively, the Federal Government viewed the securities issued by these organizations as safe and sound—if not, the government would not have exempted the GSEs from the protective regulations governing other similarly situated private entities. Thus, despite an explicit statement in every prospectus disavowing a federal guarantee, the GSEs enjoy lower financing costs than those of similarly situated private firms.[2]

The GSE debt obligations are classified as "agency securities" and have historically been issued at interest yields somewhere between AAA corporate debt and US Treasury obligations. This is despite the fact that even before their losses on subprime mortgages, the firms themselves merited a somewhat lower credit rating.[3] An estimate of the cost of this implicit federal subsidy for the debt issued by the GSEs can be derived from the spread between the interest rates paid by the GSEs for the debt they issue and the rates paid by comparable private institutions. This comparison, in turn, depends on the credit ratings, maturities, and other features of the bonds issued, as well as market interest rates and credit conditions. Quigley (2006) provides a detailed review of estimates of this spread that have been reported in different studies using different methodologies. On the basis of this kind of evidence, the Congressional Budget Office (CBO 2001) has concluded that the overall funding advantage enjoyed by the GSEs is about 41 basis points.

2. This benefit can be measured either in terms of the subsidized cost of GSE borrowing or in terms of the expected costs that would be imposed on the government if it had to make restitution to GSE bondholders and MBS investors.

3. The Congressional Budget Office estimates that without GSE status, the housing enterprises would have credit ratings between AA and A. See CBO (2001).

The implicit federal guarantee provides an analogous advantage to GSE-issued MBS compared with MBS guaranteed by other private entities. The market requires a greater capital backing for a private guarantee than for a guarantee made by Fannie Mae or Freddie Mac, and the provision of this additional capital reserve is costly to private firms. The CBO (2004) has also estimated that the advantage enjoyed by the GSEs is about 30 basis points. These subsidies could, in principle, either be passed through to mortgage borrowers in the form of lower mortgage rates or be retained as profits by the GSEs. If an equivalent subsidy were provided to a competitive industry, it could be presumed that most, if not all, of the subsidy would be passed through to final consumers. There is evidence, however, that Fannie Mae and Freddie exercise considerable market power (see Hermalin and Jaffee [1996]). However, even duopolists have incentives to pass forward part of a subsidy, and there is evidence that a part—perhaps about half—of this subsidy is passed through by Fannie and Freddie to mortgage borrowers.[4] The residual fraction of this benefit is retained by the shareholders of the GSEs. This residual arises from the competitive advantage of the GSEs over other financial institutions, which is conferred by their federal charters.

As noted, estimates of the reduction in mortgage interest rates attributable to this subsidy have some range—around, say, 40 basis points (see Quigley [2006] table 3). If the conforming limit for GSE loans were set low enough, more of the benefits of this interest rate reduction would accrue to moderate-income households. But the limit has been set generously by the Federal Housing Finance Board. In 2009, conforming mortgages could be issued for an 80 percent loan on a property selling for $625,500 ($938,250 in Alaska and Hawaii).

Even before being placed in a conservatorship, it was difficult to provide a precise dollar estimate of subsidy provided by federal taxpayers to the GSEs. An up-to-date summary of existing studies is available in chapter 6 in this volume by Lucas and McDonald. Based on the accumulating costs of the GSE conservatorships, it now seems likely that the ultimate cost will be measured in the hundreds of billions of dollars.

5.4   The FHA and VA Insurance and Guarantee Programs

5.4.1   The Great Depression Origins

Before the Depression of the 1930s, home mortgage instruments were typically of short terms (three to ten years) with loan-to-value (LTV) ratios

---

4. Differing estimates of the reduction in mortgage rates created by the subsidy has resulted in a quite contentious literature. Perhaps the lowest estimate, 7 basis points, is provided by Federal Reserve economists in Passmore, Sherlund, and Burgess (2005). A much higher estimate is provided by Blinder, Flannery, and Kamihachi (2004) in a study funded and published by Fannie Mae.

of 60 percent or less. Mortgages were nonamortizing, requiring a balloon payment at the expiration of the term. The onset of the Great Depression engendered a liquidity crisis beginning in 1930, precluding renewal of many outstanding contracts. Other borrowers were simply unable to make regular payments. The liquidity crisis affecting new mortgage loans, together with elevated default rates on existing loans, had catastrophic effects on housing suppliers as well as housing consumers.

Despite voluntary forbearance on the part of some lending institutions and mandated forbearance enacted by many state legislatures, the system of mortgage lending that existed in the early 1930s continued to contract, and many lending institutions simply failed. The establishment of the Home Owners' Loan Corporation in 1933 within the Federal Home Loan Bank System (established a year earlier) provided stop-gap refinancing for a million mortgages. Passage of the National Housing Act of 1934 established the structure of home mortgage insurance and facilitated the growth of the modern system of mortgage finance in the United States.

The 1934 act established the Federal Housing Administration to oversee a program of home mortgage insurance against default. Insurance was funded by the proceeds of a fixed premium charged on unpaid loan balances. These revenues were deposited in Treasury securities and managed as a mutual insurance fund. Significantly, default insurance was offered on "economically sound" self-amortizing mortgages with terms as long as twenty years and with LTV ratios up to 80 percent.

Diffusion of this product across the country required national standardization of underwriting procedures. Appraisals were required, and borrowers' credit histories and financial capacities were reported and evaluated systematically. The modern standardized mortgage was born.[5]

The Mutual Mortgage Insurance Fund, which was established to manage the reserve of annual premiums, was required to be actuarially sound. This was generally understood to involve very small redistributions from high-income to low-income FHA mortgagees. (See, for example, Aaron [1972].) By its original design, the FHA was clearly intended to serve the vast majority of homeowners. Initial loan amounts were restricted to be no larger than $16,000 at a time when the median house price was $5,304.[6]

Near the end of World War II, it was widely feared that the peacetime economy would return the housing market to its Depression-era performance. Indeed, housing starts in 1944 were at about the same level as they had been a decade earlier. The VA loan program, passed as a part of the GI Bill in 1944, rapidly evolved from a temporary "readjustment" program to a long-range housing program available to veterans for a decade or more after

---

5. See Green and Wachter (2005) for an extensive discussion of this history.
6. The FHA ceiling was reduced to $6,000 in 1938, but that level was still above the price of the median house at the time, $5,804.

returning to civilian life. This transformation contributed to the boom in the residential construction industry that began in the late 1940s. Ultimately, a liberal program of veterans' home loans was established in 1950 and subsequently extended. In contrast to the insurance provided by the FHA, the VA provided a federal guarantee for up to 60 percent of the face value of a mortgage loan made to an eligible veteran, subject to a legislated maximum. The VA program facilitated loans by private lenders on favorable terms with no down payments at moderate interest rates.

5.4.2   The FHA and VA Programs in the Postwar Housing Market

The two programs, FHA and VA, providing government insurance and mortgage guarantees, brought homeownership opportunities to middle-class American households in a short space of time. Figure 5.1 shows the remarkable growth of mortgage originations attributable to these programs.[7] In 1960, about $5 billion in FHA-insured mortgages and $2 billion in VA guaranteed mortgages were issued. The programs reached a peak volume in 2003, when the FHA insured about $165 billion and the VA guaranteed about $66 billion in mortgages. After 2003, the volumes of mortgage originations in both programs declined significantly, so by 2006, the FHA insured under $54 billion and the VA guaranteed under $25 billion in mortgages, a decline of two-thirds from their peak volumes recorded just three years earlier. However, in the aftermath of the subprime mortgage crisis, the combined mortgage originations of the two government programs rose to just short of $300 billion for the year 2008.

The fraction of total mortgage originations attributable to the FHA and VA also declined systematically over time until the collapse of mortgage markets in 2006. Figure 5.2 reports that the FHA mortgage origination share (based on dollar volume) declined from the peak share of about 25 percent in 1970 to under 2 percent in 2006. The VA guaranteed mortgage share has similarly declined from a peak share of almost 28 percent in 1947 to under 1 percent in 2006. However, in 2008, the share of the two government programs exceeded 20 percent of total mortgage originations, levels not seen for three decades.

The secular decline in the market share of the two programs and the precipitous volatility in both market shares and dollar volumes after 2003 raise serious policy issues for the future of the two programs. A reasoned policy response requires a sound understanding of the forces that contributed to

7. This figure and the subsequent discussion focus on the single-family insurance programs of the FHA and VA agencies. The original mission for the FHA also included multifamily housing, and starting in the 1960s, the FHA multifamily programs became significant in size and scale. Indeed, the multifamily program became quite notorious for allegations of waste, fraud, and corruption; see Vandell (1995) and Quigley (2006). However, multifamily loans never exceeded 15 percent of the total FHA portfolio, and today they are less than 10 percent. In this chapter, we consider only the single-family program.

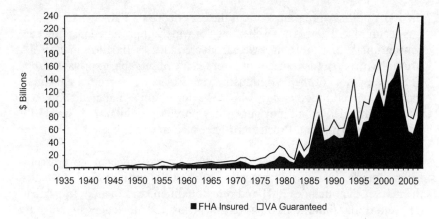

Fig. 5.1   Dollar volume of FHA and VA mortgage originations, 1935 to 2008
Source: Historical Statistics of the United States, Office of Federal Housing Enterprise Oversight (OFHEO), and Inside Mortgage Finance

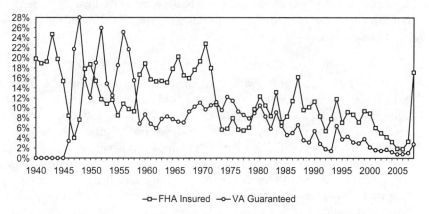

Fig. 5.2   FHA and VA mortgage originations, share of total originations, 1939 to 2008

the secular declines and the recent volatility. We first analyze the long-term factors and then the more recent contributors.

5.4.3   The Declining FHA and VA Market Shares: Long-Term Causes

The long-run decline in FHA and VA originations has arisen from two primary factors, both relating to the development of the private mortgage insurance (PMI) industry. A significant PMI industry was first developed in the United States during the housing boom of the 1920s. These insurance firms became insolvent in the early years of the Great Depression, and there were allegations of fraud and mismanagement as well. The creation of a viable PMI industry began in the late 1950s, aided by the evident success of the FHA and VA programs.[8] Until the experience of FHA/VA mortgages was accumulated, it was not well known or widely appreciated just how safe conventional home mortgages were from credit losses. Balances in the FHA Mutual Mortgage Insurance Fund were easily observable to private actors. The development of the PMI industry was also abetted by the expansion of Fannie Mae and Freddie Mac, whose charters require that credit enhancement be provided on all mortgages they purchase or guarantee with LTV ratios above 80 percent. Private mortgage insurance has been the dominant form of this credit enhancement.

Secondly, the rules governing FHA and VA coverage affect the government-insured market share as a proportion of the total insured market (that is, the market that includes PMI and other credit enhancements). In particular, fixed-dollar limitations on government-insured mortgages significantly reduced the ability of the FHA and the VA programs to serve middle- and upper-middle-income households. Figure 5.3 reports the volume of FHA and VA insured mortgages as a fraction of all insured mortgages. As the figure shows, the FHA/VA mortgage share declined quite steadily through 2006 but then rose dramatically in 2008 at the onset of the subprime mortgage crisis.

5.4.4   The Recent Collapse in FHA and VA Program Activity

Although the FHA program was initially developed to support a large part of the mortgage market, for the past quarter-century, its focus has been on lower-income borrowers. Indeed, the Housing and Community Development Act of 1981 explicitly established specific targets for serving low-income borrowers. The availability of low down payment FHA mortgages and FHA mortgages for those with a less-than-perfect credit rating has meant that the FHA's market share of originations has been larger for those traditionally disadvantaged in the homeownership market. As a result, the overwhelming fraction of FHA borrowers have obtained mortgages with LTV ratios of 95 to 98 percent or more, including a large number of borrowers with "nontraditional" credit histories or with imperfect credit records. The academic literature has documented these specific attributes of the FHA clientele. For example, Ambrose and Pennington-Cross (2000) found that FHA market shares are higher in cities with higher economic risk characteristics, while Ambrose, Pennington-Cross, and Yezer (2002) found that as local economic conditions deteriorate, conventional lenders tend to withdraw mortgage finance, in effect making the government programs the only source of credit.

Data released under the Home Mortgage Disclosure Act (HMDA) include measures of the income and race of borrowers, as well as the census tracts

---

8. In 1957, the Mortgage Guaranty Insurance Corporation (MGIC) became the first private mortgage guarantee firm established since the Great Depression.

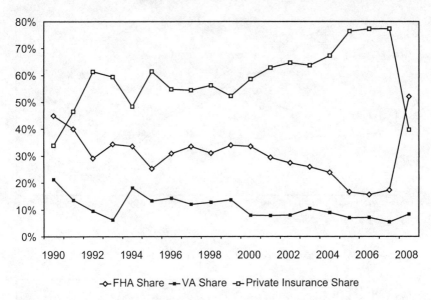

Fig. 5.3   **Insured mortgage originations by share of total insured originations**

in which they reside. By comparing government-insured and uninsured mortgage originations, it is possible to gauge how well the FHA succeeds in serving a lower-income clientele.[9] Figure 5.4 presents estimates of the government-insured share of total mortgage originations separately by race. In 1997, market shares for black, Hispanic, and white borrowers were 46, 48, and 20 percent, respectively. By 2005 and 2006, the combined FHA + VA market share for each borrower group had fallen precipitously to between 5 and 10 percent. The data for 2007, the most recent data available, show a distinct recovery for the government programs, especially among black borrowers. This no doubt reflects the recent disruption in conventional subprime mortgage markets. It can be assumed that the detailed 2008 HMDA data will show an even more dramatic recovery in the market share of the government programs.

Figure 5.5 reports the combined FHA + VA market share by the income of the census tract in which the borrower resides. In 1997, the government programs had a 16 percent share of mortgages made in upper-income neighborhoods and close to a 35 percent share of originations in low- and moderate-income neighborhoods. By 2005 and 2006, the FHA + VA share for all neighborhood categories had declined precipitously and converged to values of about 5 percent. More recent data indicate some recovery in

9. Quigley (2006) analyzed the same data for the period just before the sharp decline of the last three years. The GAO (2007a), published after the first version of this chapter had been circulated, also reports some of these data, but only during the 1996 to 2005 period.

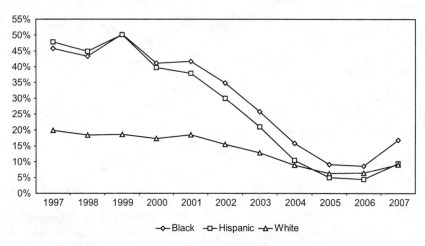

Fig. 5.4   FHA + VA share of origination by borrower race, 1997 to 2007

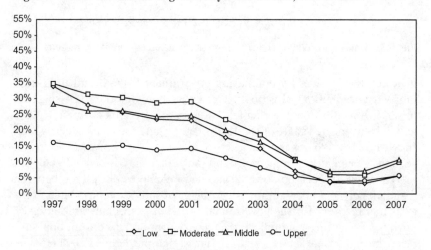

Fig. 5.5   FHA + VA market share by census tract income, 1997 to 2006

the government program share, especially for moderate- and middle-income borrowers.

Figure 5.6 reports analogous FHA + VA market share information by the fraction of minorities living in the census tract of origination. By 2005 and 2006, all these market shares had fallen rapidly to shares of about 5 percent. The data for 2007, in contrast, show a recovery close to a 10 percent market share for the government programs across all census tracts.

In summary, figures 5.4 to 5.6 indicate that however borrower characteristics are categorized, the government-insured share had simply collapsed to a few percent by 2005 and 2006 before recovering somewhat as the subprime mortgage crisis unfolded in 2007. This reinforces the patterns noted previ-

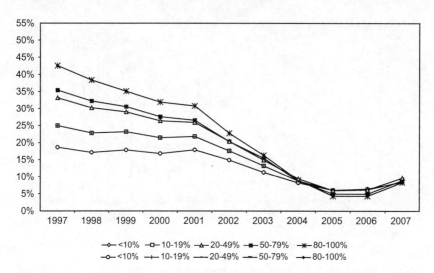

Fig. 5.6   FHA+VA share of originations by census tract percent minority population, 1997 to 2007

ously in figures 5.1 to 5.3, with FHA and VA shares falling precipitously through 2006, then rising steadily through 2007 and 2008.[10]

We now consider the factors responsible for this precipitous decline in FHA and VA originations from 2003 through 2006. We identify four specific factors: subprime lending, predatory lending, GSE competition, and the failure of the FHA to innovate its mortgage contracts. We discuss each in turn.

Subprime Lending

Figure 5.7 shows the dramatic inroads that conventional subprime lending made as a share of total home mortgage originations.[11] As recently as 2002, subprime lending represented only 7 percent of total mortgage originations, but its market share peaked at more than 21 percent by 2006. This 14 percentage point increase in market share coincides with the precipitous decline in FHA and VA lending. Correlation, of course, need not imply causation. But the subprime lenders and the government-insured lending programs share a very similar clientele—focusing on borrowers with lower credit scores, offering lower down payments, and so on. So, it

10. The aggregate data use the HUD's estimates of total mortgage originations and FHA and VA mortgage originations based on information reported by the agencies. The HMDA data, in contrast, are based on a sample of large, for-profit, and metropolitan lenders who are required to report their loan applications and loans awarded. The higher FHA+VA market share in the HMDA data arises if the surveyed lenders have a higher share of government-insured mortgages than the universe of all lenders.

11. See Murphy (2007) for a useful primer on subprime mortgages.

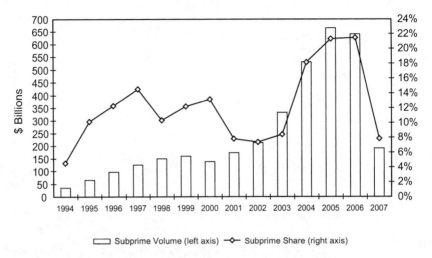

Fig. 5.7   **Subprime lending and total mortgage originations**

seems highly plausible that the expansion of the subprime loan market is the source of most of the decline in the market share of the FHA and VA programs.

The great financial distress of some subprime borrowers has been reflected in rising foreclosure rates on these mortgages. Figure 5.8 compares the foreclosure rates on FHA, VA, and conventional mortgages in recent years, based on data from the Mortgage Bankers' Association (MBA). Prior to 1998, the annual default rates for the available categories never reached as high as 2 percent. In contrast, the foreclosure rates on subprime loans, with data starting in 1998, are almost an order of magnitude higher, exceeding 9 percent annually in 2001 and approaching 14 percent of year-end 2008. In recent years, the FHA foreclosure rate has remained moderately high, above 2 percent, while the VA foreclosure rate has remained above 1 percent. The foreclosure rate on prime conventional loans, stable for many years, is approaching 2.0 percent by year-end 2008.

The growth of the subprime loan market was certainly one source of the recent decline in the FHA and VA market shares. But this raises the deeper question of why the subprime market expanded so suddenly. What skills or techniques were subprime lenders able to adopt—quite suddenly, it appears, in about 2000—that were not evident earlier? This is a key question for the government-insured programs, since it may identify the missing skill or technique that could allow them to regain a reasonable share of the lower-income mortgage market on a sustained basis. Given the relatively short history of the subprime market and the uncertainty over how (or whether) it will survive its current crisis, answers are necessarily speculative. Nevertheless, three factors appear to be crucial:

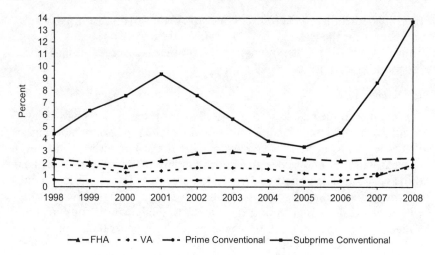

Fig. 5.8   **Foreclosure rate, year-end inventory**

1. *Technology.* Access to large bodies of information concerning current borrowers and past loan outcomes has been combined with computing power and statistical methods to extract useful information concerning likely default rates and loan costs, especially for lower-quality borrowers.

2. *Contract innovation.* The subprime mortgage markets created new "alternative" mortgage contracts (including interest-only, optional-payment, and incomplete-document loans).[12] They have also expanded the use of traditional formats (such as adjustable-rate and negative-amortization mortgages) as alternatives to the standard, fixed-rate, long-term mortgages offered by FHA and VA.

3. *Securitization.* Many of the lenders utilizing this new technology and sponsoring innovative contracts have a limited capacity to hold mortgages, so it has been essential they have access to the new and efficient techniques of mortgage-backed and asset-backed securitization for selling newly originated loans in the secondary market.

Although these factors that created the subprime mortgage boom and crisis are reasonably clear (see, for example, Quigley [2008]), it is very unclear how the mortgage market will be restructured in the aftermath of the crisis. The FHA and VA markets clearly received renewed demand during 2007 and 2008 as the subprime market crashed. In the longer run, however, the market for alternative mortgages does rest on some sensible fundamentals—technology, contract design, and securitization—so it is an interesting ques-

12. See Piskorski and Tchistyi (2007) for a discussion of the new alternative mortgages based on the concepts of security design.

tion of whether that market will continue to operate in some form as a viable competitor for the FHA and VA government insurance programs. We will return to this issue when discussing the future of government insurance programs in section 5.5.

Predatory Lending

Headlines in the business press as well as the popular press have drawn attention to predatory lending practices as well as subprime mortgages. Predatory loans generally refer to loans that the borrower would have rejected with full knowledge and understanding of their terms as well as those of available alternatives. In practice, predatory loans rely on a range of practices including deception, fraud, and manipulation that create loans with terms that are highly disadvantageous to the borrower, thus creating a high likelihood of default (to which the lender is generally immune; see Government Accountability Office [GAO] 2004 and Morgan [2007]).[13] The two key features of predatory loans are as follows: first, the borrower would not have agreed to the loan had he or she understood the terms and conditions; and second, the lender or investor earns an acceptable return, even if the borrower defaults. These features contrast with other conventional or alternative loans in which the borrower benefits from the loan and in which the lender (or loan investor) suffers a loss if the borrower defaults.

In July 2008, the Federal Reserve issued important additions to the Truth in Lending Act (TILA), and the HUD has prepared parallel changes in the rules implementing the Real Estate Settlement Procedures Act. The key component of the TILA reform is a suitability requirement that requires lenders on subprime mortgages (after October 1, 2009) to verify that the borrower is capable of making mortgage payments at the highest level the mortgage contract can require. There are also restrictions on "teaser rates," low- or no-documentation loans, and prepayment penalties.[14] In addition, subprime mortgages now require certified house value appraisals. Had those requirements been in effect earlier, predatory lending would have been reduced, and quite possibly, the subprime mortgage crisis would have been less severe.

Another useful regulatory approach would focus on disclosures and incentives that can mitigate the informational asymmetry under which inexperienced borrowers are unaware of more beneficial alternative contracts for which they may also qualify. For example, mortgage brokers often receive their full commission soon after a loan is closed. If the loan subsequently

13. Specific devices include loan flipping (repeated refinancing with excessive prepayment penalties), unexpected balloon payments, and mandatory arbitration.
14. In the original 2007 version of this chapter, we emphasized the importance of a suitability requirement to eliminate future predatory lending, as well as prohibitions against teaser rates and low-documentation loans and limitations on prepayment penalties.

defaults, there is no recourse to the broker for the commission already paid. Mortgage brokers thus have some incentive to recommend loans to borrowers, even when they suspect that the default probability is high. An incentive-compatible reform would impose a delay on the payment of origination fees and commissions to mortgage brokers, at least until the borrower creates a credible record of on-time payments. More generally, it would seem that the best way to mitigate asymmetric information is to create a standardized, nonpredatory, alternative loan and to require that all lenders making loans to lower-income borrowers disclose the availability of this loan. As noted next, this could be an important function of an expanded FHA.

The Government Sponsored Enterprises Go "Down Market"

The expansion of the GSE mortgage portfolios into riskier mortgages is a third important factor that reduced the market share of the FHA and VA government insurance programs. The GSE expansion was partly profit motivated, since the GSEs required new markets if they were to expand beyond their traditional domain of prime-conforming mortgages. But it was also regulatory based, since the GSEs faced "affordable housing goals," which required that they allocate specified shares of their lending activity to various classes of lower-income borrowers. (See Weicher [2006] and Jaffee and Quigley [2007] for detailed discussions of the goals.)

The academic literature has confirmed the "down-market" expansion of the GSEs and has found it to have a measurable impact on the traditional domain of the government-insured programs. An and Bostic (2008) presented quantitative evidence that the GSEs are increasingly targeting borrowers who would otherwise represent the higher-quality segment of FHA borrowers. Using HMDA data, they confirmed the fact that as the GSE share of originations in an underserved neighborhood expands, the FHA share declines. Their theoretical model also predicts that in response to GSE competition, the FHA will raise its underwriting standards in order to control what is now a lower-quality loan pool, on average. Most recently, An et al. (2007) have investigated the relationship between the GSE affordable housing goals and the FHA clientele. Using a sample of FHA loans, they confirmed the decline in the quality of the FHA borrowing pool. They also found that FHA borrowers exercise their refinancing options less aggressively, consistent with other studies of lower-income borrowers and those with lower credit ratings.

Analyses of the "overlap" in clientele also help measure the possible substitution between GSE and FHA loans. The HUD has commissioned several studies of this overlap, including a thorough analysis by Abt Associates (HUD 2005). The Abt analysts used microdata on borrowers and their loans to estimate two statistical models: one predicting the choice of an FHA loan and the other predicting borrower choice of a GSE loan. If the 95 percent confidence interval for an individual loan did not include a probability of 0.0

or 1.0 for either the FHA or the GSE category, then the loan was characterized as an "overlap." Based on data from 1998 to 2000, HUD (2005) found
that 10 to 14 percent of the loans made by FHA fell in the "overlap" region.
This result is consistent with the academic studies documenting substitution
between the FHA and GSE loans. The quantitative estimate does indicate
that no more than 14 percent of the FHA clients would also qualify for GSE
loans. However, the HUD analysis was based on data from 1998 to 2000. As
the GSEs have lowered their underwriting standards since then, the degree
of overlap has greatly expanded.

Failures in Contract Innovation and in Underwriting at the FHA

The previous sections indicate how subprime, predatory, and GSE
lenders have greatly reduced the market share of FHA and VA loans in
recent years. It is natural to ask why the government programs have not
responded with innovative contracts and underwriting methods of their
own in order to protect their market share. Indeed, historically, the FHA
was responsible for crucial innovations in the US mortgage market: the
fixed-payment, long-term, fully amortizing mortgage in the 1930s and the
first mortgage-backed securitization program—Ginnie Mae—in the 1970s.
In recent years, however, the FHA has shown a distinct disinclination to
innovate.

In particular, the FHA has offered no response to the new alternative
mortgages created as part of the subprime market. At least in principle, the
FHA could have created better-designed mortgages that would have mitigated or even averted the major losses. One major handicap is the FHA's out-
dated credit scoring model, which suggests that the FHA cannot adequately
judge the quality of borrowers or loans, nor can it implement risk-based
pricing by charging higher insurance fees on demonstrably riskier mortgages
(see GAO [2006a]). Given that most of the recent mortgage innovations
have involved somewhat riskier contracts, it is essential that these risks be
reflected in the insurance premiums (unless a subsidy to riskier borrowers
is an explicit policy). To be sure, the FHA requires Congressional approval
before it can carry out these and related innovations. Mobilizing Congress
to act is a time-consuming friction at the least, one that surely inhibits the
innovative process (see Weicher [2006]).

There is also a sense that the failure of the FHA to innovate reflects to
some degree the agency's philosophy. This is suggested in the report commissioned by the HUD in 1995, at a time when the FHA was facing an earlier
crisis concerning its future. A major part of that report argues that the FHA
clientele is "unique," with no significant overlap with either private mortgage insurance or the GSEs. The report dismisses what were the early signs
that the conventional mortgage market was making headway in meeting the
needs of underserved borrowers:

Only FHA allows for a combination of credit histories, cash balances, downpayments and payment ratios, which provide mortgage credit opportunities to families with past credit problems and broken income streams. Because of this, private market initiatives will grow as they attract new homeowners, but they will not significantly diminish the core business of FHA. (HUD 1995, 7–2)

A bit later, the report lists some "distinctive" FHA benefits: up to full financing of up-front loan closing costs and insurance premiums, lower down payment requirements on both home purchase and refinancing loans, higher allowances for seller-paid closing costs, and greater protections against foreclosure.

These FHA "benefits" are hardly distinctive, and they are certainly not unique.

The FHA has also resisted implementation of risk-based pricing for its insurance premiums. From its inception in 1934 through 1983, the FHA charged a flat annual insurance premium of 0.5 percent on the outstanding loan balance—very low by current standards. In 1983, the FHA switched to a 3.8 percent, one-time, up-front fee that was revenue neutral overall compared to the earlier system. As a result of worsening underwriting experience during the 1980s, the 1990 National Affordable Housing Act (NAHA) required an increase in the FHA premiums and for the first time imposed higher premiums on loans with higher LTV ratios. However, in practice, this component of risk-based pricing was quantitatively minor. The major consequence of changes mandated by the NAHA was that for the first time, FHA premiums became significantly higher than the PMI premiums a borrower would pay if he or she qualified for both insurance programs. Since rational borrowers who are eligible for both FHA and PMI loans would always choose the lower-cost PMI option, the FHA argues that at least in principle, there is no effective overlap between the FHA and PMI clientele.

In summary, it appears that two of the three forces that lead to the dramatic growth in subprime lending, technology and contract innovation, are missing—seemingly intentionally missing—from the current FHA strategic plan. Furthermore, even the third factor, securitization, for which the FHA was once the leader with its Ginnie Mae program, is at risk for the first time. The Ginnie Mae program will not able to maintain a liquid market for its mortgage-backed securities unless its supply of raw material—newly originated FHA and VA mortgages—were to expand.

5.4.5   FHA Single-Family Program Subsidies

The mortgage insurance fund for FHA's single-family housing insurance program has remained solvent continuously, and with the exception of a few brief intervals, the fund has remained actuarially sound as well. The

FHA has also reported under the budget accounting rules specified in the Federal Credit Reform Act of 1990 (FCRA) that the program provides a net surplus to the government; that is, the program is estimated to provide a *negative* subsidy to general taxpayers—as much as $1.5 billion during fiscal year 2003. This is an important factor, because the FHA is a "discretionary" program and otherwise would require an annual appropriation for any explicit subsidy costs.

The Congressional Budget Office, however, has challenged the FCRA method and contends that the Mutual Mortgage Insurance program actually requires a positive federal subsidy when the actuarial costs are computed appropriately (see CBO [2003] and [2006]). There are two main elements of contention. The first element is that the FCRA method excludes administrative expenses from the subsidy computation. Indeed, were administrative costs included, the FCRA method indicates that the FHA received a modest subsidy from federal taxpayers in fiscal year 2007.

The second element is that expected future losses from insurance activity are computed as a single average present value under the FCRA method. This ignores the dispersion of possible losses, including the likelihood that the greatest losses will occur when the economy is in a recession. The CBO contends that the covariation of potential realized losses and weak states of the overall economy requires that a "risk premium" be added to the computation. The CBO quantifies this risk premium as the difference between the insurance premiums charged by the private mortgage insurance industry and the premiums charged by the FHA on comparable mortgages. Using this benchmark, the CBO estimates that the FHA program actually received a taxpayer subsidy of about $2 billion for fiscal year 2007 (compared to the small surplus computed using the FCRA method).

The FHA disagrees with the principle behind the CBO's risk premium adjustment. In the FHA view, the federal guarantee that backs its insurance and the FHA's privilege to borrow from the US Treasury at risk-free interest rates are fundamental features of the program, which allow the FHA to operate with vastly lower capital ratios than its PMI competitors. The quid pro quo is that the FHA program serves a much riskier clientele. In the FHA view, an accurate actuarial computation of its expected losses relative to the premiums charged is the proper basis for determining the cost, if any, that the program imposes on the federal budget.

The proper computation of the program's subsidy is important if Congress is to make sensible appropriations for the FHA programs in comparison with all other discretionary government expenditures and also in the evaluation of alternative means for subsidizing housing (for example, in comparing HUD voucher programs and FHA mortgage insurance). A proper computation of the subsidy amount would also help to avoid unexpected and quite unpleasant budgetary surprises, which may occur when any insurance program suddenly suffers losses that exceed its revenues.[15]

5.5   Options for the FHA Single-Family Insurance Program

The large decline in the volume of FHA and VA mortgage originations between 2003 and 2006 raises fundamental questions about the future of the agencies. The plummeting share of FHA and VA in total originations led to suggestions that the agencies simply be closed. This action would have recognized the apparent success of private mortgage insurance in insuring risky mortgages. Thus, while the FHA programs may have increased homeownership historically among the eligible population,[16] the elimination of the FHA might simply induce private lenders to be more aggressive in supplying credit to this segment of the market. The crash of subprime lending since 2007 has, of course, provided new life to the FHA and VA programs. There remains, however, the long-term question of what the proper role will be for the government programs as a restructured mortgage market emerges in the aftermath of the subprime crisis.

5.5.1   An Expanded Role for the FHA with Alternative Mortgages and Risk-Based Pricing

One approach would allow the FHA to continue to function in its historical manner, but to require that it become much more aggressive in using technology to improve its underwriting policies for higher-risk borrowers, and to incorporate risk-based pricing in federal mortgage products. This would entail an expanded legislative mandate for the agency, increasing loan limits, eliminating statutory down-payment requirements, and encouraging risk-based pricing of mortgage products. These directions have been endorsed by the various interest groups that would benefit from more robust and liquid housing markets.[17] However, concerns have also been raised that the FHA will not have the expertise to manage a more creative underwriting program

15. As a case in point, Congress recently had to appropriate more than $20 billion to the Federal Flood Insurance (FFI) program to cover the unexpected losses created by Hurricane Katrina, an amount equal to the total insurance premiums, net of administrative expenses, collected since that program's inception in 1968; see Government Accounting Office (2006b). In other words, the premiums charged over the program's forty-year history actually represented more than a 50 percent subsidy. This subsidy had gone unrecognized, because the program had broken even on a cash flow basis over its entire history until the 2005 hurricane. But this represented only good luck; no previous flood had struck a major metropolitan center—hardly the basis for sensible actuarial budgeting.

16. See Quigley (2006) for a further discussion of the dramatic effect of the FHA program in expanding homeownership among its clientele households.

17. Some of these measures have been introduced into legislation (e.g., the "Expanding American Homeownership Act," H.R. 1752, and H.R. 5121) and have been debated in the House of Representatives but not in the Senate.

entailing more complicated and riskier loans, and that risk-based pricing will eliminate what some consider the current beneficial pattern of cross-subsidization of riskier borrowers by safer borrowers (See GAO [2007b] and Inside Mortgage Finance [2007a, 2007b]).

5.5.2 Demonstrable FHA Alternative to Predatory and Subprime Loans

An alternative approach, not inconsistent with the preceding proposal, is to expand the role of the FHA by focusing on its potential to mitigate predatory lending. As previously noted, the July 2008 Federal Reserve expansion of the Truth in Lending regulations is a major step forward. These regulations, if enforced, will no doubt reduce the extent of predatory lending, but it is equally clear that they would also reduce the incidence of alternative mortgages that are beneficial to borrowers and lenders.

Arguably, the operation of a "fully competitive" market could itself protect less informed market participants. However, the wide range of consumer protection legislation enacted in the United States suggests that policymakers are frequently not confident that competitive markets can be depended on to perform this role. Even within the financial markets, the US government has historically taken vigorous action to protect consumers. For example, in stock market trading, the SEC regulates brokers and mutual funds, requiring them to obtain "best execution" for their customers, even though, at least in principle, "perfect competition" would achieve the same end. Similarly, brokers are held to a "suitability" standard by the National Association of Securities Dealers (NASD) in mediating retail stock transactions. Government intervention in these ways no doubt reflects some paternalism, but as Sunstein and Thaler (2003) argue, financial decisions by consumers often reflect framing and other behavioral factors, with the result that an element of low-cost paternalism might be judged to be highly beneficial overall.

Consumer protection has also long been a rationale for housing and mortgage market legislation (see US Department of Treasury [2000]). For example, the Truth in Lending Act (Regulation Z of the Federal Reserve Act) has long specified very precisely how the terms of installment loans, including mortgage loans, must be disclosed to borrowers. For another example, the Real Estate Settlement Procedures Act (RESPA) regulates the behavior of the parties to a home purchase transaction and specifies in detail the disclosures required by lenders to borrowers. Finally, the Home Owner and Equity Protection Act (HOEPA) requires special disclosures concerning prepayment penalties, balloon payments, and negative amortization on certain refinancings and home equity loans.

These detailed regulations illustrate the fact that Congress has not been shy to take a paternalistic stance when it felt poorly informed borrowers were disadvantaged. It appears that the details of modern mortgage contracts are sufficiently technical and specialized that it is more efficient to regulate predatory lending with specific legislation.

An aggressive and innovative loan demonstration by the FHA can be an efficient and effective means to reverse the inroads that predatory lenders had achieved as a result of the inherently complex nature of the new mortgage contracts. Suppose, for example, legislation enabled the FHA to offer risk-based pricing and adjustable rate mortgages, and at the same time, the FHA was directed to develop new alternative mortgage contracts that would offer competitive terms to those currently eligible for FHA financing but who had previously been attracted to the private subprime market and at least in some instances by predatory lenders.

Disclosures concerning these new alternative FHA mortgages could be of potential value in deterring predatory lending to lower-income home purchasers. Comparable actions by government entities can be found in other markets. The student loan market provides some comparison, but the Direct Loan Program provided through the US Department of Education does not compete head-to-head with loans offered by banks and other private lenders.[18] A more appropriate example at the federal level is the United States Postal Service, which provides mailing services that compete with private suppliers such as Federal Express and the United Parcel Service. And at the state level, the Departments of Insurance in a number of states provide comprehensive information on the auto insurance and homeowner insurance options available to consumers based on the rate filings of their registered insurers.[19]

To apply this technique to the subprime mortgage market, the FHA would have to offer a borrower one or more alternative mortgages for consideration well in advance of a scheduled house closing. To allow the FHA to prepare these loan offers, information about borrower creditworthiness, assets, home appraisal, and so on would have to be transmitted to the FHA in advance of a contemplated mortgage transaction by any lender about to make a loan to a household eligible for FHA financing. The concept of requiring lenders to make unique disclosures prior to a loan is already a core component of the HOEPA. The FHA would be directed to use this information to produce one

18. The federal student loan programs operate in two forms. The Direct Loan programs use government funds, and the loans are originated and serviced by the US Department of Education. The Federal Family Education Loan (FFEL) programs use funds provided by a bank or other participating lender, but the loans are government guaranteed, and the key loan terms, including the interest rate, are identical to the Direct Loan programs. Both of these programs compete with fully private market loans that are available from banks and other lenders. Private market student loans, in turn, come in different versions, including those where the student is "certified" by his or her university versus loans that do not require such certification.

19. For example, in California, auto insurance premiums are regularly published by the state government. See http://interactive.web.insurance.ca.gov/survey/survey?type=autoSurvey &event=autoSearch. For Berkeley, California, for example, the highest rates reported for standard coverage are more than double the lowest rates.

or more specific loans for consideration by the contracting household. These terms would be transmitted to the household in a side-by-side comparison with those offered by the subprime lender. Mortgage contracts would not be enforceable unless the contracting household had explicitly declined the terms of an FHA mortgage in favor of a loan supplied in the private market. This requirement, together with the suitability rules described earlier, patterned after those of the NASD, could provide powerful deterrents to predatory lending.

These disclosure requirements would provide the borrower with an explicit alternative in the form of an available FHA loan, as well as the full set of information suggested by Congress:

> This new disclosure should include a table clearly displaying a full pay- ment schedule over the life of the loan, all fees associated with the loan, an explanation of the "alternative features" of the loan (i.e. negative amortization) and a full explanation of the risks associating with taking advantage of those features, including the timeframe in which borrow- ers were likely to feel the negative effects of those risks. (Joint Economic Committee 2007, p. 18)

Implementation would require FHA-eligible households to consider and reject the terms of competitive FHA mortgages before contracting for alternative mortgage finance in the private market. In making this decision, borrowers would have the full set of mortgage information, and they would have a specific alternative to consider. If, after consideration of the terms proffered, a household chose alternative mortgage finance, it would not be on the basis of incomplete information or the misrepresentation of alterna- tives. This is probably the best one can hope for in guiding the choices of others in a market economy.

5.5.3   Merging the GSE Activities into the FHA/Government National Mortgage Association (GNMA) Nexus

Finally, the breakdown in the mortgage markets following the subprime crisis might provide the opportunity to reposition the primary mortgage securitization business of the GSEs within a government entity. This activity could be operated inside the HUD as a middle-income mortgage guarantee business, parallel to the FHA and GNMA; see Jaffee (2009a, 2009b). Alternatively, this securitization activity could be operated as a new government-owned corporation, which could provide more flexibility. The exemplary history of the FHA provides a basis for believing that the business of guaranteeing and securitizing mortgages—in particular, relatively high- quality mortgages—could be efficiently carried out by a government entity, especially if it were afforded the flexibility inherent in a government-owned corporation. The key benefit, in the context of the subprime mortgage cri- sis, is that the new program would provide a strong government safety net against current and future systemic market failures. We should expect that major innovations in mortgage finance would arise and be carried out in the private mortgage markets. Thus, it would be critical that any new government programs not be subsidized so that they would not crowd out efficient private market initiatives.

References

Aaron, H. J. 1972. *Shelter and subsidies: Who benefits from Federal housing programs?* Washington, DC: Brookings Institution.

Ambrose, B., and A. Pennington-Cross. 2000. Local economic risk factors and the primary and secondary mortgage markets. *Regional Science and Urban Economics* 30 (6): 683–701.

Ambrose, B., A. Pennington-Cross, and A. Yezer. 2002. Credit rationing in the U.S. mortgage market: Evidence from variation in FHA market shares. *Journal of Urban Economics* 51 (2): 272–94.

An, X., and R. Bostic. 2008. GSE activity, FHA feedback, and implications for the efficacy of the affordable housing goals. *Journal of Real Estate Finance and Economics* 36 (2): 207–31.

An, X., R. W. Bostic, Y. Deng, and S. A. Gabriel. 2007. GSE loan purchases, the FHA, and housing outcomes in targeted, low-income neighborhoods. In *Brookings-Wharton Papers on Urban Affairs: 2007,* ed. G. Burtless and J. R. Pack, 205–40. Washington, DC: Brookings Institution.

Blinder, A., M. Flannery, and J. Kamihachi. 2004. The value of housing-related government sponsored enterprises: A review of a preliminary draft paper by Wayne Passmore. *Fannie Mae Papers* 3 (2).

Congressional Budget Office (CBO). 2001. *Federal subsidies and the housing GSEs.* Washington, DC: Government Printing Office (GPO).

———. 2003. *Subsidy estimate for FHA mortgage guarantee.* Washington, DC: GPO.

———. 2004. *Updated estimates of the subsidies to the housing GSEs.* Washington, DC: GPO.

———. 2006. *Assessing the government's costs for mortgage insurance provide by the Federal Housing Administration.* Washington, DC: GPO.

Green, R., and S. Wachter. 2005. The American mortgage in historical and international context. *Journal of Economic Perspectives* 119 (4): 93–114.

Hermalin, B., and D. Jaffee. 1996. The privatization of Fannie Mae and Freddie Mac: Implications for mortgage industry structure. In *Studies on privatizing Fannie Mae and Freddie Mac,* ed. US Department of Housing and Urban Development (HUD), 225–302. Washington, DC: HUD.

Inside Mortgage Finance. 2007a. MBA calls for cautious approach to FHA reform, even as new bills tout remedies to program's ills. April 6.

———. 2007b. Optimism remains high on FHA reform despite critical HUD IG, GAO Reports. March 23.

Jaffee, D. 2009a. Reforming Fannie and Freddie. *Regulation* 31 (4): 52–57.

———. 2009b. Monoline Regulations to Control the Systemic Risk Created by Investment Banks and GSEs. *The B.E. Journal of Economic Analysis & Policy* 9 (3), Symposium, article 17. Available at http://www.bepress.com/bejeap/vol9/iss3/art17.

Jaffee, D., and J. M. Quigley. 2007. Housing subsidies and homeowners: What role for government-sponsored enterprises? *Brookings-Wharton Papers on Urban Affairs: 2007,* ed. G. Burtless and J. R. Pack, 103–49. Washington, DC: Brookings Institution.

———. 2008. Mortgage guarantee programs and the subprime crisis. *California Management Review* 51 (1): 117–43.

———. 2009. The government sponsored enterprises: Recovering from a failed experiment. Berkeley Program on Housing and Urban Policy Working Paper no. W09-001.

Joint Economic Committee. 2007. Sheltering neighborhoods from the subprime foreclosure storm. Report of the US Congress Joint Economic Committee, April 11.

Morgan, D. P. 2007. Defining and detecting predatory lending. Federal Reserve Bank of New York Staff Report no. 273, January.

Murphy, E. 2007. Subprime mortgages: Primer on current lending and foreclosure issues. Congressional Research Service Report, Order Code RL33930. Washington, DC: CRS.

National Association of Realtors. 2007. Proposed statement on subprime lending. Submitted to the Controller of the Currency, May 7.

Passmore, W., S. M. Sherlund, and G. Burgess. 2005. The effect of housing government-sponsored enterprises on mortgage rates. *Real Estate Economics* 33 (3): 427–63.

Piskorski, T., and A. Tchistyi. 2007. Optimal mortgage design. Paper presented at the National Bureau of Economic Research (NBER) Real Estate conference. 25 July, Cambridge, Massachusetts.

Quigley, J. M. 1998. The taxation of owner-occupied housing. In *The encyclopedia of housing,* ed. W. van Vliet, 579–81. Thousand Oaks, CA: Sage Publications.

———. 2006. Federal credit and insurance programs: housing. *Federal Reserve Bank of St. Louis Review* 88 (4): 281–310.

———. 2008. Compensation and incentives in the mortgage business. *Economists' Voice* 5 (13): 1–3.

Sunstein, C., and R. Thaler. 2003. Libertarian paternalism is not an oxymoron. *University of Chicago Law Review* 70 (4): 1159–202.

United States Department of Housing and Urban Development (HUD). 1995. *An analysis of FHA's single-family insurance program.* Washington, DC: HUD.

———. 2005. *A study of market sector overlap and mortgage lending.* Washington, DC: HUD.

United States Department of the Treasury. 2000. Predatory lending. Report no. 3076. Available at: http://www.ustreas.gov/press/releases/report3076.htm.

United States Government Accountability Office (GAO). 2004. Consumer protection: Federal and state agencies face challenges in combating predatory lending. GAO-04-412T. Washington, DC: GAO.

———. 2006a. Alternative mortgage products. GAO-06-1021. Washington, DC: GAO.

———. 2006b. National Flood Insurance Program. GAO-07-169. Washington, DC: GAO.

———. 2007a. Federal Housing Administration: Decline in the agency's market share was associated with product and process development of other mortgage market participants. GAO-07-646. Washington, DC: GAO.

———. 2007b. Modernization proposals would have program and budget implications and require continued improvements in risk management. GAO-07-708. Washington, DC: GAO.

United States Office of Management and Budget. 2008. *Budget of the United States government, analytical perspectives, fiscal year 2009.* Washington, DC: GPO.

Vandell, K. D. 1995. FHA restructuring proposals: Alternatives and implications. *Housing Policy Debate* 6 (2): 299–393.
Weicher, J. 2006. Commentary. *Federal Reserve Bank of St. Louis Review* 88 (4): 311–22.

Comment   Susan M. Wachter

Authors Jaffee and Quigley focus their chapter on an analysis of federal programs that provide insurance and housing credit guarantees. After a description of a variety of federal government programs, including the federally-chartered government sponsored enterprises (GSEs) Fannie Mae and Freddie Mac, they concentrate specifically on the changes and challenges to the mortgage insurance and guarantee programs managed by the Federal Housing Administration (FHA). They offer specific, policy-oriented recommendations to bolster the FHA's declining market share.

After the Great Depression, the FHA pioneered the introduction of the thirty-year self-amortizing fixed rate mortgage, the standard mortgage that prevailed in the United States for decades. The FHA and Fannie Mae, and its predecessor the Home Owners' Loan Corporation (HOLC)—a federal entity—succeeded in reviving a mortgage market then in collapse due to the prevalence of "bullet" loans. After World War II, loans insured by the FHA lost market share to similarly structured nongovernment or "conventional" loans. The FHA's role evolved to serve lower income households who lacked the 10 percent down payment required by the conventional prime market. With the explosion (now implosion) of subprime over the past decade, FHA's market share decreased even further until 2008 when, in response to the collapse of subprime, FHA market share increased to its current 25 percent level. The ongoing subprime mortgage market crisis (similar to the Great Depression, centered on loans that require refinancing at a time when financial markets seize up) makes the role of the FHA newly relevant.[1]

A large segment of the Jaffee and Quigley chapter is devoted to a comprehensive and very useful description of all federal housing programs. The chapter sets out an historical and contextual analysis of the evolution of housing programs over time, pointing to the elimination of supply-side public housing in favor of demand-side housing vouchers. The chapter contrasts this—and other directly funded programs that have lost federal support—with the growth of programs indirectly funded through federal tax expenditures, including the homeowner deduction and the low income

Susan M. Wachter is the Richard B. Worley Professor of Financial Management and professor of real estate and finance at The Wharton School, University of Pennsylvania.
    1. For additional discussion on the FHA, see Green and Wachter (2007).

housing tax credit. Direct federal funding for all housing programs has declined significantly over time. Why is this so? What have we lost or gained? The authors do not take on these questions or the overarching question of what is the appropriate role of federal government in housing. Such a perspective might have helped as they transition into conclusions for the programs which they do delve into in more detail.

The major part of the chapter is focused on federal support for housing credit. After a description of the history of the GSEs, the authors take on the controversy of the source of GSE funding. They soundly come down in favor of funding with pass-through securities with limits on portfolio lending rather than through expanded portfolio lending. They point out that taxpayers bear contingent liability for the latter if the GSEs take on interest-rate risk. The Office of Federal Housing Enterprise Oversight (OFHEO) did in fact put retained mortgage portfolio limits in place, in part in response to the GSE's accounting difficulties; only to lift these as the mortgage market deteriorated in 2008.

The authors also take the position that the implicit subsidy received by the GSEs could be better "spent" from a distributional perspective if the GSEs were forced by lower conforming loan limits to lend to a lower income portion of the market. Recent legislation has lifted conforming loan limits.

In the aftermath of the subprime crisis, legislators have looked to the GSEs as well as to the FHA to expand their roles. The authors argue for an expanded role for the FHA and for a more limited role for the GSEs. It may be that now is the time to rely on the FHA and Ginnie Mae, which securitizes FHA mortgages. Nonetheless, it would have been useful for the authors to take this question on explicitly. These institutions and their markets are linked and both the FHA insured mortgages and the GSEs' "agency" mortgage-backed securities (MBS) market have secure funding sources, an important distinction, given the seizing up of the private sources of "private label" funding for subprime mortgages. Moreover, except for the discussion of interest rate risk, the authors do not directly take on the question of burgeoning mortgage default risk and how it relates to the growth of the subprime market and the private label mortgage-backed securities market and the market for MBS derivatives, Collateralized Debt Obligations (CDOs). Nonetheless, the authors are prescient in their implicit reliance on government guaranteed FHA rather than on the Fannie/Freddie model, since, through conservancy, they have become government guaranteed mortgage companies as well.

The authors' recommendations are timely because they offer their view of what long-term policy dealing with subprime should be. The essence of their recommendation is to expand the FHA's market share by reshaping the FHA to take on some aspects of the subprime market, in order to allow the FHA to compete with this market. To understand the impact of this policy suggestion, it is useful to point to the key differences in these two mortgage markets as currently designed.

Subprime mortgages are designed for borrowers with impaired credit records. Unlike FHA insured and GSE guaranteed mortgages, subprime mortgages "price" risk. On the other hand, for borrowers who meet the risk thresholds of the FHA and the GSEs, a more or less uniform mortgage rate is charged for accepted loans. That is, risk-based pricing is limited and lower risk borrowers cross-subsidize higher risk borrowers.

The authors attribute the decline in FHA loans to four factors: subprime lending, predatory lending, GSE competition, and the failure of the FHA to offer innovative mortgage products. The developments that they point to as helping conventional markets are advances in underwriting technology and growth in private mortgage securitization, in addition to GSE market share growth.

The simple explanation for the FHA decline in market share, however, is apparent in the graph shown in figure 5C.1: FHA market share declined as subprime market share grew (GAO 2007). Why subprime took market share away from the FHA is not directly addressed. Two obvious explanations are that subprime lending criteria were liberal to nonexistent and that short-run mortgage payments (before teaser rates adjusted) were lower and more "affordable."

The authors offer a normative policy analysis and a fundamental repurposing of the FHA. The new purpose in short is "to counter the growth of subprime and predatory lending associated with subprime." They suggest that an aggressive and innovative loan demonstration by the FHA can be an efficient means of redressing the extent of predatory lending, especially to lower income clientele.

To do so, they propose legislation that would enable the FHA to develop mortgage contracts that would offer competitive terms to those attracted to the subprime market, but also eligible for FHA funding. The authors mention the incorporation of innovative tools, including teaser rates, as well as risk-based pricing. In order to assist borrowers who are unaware of alternatives and therefore are subject to predatory pricing, the authors recommend that the FHA offer one or more alternative mortgages for consideration at least several days before a scheduled house closing; the terms of the mortgage would be transmitted to the borrower in a side-by-side format, which compares the FHA mortgage to the subprime mortgage being offered. Mortgage contracts would not be enforceable unless the borrower household explicitly rejected the FHA mortgage in favor of the private, subprime mortgage. The authors couple this policy approach with an additional recommendation that mortgage lenders be required to abide by a duty of suitability similar to the system upheld in the stock-broker industry. Together they believe these requirements would be a powerful deterrent to predatory lending. They argue that this approach could militate against informational

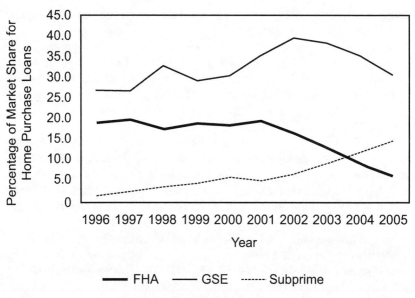

Fig. 5C.1   Market participants' share of home purchase mortgage market: 1996 to 2005

Source: Government Accountability Office (2007).

asymmetry, particularly for inexperienced borrowers who are unaware of alternative, more beneficial mortgage contracts for which they also qualify. The authors thus suggest that the best way to redress asymmetric information for the buyer is to create a standardized FHA loan comparable to subprime and require that this loan be disclosed by all lenders extending loans to lower income clientele.[2]

While of great value, such a recommendation raises questions, especially in light of the subprime crisis. If the FHA were really to compete would it have to offer the teaser rate adjustable-rate mortgages (ARMs) that have been at the center of the subprime crisis and arguably were a major source of the growth in subprime and loss of FHA market share? It may very well be that the growth of these loans, in particular, allowed subprime to outcompete the FHA, since these loans were affordable in a period of rising housing prices, when other loans were not.

Or let us assume that such loans are ruled out because they could not meet a standard of suitability.[3] Would the FHA's role be to match the subprime

2. The authors' suggestions are similar to those given in Barr, Sendhil, and Shafir (2008), where it is argued that borrowers should be presented with an "opt-out mortgage plan" to mitigate the problem of asymmetric information. Borrowers would receive a standard set of mortgages with easily understandable terms and strong underwriting. A borrower would then have to explicitly "opt-out" of the mortgage if they chose not to participate.

3. For a discussion on the relative benefits of suitability versus a standard, see Wachter (2003) and Engel and McCoy (2002).

market's pricing for allowable loans? But of course the subprime loans that were being made during the run-up to the mortgage crisis were not fully pricing risk. Subprime loans were higher risk without bearing sufficiently higher return to cover the risk.

If the FHA had gone this way, it would have required immediate taxpayer support and a bailout, undermining the current circumstances under which the FHA has been used as a platform to assist the struggling mortgage market and borrowers in distress. The history of financial markets suggests that episodes of mispricing and underpricing of risk are not avoidable. Markets appear to be backward-looking in terms of their assessment of risk. In good times risk is assumed to be low and after a crisis, risk is reevaluated and lending rates spike. The subprime lending industry appears to have followed this pattern. Going forward, should the FHA attempt to compete and follow market-pricing patterns? If it does not, then these parallel mortgages will be irrelevant, and once again the FHA will lose market share. If it does then the FHA too will be subject to mispricing, adding to market volatility.[4]

The ultimate questions are how much risk and volatility do we want in our mortgage finance system? Wall Street will price any risk and procyclically misprice risk, especially in the absence of price discovery mechanisms. The private label securitization system discouraged standardized, liquid MBS and CDOs that would have enabled short sellers to trade and to take the other side of bets that were wrongly made. Investors in these instruments took on great risk, which was not compensated by higher required returns. When they did so, they also exposed borrowers and the overall economy to increased house price volatility and risk. Such lending financed through MBS, even with diversified loan portfolios, is entirely exposed to systemic risk. Negatively amortizing and teaser rate mortgages that require refinancing to avoid certain default have risk that is correlated, engendering systemic risk similar to that created by the mortgages prevalent during the Great Depression. The procyclical easing of lending standards and underpricing of risk is an endemic problem, not likely to be corrected by the useful but limited solutions put forth here.

References

Abraham, J. M., A. Pavlov, and S. Wachter. 2008. Explaining the United States' uniquely bad housing market. *Wharton Real Estate Review* 12 (Fall).

Barr, M. S., S. Mullainathan, and E. Shafir. 2008. Behaviorally informed home mortgage credit regulation. UCC08-12. Harvard University, Joint Center for Housing Studies.

Engel, K., and P. McCoy. 2002. A tale of three markets: The law and economics of predatory lending. *Texas Law Review* 80 (6): 1255–382.

4. For discussion and evidence on why and how markets with nonrecourse lending tend to underprice risk, see the following references: Abraham, Pavlov, and Wachter (2008); Green et al. (2008); Green and Wachter (2007); Pavlov and Wachter (2008, 2006, and 2009); and Wachter (2003).

Green, R., R. Mariano, A. Pavlov, and S. Wachter. 2008. Misaligned incentives for mortgage lending in Asia. In *Financial sector development in the Pacific Rim,* ed. T. Ito and A. K. Rose, 95–117. Chicago: University of Chicago Press.

Green, R., and S. Wachter. 2007. The housing finance revolution. Paper presented at the Federal Reserve Bank of Kansas City symposium, Housing, Housing Finance, and Monetary Policy. 30 August–1 September, Jackson Hole, Wyoming.

Pavlov, A., and S. Wachter. 2006. The inevitability of marketwide underpricing of mortgage default risk. *Real Estate Economics* 34 (4): 479–96.

———. 2008. Subprime lending and house price volatility. University of Pennsylvania, Wharton School. Manuscript, April.

———. 2009. Mortgage put options and real estate markets. *Journal of Real Estate Finance and Economics* 38 (1): 89–103.

United States Government Accountability Office (GAO). 2007. Federal Housing Administration: Decline in the agency's market share was associated with product and process developments of other mortgage market participants. GAO-07-645. Washington, DC: GAO.

Wachter, S. 2003. Price revelation and efficient mortgage markets: Commentary. *Texas Law Review* 82 (2): 413–21.

6

Valuing Government Guarantees
Fannie and Freddie Revisited

Deborah Lucas and Robert McDonald

6.1 Introduction

The federal government explicitly guarantees a portion of deposit obligations of commercial banks and thrifts through deposit insurance, and is thought to provide protection beyond this legal obligation for institutions considered "too big to fail." Although not explicitly guaranteed until recently, Fannie Mae and Freddie Mac also have been longtime beneficiaries of similar federal protection of their debt securities against default.

Despite the perception that Fannie and Freddie derive value from the implicit guarantee and pose significant risk to the government, quantifying the federal exposure is difficult and there is substantial disagreement in the literature about magnitudes. In general, spread-based estimates of guarantee value for Fannie and Freddie are significantly higher than options-based estimates. Spread-based estimates capitalize the difference between the interest expense of Fannie and Freddie and that of similarly rated financial institutions.[1] Using this approach, Passmore (2005) reports a present value over twenty-five years in the range of $122 to $182 billion as the subsidy to Fannie and Freddie. At the other extreme, in a study commissioned by Fannie

Deborah Lucas is the former Donald C. Clark HSBC Professor of Consumer Finance at the Kellogg School of Management, Northwestern University, and is currently Associate Director of Financial Analysis at the CBO and a research associate of the National Bureau of Economic Research. Robert McDonald is the Erwin P. Nemmers Distinguished Professor of Finance at the Kellogg School of Management, Northwestern University.

We thank Alan Marcus and Dwight Jaffee for helpful suggestions and comments on an earlier draft. All errors remain our own.

1. In CBO (2001), based on the analysis of Ambrose and Warga (2002), the comparison is made using a "stand-alone" rating for Fannie and Freddie, which reflects their risk to the government. As of April 2008, the GSEs had a stand-alone rating of AA– from S&P. See also Nothaft et al. (2002).

Mae using an options pricing approach, Stiglitz, Orszag, and Orszag (2002) conclude that the cost of an implicit guarantee to the government does not exceed $200 million. In a recent paper also using an options pricing approach (Lucas and McDonald 2006), we estimate a present value cost over twenty-five years of $28 billion for the two enterprises, still an order of magnitude lower than in Passmore (2005).[2]

There are several possible explanations for the higher subsidy values generally implied by spread-based analyses. One is that the guarantee may be valued by investors in government-sponsored enterprises (GSE) securities not just because of the direct value of protection from default risk, but also because of other benefits such as increased liquidity, or because they satisfy regulatory restrictions. Thus, the reduction in the GSEs' borrowing costs may exceed the cost of expected defaults to the government. Whether these other benefits to GSE stakeholders should be included in a calculation of government cost depends on the question at hand. From a broad opportunity cost perspective, since other financial institutions would pay to obtain the same privileges, they are part of the cost. To answer the narrower question of the expected cost of defaults, it is probably appropriate to exclude the value of these sorts of additional benefits.

The theoretical model developed here suggests another reason that spread-based models overestimate guarantee values: they do not correct for the more conservative optimal default policy of an insured firm. To preserve the ability to borrow at a risk-free rate in the future, we show that a guaranteed firm will choose to make debt payments in some states of the world where an otherwise identical uninsured firm would default, lowering the cost to the government relative to what a spread-based estimate would imply. This finding is related to a large body of earlier work on risk taking, charter value, and bank regulation (see, e.g., Demsetz, Saidenberg, and Strahan [1996] and the references therein). As far as we know, however, this analysis is the first to highlight the implications for credit spreads as potentially biased estimators of subsidy value.

A further possibility is that simple options-based models fail to capture important dimensions of risk, and thereby underestimate the cost and risk to the government of providing insurance. To explore this possibility, we consider several possibilities that have not been taken into account in past options-based estimates for Fannie and Freddie. First, we develop a theoretical model to examine whether and how the presence of a guarantee may affect the statistical relation between equity and asset value, and hence affect the imputation of asset value and volatility. We then calibrate and simulate a generalized version of the model to consider its quantitative implications, and to incorporate a process for the evolution of assets that includes a jump as well as a diffusion component. In light of episodes such as Fannie's

2. See also CBO (2004), Feldman (1999), and Hubbard (2004).

accounting restatements and subsequent fall in share price and the spike in credit losses following the wave of subprime defaults, we also explore the sensitivity of options-based estimates to initial conditions for equity value and volatility. In all variations, we report insurance value in terms of an annual premium as well as reporting a present value, making costs easier to interpret and normalizing for the estimation horizon.

The simulation results suggest that an insurance premium of 20 to 30 basis points (bps) would have been fair compensation for the default risk assumed by the government at year-end 2005. Cost estimates of this magnitude are still smaller than from some spread-based analyses, but they are in line with others—for instance, the Congressional Budget Office (CBO) (2001) reports a GSE borrowing advantage of 41 bps over comparable nonguaranteed financial institutions. The results also show that the fair premium rate increases rapidly with the leverage ratio, suggesting a much higher fair rate following the decline in asset values starting in late 2007.

The remainder of the chapter is organized as follows. Section 6.2 provides a brief description of Fannie and Freddie, their risk exposure, and the regulatory environment. In section 6.3 we present the valuation model and discuss the effect of the government guarantee on the dynamic relation between the underlying assets and the value of equity. Section 6.4 describes the calibration used to quantify the value of the guarantee, and reports the results of sensitivity analysis. Section 6.5 concludes.

6.2 Background

Fannie Mae and Freddie Mac are government-sponsored enterprises (GSEs) that were created by Congress to provide liquidity and stability in the home mortgage market. They also are required to meet modest goals for low-income lending. The GSEs are hybrids of private corporations and federal entities. Although their debt securities explicitly state that they do not bear a government guarantee, their many federal ties and critical role in the housing and financial markets suggest otherwise. As a consequence, the GSEs raise capital through debt financing at a narrower spread over Treasury rates than similarly rated financial institutions, an advantage that is generally viewed as an unbooked federal subsidy.

Fannie and Freddie participate in the mortgage market in two distinct ways. One is by buying mortgages and financing the purchases with debt issues. Those on-balance-sheet holdings expose the enterprises to default, interest rate, and prepayment risk. The interest rate and prepayment risk is partially hedged with the use of derivatives and dynamic hedging strategies (see Jaffee [2003]). They also securitize mortgages, an off-balance-sheet activity in which Fannie and Freddie assume default risk by issuing a credit guarantee.

The rapid growth of on-balance-sheet holdings in the 1990s increasingly raised concerns about the government's risk exposure, specifically about unhedged interest rate and prepayment risk (Frame and White 2005). Following the discovery of accounting irregularities at Fannie Mae,[3] its on-balance-sheet growth was temporarily slowed by a consent order from their regulator that limited its mortgage portfolio to $727 billion, down from the $904 billion it held at year-end 2004. Fannie's mortgage-backed security (MBS) outstanding continued to grow, and reached $1.77 trillion as of November 2006. The consent decree was lifted in late 2007, after which growth in its on-balance-sheet obligations resumed. At year-end 2005, the time we focus on for the base case analysis of guarantee values, Freddie Mac had a comparable exposure to Fannie Mae, with $710 billion of mortgages held on balance sheet, and $1.34 trillion in MBS outstanding.

With the sharp downturn in the housing market that began in 2007, concerns about default risk—previously thought to be a minor concern—caused the stock price of both companies to plummet. Fair value estimates reported by the GSEs in early 2008 indicated that Freddie has negative equity value, and that Fannie was barely solvent. In July 2008, Congress granted Treasury the authority to infuse funds into the entities as needed over the next eighteen months, effectively making the implicit guarantee explicit, and incurring a present value cost to taxpayers estimated by the Congressional Budget Office (CBO) to be $25 billion (CBO 2008). Treasury used this authority two months later to take both GSEs into federal conservatorship.

An independent regulator oversees the operations of the GSEs, but their activities are primarily constrained by statute.[4] By law, assets consist primarily of conforming mortgages, and the enterprises must meet minimum capital requirements.[5] Typically both firms maintain slightly more than the regulatory minimum capital, although capital on occasion has been a binding constraint. As for commercial banks with deposit insurance, economic theory predicts that to maximize the value of the implicit guarantee the enterprises would manage liabilities to keep capital close to the regulatory minimum.

Historically, the stock of both firms consistently outperformed the overall market. Even before the recent turmoil in the housing market, however, stock price volatility had increased and returns declined. Whether the historically high returns can be attributed to unanticipated growth in the implicit subsidy

---

3. Fannie Mae was found by the Securities and Exchange Commission (SEC) to have overstated profits by an estimated $9 billion starting in the late 1990s.

4. Created in 1992, the Office of Federal Housing Enterprise Oversight (OFHEO), an independent entity within the Department of Housing and Urban Development, had limited regulatory authority over Fannie Mae and Freddie Mac. The Housing and Economic Recovery Act of 2008 created a new and stronger regulator to supersede OFHEO, the Federal Housing Finance Agency (FHFA). The FHFA now has oversight responsibility for the Federal Home Loan Banks as well as for Fannie and Freddie.

5. Current legislative proposals would increase the conforming mortgage limits in high-cost states, allowing GSE holdings of mortgages previously considered jumbo loans.

is a matter of some debate. Many observers contend that GSE stockholders benefit from their special status, but the enterprises counter that competitive pressure forces any cost advantage to be passed through to borrowers (Naranjo and Toevs 2002). To the extent that rents are captured by stockholders, returns should be affected by unanticipated changes in the value of the perceived guarantee, and Seiler (2003) presents some evidence of this effect. In any event the stock returns on the two firms are highly correlated, suggesting that they are affected by common risk factors including common regulatory risk.

6.3   Modeling Guarantee Value

We take an options pricing approach to modeling the dynamics of guarantee value and risk exposure. The model is based on the fundamental insight of Sharpe (1976) and Merton (1977), that insurance can be valued as a put option on the assets of the firm. To illustrate the basic idea of how the guarantee is valued, and to understand its effect on the relation between observed equity valuations and the unobserved value of operating assets, we begin by analyzing a simple closed-form model where debt is adjusted at fixed intervals as long as the firm remains solvent.

For a firm with guaranteed debt, equity value has two components. The first, analogous to the equity of a levered firm without a guarantee, is a call option on the operating assets of the firm. The second component is the value of the guarantee itself, which is the present value of the (uncertain) stream of savings from being able to borrow at the risk-free rate, rather than at a risk-adjusted rate. The theoretical model is used to explore how the presence of a guarantee affects the dynamics of equity returns and their relation to the dynamics of operating assets. Since the options pricing approach imputes the value and volatility of operating assets from the value and volatility of equity, understanding this relationship is critical to correctly imputing guarantee value.

To examine the value of the guarantees quantitatively, in section 6.3.3 we numerically implement a more complex version of the theoretical model using an approach similar to that of credit analysis firm KMV (as described in Crosbie and Bohn [2003]). It allows for externally financed asset growth, debt adjustment over time, a state-contingent bankruptcy trigger, and state-contingent conditional volatility. Expanding on the related analysis in Lucas and McDonald (2006), we incorporate a jump process, add new internal consistency checks motivated by the theoretical analysis, and investigate a wider range of parameter values, particularly the sensitivity to initial capital. The value of government insurance is calculated using a Monte Carlo simulation with risk-neutral probabilities. We also track the corresponding actual distribution of assets, liabilities, and defaults, in order to report the implied distribution of insurance payouts.

6.3.1 Single-Period Guarantee

We first consider the effect of a guarantee for a firm with a one-period debt contract, where a period has a length T. Consider two firms, one with insured debt and one with uninsured debt. Superscripts "I" and "U" denote quantities associated with the insured and uninsured firm, respectively; quantities without superscripts are the same for both. Suppose that at time 0 each promises the same debt payment at maturity T, $D_0(T)$, and have the same initial value of operating assets, $A_0(0)$. For consistency with a multi-period model, we use the notation $A_i(s)$ to denote the value of assets at time $iT + s$. In the single-period model, $i = 0$. The only source of uncertainty is the value of operating assets, which evolve stochastically over time.

At time 0, the equity value of the going concern is the present value of the expected payoff to equity holders. Let $E_0[.]$ denote the expectation conditional on time 0 information under the risk-neutral measure. Because both firms have the same physical assets and the same promised debt repayment, the market value of equity of both firms is: $E_0(0) = e^{-rT} E_0[\max(0, A_0(T) - D_0(T))]$, where r is the risk-free rate. Between times 0 and T, the equity values remain the same: both claims are a call option on the same underlying assets, with identical strike price and maturity.

Unlike for equity, the present value of the debt of the two firms prior to maturity is not equal. At any time $t \leq T$, the value of insured debt is simply the present value of the promised payment: $D_0^I(t) = e^{-r(T-t)}D_0(T)$. The realized payment on uninsured debt will be the promised amount, $D_0(T)$, or the asset value at time T, $A_0(T)$, whichever is less. Hence the value of uninsured debt is the present value of the *expected* payment to debt holders: $D_0^U(t) = e^{-r(T-t)}E_t[\min(A_0(T),D_0(T))]$.

The value of the T-period guarantee made at time 0, $G_0(0)$ is the difference between the initial value of the insured and uninsured debt:

(1) $$G_0(0) = e^{-rT} D_0(T) - e^{-rT} E_0[\min(A_0(T), D_0(T))]$$
$$= e^{-rT} E_0[\max(D_0(T) - A_0(T),0)].$$

The expression on the right-hand side of equation (1) is the value of a put option on the operating assets of the firm, where the strike price is the promised payment on debt. When assets are lognormally distributed, the value can be computed using the standard Black Scholes formula for a put option.

We assume that the guarantee value accrues to equity holders.[6] Thus at time 0, after the guarantee is announced but before debt is issued, the market

---

6. To the extent that Fannie and Freddie are able to act as duopolists rather than as competitors, we expect the guarantee value to accrue to their equity holders rather than to mortgage borrowers or other stakeholders. Some of the benefit may be passed to borrowers in the form of lower rates. As long as the pass-through is a constant proportion of guarantee value, the implications for imputing equity value are similar.

value of equity is $G_0(0) + E_0(0)$. Since we assume that the scale of operating assets is not affected by the presence of a guarantee, $G_0(0)$ can be thought of as being immediately distributed either via a dividend, a share repurchase, or equivalently, as a reduction in the initial investment required from the original equity holders. Following the cash distribution, equity price dynamics, as described previously, are identical to that of the uninsured firm.

For the government—both from a production cost and opportunity cost perspective—the value of the guarantee is also $G_0(0)$. The guarantee is equivalent to the government writing a put option worth $G_0(0)$, and the firm would be willing to pay up to $G_0(0)$ for the insurance.

6.3.2 Repeated Debt Guarantees

The debt guarantee as just modeled is static: the firm issues debt and then at time T either pays the debt in full or the government makes up the shortfall. This description of the guarantee is overly simplified along several dimensions. First, if the insured firm does not go bankrupt at time T, it will likely have the opportunity to issue additional guaranteed debt. Second, whether or not the insured firm will declare bankruptcy depends on the market value of assets, which is inclusive of current and anticipated future guarantees. Third, the insured firm may readjust its capital structure over time. For example, if assets appreciate the firm may issue more guaranteed debt, whereas if assets fall the firm may buy back some of the guaranteed debt. Such behavior will affect the value of the guarantee and its relation to the value of equity and operating assets. In this section we derive the value of a debt guarantee of an ongoing firm, taking into account these considerations.[7]

Operating Asset Dynamics

We distinguish between "operating assets," which denote the financial and physical assets of a firm, and "market assets," which in addition includes the value of credit guarantees. As in Merton (1977) and Merton (1976), we assume that the evolution of firm operating assets over time has three components: an expected return, a random component that is lognormally distributed, and (in the simulations only) a discrete jump in value. Specifically, under the risk-neutral distribution, the percentage change in assets over time is given by the process:

$$(2) \qquad dA_t = (r - \lambda k - \delta) A_t dt + \sigma_A A_t dZ_t + A_t dq$$

where A_t is the asset value, σ is the volatility parameter, dZ_t is a Brownian motion, dq is a random variable that over the interval dt is zero with

---

7. For tractability, we take the risk of operating assets as exogenous, but the presence of a guarantee can also affect the characteristics and dynamics of operating assets (see Keely [1990]).

probability $1 - \lambda dt$ and $Y - 1$ with probability λdt and $k = E(Y - 1)$. The dq term permits the value of assets to jump discretely with probability λdt over an interval dt. The jump takes assets from A_t to YA_t, so the percentage change is $(Y - 1)$. Subtracting λk from r corrects the drift for the average effect of jumps. Formulations like equation (2) appear regularly in the literature on debt valuation and bankruptcy.

Valuing a Repeated Guarantee

Here we derive the value of a debt guarantee for a firm with a stationary target debt-to-operating asset ratio. The firm periodically issues debt to fixed, one-period maturity T, setting the amount of new debt to achieve its target debt ratio. Each period the firm also chooses whether or not to declare bankruptcy so as to maximize the value of equity. For tractability we take the target leverage ratio as given, but a similar policy could arise in response to a regulatory capital requirement, or as an optimal policy in a stationary environment in the presence of fixed adjustment costs. Also for simplicity we assume that the value of operating assets does not jump; that is, $Y = 1$ in equation (2).

We denote the value of a quantity X at time $mT + t$ as $X_m(t)$. We also denote the risk-neutral expectation at time mT conditional on information at that time as E_m. We can then express the constant target debt ratio as γe^{rT}, so that for $m = 0, 1, \ldots,$

$$(3) \qquad\qquad D_m(T) = \gamma e^{rt} A_m(0).$$

The equity value and the default decision for the guaranteed firm will depend on the expected value of current and future credit guarantees. To calculate these quantities, we need to calculate expectations conditional on future solvency. Let $p_m^j(0)$ denote the risk-neutral probability, conditional on information at time mT, that firm $j = \{I, U\}$ is not bankrupt at time $(m + 1)T$. Further, let $\lambda_m^j(0)$ be the expectation of the asset growth rate conditional on no bankruptcy at time $(m + 1)T$. Then define $\psi_m^j(0) \equiv \lambda_m^j(0) \times p_m^j(0)$ and let $\phi_m^j(0) = e^{-rT} \psi_m^j(0)$. In the analysis of a stationary equilibrium we drop the time subscripts. These values will depend on the specific condition in any period that determines whether the insured firm declares bankruptcy.

As in the one-period case, we compare the value of the guaranteed firm with that of a similar uninsured firm, where both have the same operating assets and target debt ratio, given by equations (2) and (3). For the guaranteed firm, the guarantee remains in place as long as the firm does not experience a default. If the firm does default, we assume that the value of future debt guarantees is lost forever to current stakeholders. To maintain equivalence of operating assets, we assume that the guarantee value, which is realized through higher proceeds at the time of each debt issue, is paid out immediately as a dividend to the equity holders of the guaranteed firm.

We denote the cum dividend equity value at time mT as $E_{m-1}(T)$, and the ex-dividend equity value as $E_m(0)$.

The one-period guarantee value, and hence the incremental dividend received by the equity holders of the insured firm, is a constant proportion, g, of asset value. This follows from the assumption that the amount of newly issued debt is a constant fraction of current asset value, and that the value of a one-period guarantee depends only on the stationary default rule of the *uninsured* firm. Using equations (1) and (3), the proportional guarantee value at a debt reset time mT is

$$(4) \quad g = \frac{G_m(0)}{A_m(0)} = \frac{D_m^I(0) - D_m^U(0)}{A_m(0)} = E_m\left[\max(\gamma - \frac{e^{-rT}A_m(T)}{A_m(0)}, 0)\right].$$

This can be rewritten, using the Black Scholes formula for a put option and the notation defined in equation (4) as

$$(5) \qquad\qquad g = (1 - p_m^U(0))\,\gamma - (1 - \phi_m^U(0)).$$

Consider a guaranteed firm, which will continue to operate until it declares bankruptcy, at a debt reset date mT. If the firm is solvent, it will issue guaranteed debt maturing at $(m + 1)T$. What is the solvency condition at time mT that maximizes equity value? If the firm remains in business, equity holders will receive a call option on the operating assets, and a claim to the present value of current and future dividends generated by the guarantee. Thus, equity holders will pay off the debt coming due, $D_{m-1}(T)$, as long as the value of operating assets plus the guarantee value exceeds the promised debt payment.

Notice that for a comparable uninsured firm, the bankruptcy condition is $A_m(T) > D_{m-1}(T)$. The call option on the operating assets has the same value as for the insured firm, but there is no additional value from the ongoing guarantee. Thus, there are states of the world where an insured firm continues to operate to preserve future guarantee value, but an uninsured firm declares bankruptcy. The different solvency conditions imply that the value to the firm of the current one-period guarantee, $gA_m(0)$, is no longer equal to the one-period production cost for the government. The former depends on the default policy of the uninsured firm, whereas the latter depends on the more conservative default policy of the insured firm. The additional losses absorbed by the insured firm's equity holders generate a commensurate reduction in cost to the government of the guarantee.

These considerations suggest that to find the value of the guarantee to the insured firm, it is convenient to characterize it in terms of two components. The first is the present value of the incremental dividend stream generated by the guarantee, $\Gamma A_m(0)$. On average, operating assets will grow at their expected rate conditional on the insured firm remaining solvent. Thus, the value of the dividend stream associated with the perpetual guarantee, starting with current asset value A, is:

$$(6) \qquad \Gamma A = gA \sum_{i=0}^{\infty} e^{-riT} [\psi^i]^i = \frac{gA}{(1 - \phi')}.$$

The second component, $HA_m(0)$, is the cost to equity holders of paying off the debt in states of the world where an uninsured firm would declare bankruptcy. At time mT, the expected difference between $gA_m(0)$ and the one-period guarantee production cost of the government is:

$$(7) \qquad \int_{A_{m(0)}(\gamma e - \Gamma + H)}^{\gamma e^{rT} A_m} [\gamma^{rT} A_m(0) - \alpha] f(\alpha | A_m(0)) d\alpha = \eta A_m(0)$$

where $f(\alpha | A_m(0))$ is the probability density of firm asset value at time $(m + 1)T$ conditional on asset value the previous period, and η denotes the cost differential as a fraction of asset value. Like guarantee value, the present value of the cost differential depends on the expected future growth rate of assets, conditional on the probability that the firm remains solvent:

$$(8) \qquad HA = \eta A \sum_{i=0}^{\infty} e^{-riT} [\psi^i]^i = \frac{\eta A}{(1 - \phi')}.$$

Thus, at mT, if the insured firm is solvent, its equity value exceeds that of the uninsured firm by

$$(9) \qquad A_m(0)[\Gamma - H].$$

It follows that one reason previous studies that estimated subsidy cost on the basis of interest rate spreads reported higher costs than derivative-based estimates is that they implicitly set H to 0 in equation (9). The size of the bias, however, is difficult to assess. To the extent that the comparison firms were banks with subsidized federal deposit insurance and access to FHLB advances, it is not clear whether the GSEs or banks have a greater incentive to default conservatively to preserve the value of subsidized insurance.

Asset Value and Volatility

We can observe the value and volatility of market equity, dividend policy, promised debt repayment, debt maturity, and the risk-free rate, but must infer the value and volatility of assets. The problem of finding the value and volatility of market assets is conceptually similar to that considered in Marcus and Shaked (1984), who modeled the value of Federal Deposit Insurance Corporation (FDIC) insurance in a one-period setting using an options pricing model. As discussed earlier, the value of equity for the guaranteed firm is a call option on market assets, which include both operating assets, with dynamics given by equation (2), and the value of future guarantees. Using equation (9), market assets on a debt reset date mT can be written as:

$$(10) \qquad A_m(0)^* = A_m(0)[1 + \Gamma - H].$$

Looking forward to the next reset date, the volatility of market assets is proportional to that of operating assets: $\sigma_{A^*} = \sigma_A[1 + \Gamma - H]$. Further, the continuation condition that maximizes equity value for the insured firm at each debt reset date is:

$$(11) \qquad\qquad A_m(0)[1 + \Gamma - H] \geq D_{m-1}(T).$$

Then the relation between the distribution of equity returns and asset returns can be found following Merton's approach as the simultaneous solution to two nonlinear equations, but with $A_m(0)^*$ in place of $A_m(0)$, and with the dividend yield, δ^*, expressed as a share of $A_m(0)^*$ rather than as a share of operating assets. Let $C(A,D,\sigma_A,\delta,T)$ denote the Black-Scholes value of a European call option with underlying assets A, promised debt payment D, asset volatility σ_A, dividend yield on market assets (δ^*), and time to maturity T. Then the value of equity for an insured firm is:

$$(12) \qquad\qquad E_m(0) = C(A_m(0)^*, D_m(T), \sigma_{A^*}, \delta^*, T).$$

The value and volatility of market assets is found by solving equation (12) simultaneously with:

$$(13) \qquad\qquad \sigma_{A^*} = \sigma_E/(N(d_1)A_m(0)^* e^{-\delta^* T}/E_m(0))$$

where

$$(14) \qquad d_1 = [\ln(A_m(0)^*/D_m(T)) + (r - \delta^* + .5\sigma^2_{A^*})T]/(\sigma_{A^*}T^{.5})$$

$$d_2 = d_1 - \sigma_{A^*}T^{.5}.$$

Equation (13) comes from the relation, $\sigma_E = (\partial E/\partial A)(A/E)\,\sigma_A$.

Discussion

The preceding analysis is useful for understanding the relation between the value and volatility of operating assets, equity, and a government guarantee on debt. The most straightforward conclusion that emerges is that the market value of debt plus equity exceeds the value of operating assets by the value of the present value of expected guarantee payments. Expected recoveries in the event of default, which depend only on the value of operating assets, must be adjusted discretely downward for this effect. The bankruptcy trigger must also be adjusted to take into account the effect of guarantee value on behavior. However, inferences about the volatility of operating assets made on the basis of stock price volatility, using the framework of equations (12) and (13) and using observations of equity prices on debt reset dates, are basically the same for a firm with or without a guarantee.

This analysis abstracts from what happens between reset dates. As the value of operating assets evolves, so too does the probability of solvency and the expectation of asset value on the next reset date, and hence the expectation of the present value of future guarantees. The fixed proportionality of guarantee value to asset value at the next reset date, however, implies that the dynamics between reset dates are also unaffected by the presence of the guarantee.

In fact, government policy may not be stationary, and the value of the guarantee may be perceived by the market as changing over time with economic and political events or as a function of the financial situation of the GSEs. Whether this would make equity value more or less volatile relative to operating assets is unclear, as it would depend on the correlation between the strength of the guarantee and the objective situation of the firm, among other things. Clearly the model can be modified to take other hypotheses into account, but in its stationary form provides a neutral starting point or "guarantee irrelevance theorem" for thinking about these effects.

6.3.3 Monte Carlo Valuation of the Guarantee

Here we employ a discrete time version of equation (2) that is suitable for simulation. The calibrated model accommodates more complex assumptions about liability management and default behavior, and allows us to explore the effect of a variety of regulatory policies on guarantee cost.

Under a risk-neutral representation in discrete time, operating assets evolve according to:

$$(15) A_{t+h} = (1 + I_{J,t}\omega)A_t \text{Exp}\left[\left(r_f - p_j\omega + \theta_t - \delta\frac{E_o}{A_o} - .5\sigma_A^2\right)h + \sigma_{A,t}\varepsilon\sqrt{h}\right],$$

where h is the time step, t subscripts represent time, E is equity, r_f is the risk-free rate, θ_t is externally financed firm asset growth, δ is the dividend yield on equity (hence $\delta E_0/A_0$ is taken to be the dividend yield on assets), $\sigma_{A,t}$ is the possibly time-dependent volatility of operating assets, ε is a draw from a standard normal distribution, $\omega = Y - 1$ is the nonstochastic jump size, $I_{j,t}$ is an indicator that a jump has occurred, pjh_j is the probability of a jump over an interval of length h. The actual evolution of operating assets is identical except that r_f is replaced by the expected return on assets r_A.

Here A_t represents the value of all of the firm's operating and investment activities, both on and off balance sheet. It includes the mortgage portfolio, the MBS business, derivative market activities, and so forth. Asset value is affected by a variety of factors, including interest rate, credit, and other risks. Unhedged interest rate risk on the retained portfolio, and the associated prepayment and extension risk that arise due to the prepayment option on residential mortgages, until recently has been considered the greatest source of risk. Credit risk arises both from mortgages held on balance sheet, and from the MBS they guarantee. This risk is mitigated by the collateral value of the underlying real estate. The remaining risks—political, accounting, fraud, liquidity, model, counterparty, and so forth—are potentially important but difficult to quantify. Political risks include the possibility of legislation that restricts growth or increases competition, reducing franchise value. Accounting misrepresentations or fraud may cause downward jumps in perceived asset value, and can prolong the time between when a problem arises and is recognized, increasing the severity of losses.

Importantly, this measure of operating assets represents the true financial condition of the company, and we take it to be the recovery value in bankruptcy. The market value of assets, however, also includes the value of current and future expected guarantees, G_t. As suggested by the analysis of section 6.3.2, we assume that the guarantee value is a constant proportion of the market value of assets:

$$(16) \qquad A_t^* = (1 + \Gamma - H)A_t.$$

We do not, however, attempt to identify the two components of guarantee value separately.

To summarize the different roles of operating assets and market value assets in the calibrations: operating assets are identified with the recovery value of the firm in bankruptcy. Market value assets determine the continuation condition for the firm. The procedure for setting the initial conditions identifies the initial market value of assets, as described in a later section.

Liabilities

Representing debt as having a single fixed maturity, as we did in sections 6.3.1 and 6.3.2, abstracts from the possibility of more complex debt rebalancing strategies and future growth opportunities. Closed-form solutions for the value of debt under optimal or stationary debt policies have been derived for a few special cases (e.g., Leland 1994; Collin-Dufresne and Goldstein 2001), but those do not allow for state dependent changes in debt policy or continuation rules. To allow for more complicated patterns of behavior we choose instead to specify a liability process that allows for gradual adjustment of debt toward a target ratio, with asymmetry in the upward and downward speed of adjustment reflecting the relative difficulty of reducing debt when asset value falls. Book liabilities, L, evolve according to:

$$(17) \qquad L_{t+h} = L_t e^{(r_d + \gamma \theta_t)h} + I_t \alpha_t h(\lambda^* - L_t e^{r_d h} / A_t)A_t,$$

where α_t is the annual rate of adjustment, which may be state dependent, λ^* is the target liability to operating asset ratio, and I_t is an indicator variable that equals one in a period where liabilities are adjusted, and 0 otherwise. Liabilities grow at a rate r_d to cover promised interest.[8] In addition, a fraction γ of externally financed growth is supported by debt. This representation applies to both the actual and risk-neutral calculations, but the realized paths differ because the return on debt and externally financed growth take

---

8. An alternative would be to reduce assets by the amount of a periodic interest payment, which would reduce the scale of the enterprises over time relative to what is assumed here.

on different values in each instance, and the ratio of assets to liabilities displays different dynamics. Although computationally it would be straightforward to add volatility to liabilities, we assume instead that the estimated volatility of assets implicitly captures volatility arising from all sources including liabilities.

The promised interest rate, r_d, depends on what one assumes about the strength of the government guarantee. If it were completely firm, and abstracting from other differences between Treasuries and agency securities, then setting r_d equal to r_f would be appropriate. In the calibrations we assume a positive rate spread that is somewhat smaller than the average observed in the data. This is consistent with our view that the guarantee is not risky, but that there are some other features that make Treasury debt more valuable than agency securities.

Insolvency Trigger

Consistent with the analysis in section 6.3.2, we assume that the solvency condition depends on the market value of assets relative to book liabilities. As in Merton (1977), we assume that bankruptcy only occurs during periodic audits. If the solvency condition is not met, the auditor closes the firm and makes a guarantee payment to debt holders.

Several insolvency triggers have been proposed in the literature. One that is roughly consistent with observed bankruptcy experience is to liquidate the firm when the market value of assets falls below the level of current liabilities, plus half of the book value of long-term liabilities. Another is that the market value of assets falls below a fraction of the total book value of liabilities. We use the latter type of rule, since distinguishing between the long- and short-term liabilities of Fannie and Freddie is complicated by the frequent maturity conversions taking place through derivatives market transactions. Given this rule, we are interested in finding the bankruptcy trigger value—the proportional gap between assets and liabilities—that maximizes the value of equity. In simulations we calculate the guarantee cost and the value of equity for a range of bankruptcy triggers and we report the results for which the value of equity is maximized.

In practice, frictions are likely to increase the guarantee cost. A drawn-out reorganization or closure process, or regulatory forbearance, can add to guarantee costs by allowing a failing firm to continue operating. This effect can be exacerbated if asset volatility increases with financial distress. This could occur, for instance, if there is a correlation between conditions that cause distress and overall market volatility; if distress raises the cost of hedging; or if management deliberately takes more risk to try to make up for past losses. This increase in volatility may not be easily discernable in historical data, both because its occurrence is a low probability event, and because it is likely to persist for relatively short periods of time when it does occur. In Lucas and McDonald (2006) we found this to be a significant potential driver of guarantee cost, and we also incorporate it into these estimates.

Equity

Equations (15) and (17), which govern the evolution of firm operating assets and book liabilities, respectively, implicitly define the cash flows to equity. Those consist of the dividend payment each period, and cash raised from subsequent debt issues not used to finance exogenous asset growth. Exogenous asset growth not assumed to be debt financed further implies a negative cash flow to initial equity holders, or equivalently an equity issue.

The time 0 value of equity is the present value of all future cash flows to equity. That value is computed in the Monte Carlo simulations under the risk-neutral measure, by discounting cash flows at the risk-free rate. As a proxy for cash flows beyond the simulation horizon T, the terminal value of equity at time T is approximated by $A_T - L_T$. This neglects the value of the guarantee after time T, but that effect becomes small as T increases. Calculating the implied equity value using this approach provides a valuable check on the internal consistency of the model, since it can be compared to the observed equity value used to determine the initial value of assets and liabilities.

Deriving Initial Conditions and Accounting for Guarantee Value

The initial market value and volatility of firm assets must be estimated since these quantities are not directly observable. The analysis of section 6.3.2 suggests that we can do this using Merton's framework, where equity can be valued as a call option on the firm's market assets. Specifically, we use equations (12) and (13), calibrated with market and balance sheet data from Fannie and Freddie, to estimate the initial market value of assets and their volatility.[9] What is tricky conceptually is to choose a horizon for debt, since liabilities follow equation (17) and there is no specific maturity date. We use the reported average effective maturity of debt as a proxy, and consider the sensitivity of the results to varying the assumed debt maturity.

We use the estimated asset volatility and asset value to compute the cost of the guarantee. As part of the estimation, we also compute the market value of equity for Fannie and Freddie. This later serves as an internal consistency check against the equity value derived from estimated discounted cash flows accruing to equity.

6.4   Calibration and Results

The model in the base case is calibrated to year-end 2005, a time when the reported financial condition of both firms was strong. We will then look at how the estimated cost of the guarantee to the government changes as

---

9. We also used this approach for deriving initial conditions for asset value and volatility in Lucas and McDonald (2005). Marcus and Shaked (1984) show that the same equations can be used to estimate the value of the government guarantee, and use that insight to estimate the value of deposit insurance for US banks.

their financial condition deteriorates, and the sensitivity to other parametric assumptions and policy variables.

Three critical inputs for guarantee valuation are market value equity, equity volatility, and liabilities. Table 6.1 reports these statistics, along with the other parameters used for the base case. Data acquisition for 2005 was complicated because Fannie Mae delayed in filing financial reports since it had to restate its financial statements through 2004. As of December 2006 it had not filed any further financial reports. Fannie did, however, provide monthly information on the size of their mortgage portfolio and MBS outstanding. We have imputed some of the missing information for Fannie by relying on Freddie's disclosures. Specifically, we estimate book liabilities for Fannie and assume that the ratio of liabilities to retained mortgages is the same for both firms.

We infer base case equity volatility using historical implied annualized thirty-day volatility from option prices. The series are shown for Fannie Mae and Freddie Mac in figures 6.1 and 6.2. Both series are graphed against thirty-day implied volatility for the Standard and Poor (S&P) 500 index (the VIX index) in order to highlight changes in volatility, which are firm specific rather than market-wide. Implied volatility for both firms ranges from 20 percent to 60 percent, with an average of about 30 percent, our base estimate for both firms. Implied volatility in 2006 and 2007 remained at similar levels.

Estimates of guarantee value are based on 50,000 Monte Carlo runs, for ten- and twenty-year horizons. As in Lucas and McDonald (2006), asset volatility is assumed to increase to four times its normal level when assets fall to 101 percent of liabilities, representing increased volatility in periods of financial distress. Management and regulatory decisions (debt adjustment and solvency determination) are evaluated at a quarterly frequency, while assets returns are calculated at a monthly frequency. Several variables are parameterized differently than in our previous study. The ability to adjust down liabilities is more constrained, a change that achieves greater consistency between observed and computed equity values. We set exogenous asset growth to zero (in contrast to the 6 percent previously assumed), because it seemed in 2005 unlikely that future growth would match historical rates. Liabilities still grow on average at about 9 percent annually, however, because of the assumption that interest accumulates as increased debt and because the expected return on assets exceeds the dividend rate, creating growth from retained earnings that, on average, causes the target debt level to grow.

As discussed in the previous section, using equations (12) and (13) to estimate initial asset value and asset volatility is problematic because it requires a fixed debt maturity as an input. Nevertheless, it is a useful starting point for estimation. In 2004, the last year for which we have obtained average maturity data, Fannie's effective debt maturity was 2.65 years and Freddie's was 3.05 years. Since the agencies normally match the duration of assets and

Table 6.1   **Base case parameter values, year-end 2005**

Short name	Value	Description
Fannie Mae		
FLinit	$744	Initial imputed book value of liabilities ($ billions)
MVEquity	$48,750	Initial market value of equity ($ millions)
Dividend yield	0.028	
Freddie Mac		
FLinit	$727	Initial book value of liabilities ($ billions)
MVEquity	$47,056	Initial market value of equity ($ millions)
Dividend yield	0.03	
Common values		
FAvol_h	FAvol*4	Firm asset volatility in high volatility state
rf	0.045	Risk free rate
rd	0.0475	Promised return on debt
FAer_a	0.053	Firm assets expected return (actual)
FAer	0.045	Firm assets expected return (risk-neutral)
FLrate_d	0.03 / 4	Quarterly adjustment of liabilities to lower target
FLrate_u	0.8 / 4	Quarterly adjustment of liabilities to higher target
growth	0.0	Externally financed growth if enough capital
growth_debt	1	Proportion of external financing that is debt
trig_volh	1.01	Trigger of assets/liabilities for higher volatility
look	4	Frequency of checking bankruptcy trigger per year
look_l	4	Frequency of updating debt
FLFAtarget	.93	Target liability to asset ratio
newFLFA	1	Proportion of debt financed exogenous asset growth
nmonte	50,000	Number of Monte Carlo simulations
nyear	10	Number of years in each simulation run
nfreq	12	Time steps per year

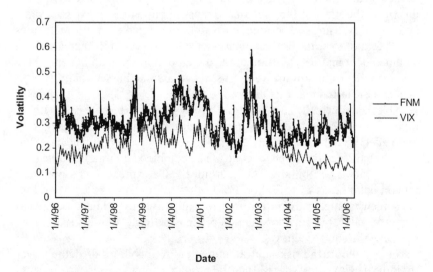

Fig. 6.1   **Implied volatility for Fannie Mae and for the S&P 500 (VIX), 1996 to 2006**
Source: Optionmetrics and Yahoo.

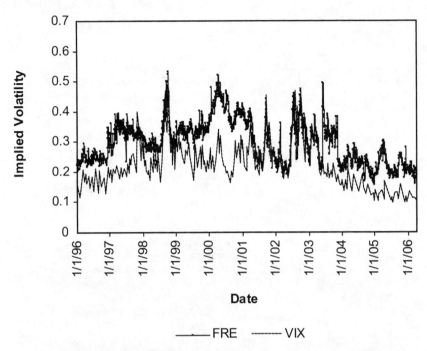

Fig. 6.2   Implied volatility for Freddie Mac and for the S&P 500 (VIX), 1996 to 2006
Source: Optionmetrics and Yahoo.

liabilities, it seems likely that their effective maturity of debt increased over the next year with the lengthening effective maturity of mortgages. Table 6.2 illustrates the effect of the debt maturity assumption on implied asset value and volatility, using the parameter assumptions in table 6.1, for maturities of 2.5, 5, and 7.5 years. Both implied asset value and volatility increases with assumed debt maturity. Although the increases appear small in percentage terms, model estimates are very sensitive to assumed asset volatility, and hence to the initial maturity assumption.

Table 6.3 reports the guarantee and equity values in the base case with no jumps in asset value, and using initial conditions assuming Fannie's (Freddie's) effective debt maturity is 2.65 (3.05) years. The default trigger is that which maximizes the value of equity. The combined guarantee value over twenty years is $65 billion. The guarantee value expressed as a premium rate on liabilities is 23 to 27 bps. For both firms, the implied equity values are somewhat higher than the observed values used to estimate asset volatility and value, but small changes in parameters (e.g., volatility) can easily reconcile the equity values.

We also report the risk-neutral and actual probabilities of default over the indicated horizon. The risk-neutral probability is inferred from observed prices and model assumptions. If the assets have a positive risk premium,

Table 6.2   Implied asset value and volatility as function of assumed debt maturity

	Fannie	Freddie	Fannie	Freddie	Fannie	Freddie
Horizon (yrs)	2.5	2.5	5	5	7.5	7.5
Asset value	797.0	778.4	800.4	781.2	803.1	780.9
Asset vol	.0208	.0185	.0225	.0204	.0238	.0230

Table 6.3   Base case 2005 guarantee value estimates

	Fannie	Freddie	Fannie	Freddie
Horizon	10	10	20	20
Guarantee cost ($ billions)	14.46	9.16	35.49	29.50
Premium rate (bp)	20.53	16.46	27.01	22.91
Implied equity value ($ billions)	49.99	45.40	55.78	48.73
Default prob. (risk-neutral)	0.19	0.18	0.34	0.34
Default prob. (actual)	0.050	0.033	0.084	0.059
Default trigger (L/A)	1.08	1.07	1.13	1.11

the risk-neutral probability is an upper bound on the physical probability of default. Identifying a physical probability of default requires making an additional assumption about the required rate of return on assets. We follow Lucas and McDonald (2006) and assume a required rate of return on assets 80 basis points greater than the risk free rate in the base case. Given the implied physical probabilities, we can also compute value at risk (VaR). Under the base case assumptions, we compute a VaR over twenty years at the 5 percent level for Fannie (Freddie) of $165 billion ($112 billion). At the 1 percent level the VaR increases to $252 billion ($201 billion).

Table 6.4 shows the effects of exogenously varying the default trigger rather than setting it at a value maximizing level as in the base case in table 6.3. As the default trigger increases from 1.0, there is a rapid increase in equity value and an increase in the premium rate. (With continuous monitoring and no bankruptcy costs, at a trigger of 1.0 there would be a zero default premium paid on bonds because bondholders would have 100 percent recovery. Because bankruptcy can only occur at discrete times, bondholders do on average suffer a loss when bankruptcy occurs.) As the trigger increases from 1.0, equity values increase, the premium rate increases, and the probability of bankruptcy declines. The last two observations are reconciled by the greater severity of defaults when the trigger level is higher.

Since the true risk premium associated with assets is subject to considerable uncertainty, table 6.5 reports, for the base case for Fannie, the sensitivity of the reported actual bankruptcy probability to the assumption about

Table 6.4   Effect of changing the bankruptcy trigger

Trigger	Equity value	Risk-neutral bankruptcy probability	Actual bankruptcy probability	Premium rate (bp)
		Fannie Mae		
1.00	42.57	70.26	24.83	14.17
1.03	48.85	58.12	17.84	21.17
1.06	52.79	48.58	13.68	24.74
1.09	54.87	41.42	10.98	26.42
1.12	55.69	35.85	9.04	27.01
1.15	55.60	31.27	7.48	26.90
		Freddie Mac		
1.00	38.24	67.38	17.11	11.57
1.03	43.85	54.33	11.77	18.09
1.06	47.01	44.57	8.67	21.22
1.09	48.41	37.49	6.86	22.65
1.12	48.71	31.75	5.51	22.83
1.15	48.17	27.22	4.45	22.46

Note: All parameters are those given in table 6.1.

Table 6.5   **Sensitivity of physical default probability to asset risk premium (Fannie Mae)**

Risk premium (bp)	Physical bankruptcy probability
0	34.22
20	25.83
40	18.83
60	12.99
80	8.40
100	5.22
120	3.11
140	1.73

Note: All parameters are those given in table 6.1 with a twenty-year horizon.

the risk premium on assets. When the risk premium is zero, the bankruptcy probability is the same as the risk-neutral default probability reported in table 6.3, and when the risk premium is 80 basis points, it is the same as the actual default probability reported in table 6.3. It is important to keep in mind that our cost estimates of the credit guarantees do not depend on the assumption about the risk premium.

Next, we consider the effect of discrete jumps down in asset value, where trend growth is adjusted up so that average asset growth is the same as the table 6.3 calculations. The probability of a jump is taken to be 3 percent per year, and the jump size is 5 percent. The results are reported in

Table 6.6   **2005 Guarantee value estimates with jumps**

	Fannie	Freddie	Fannie	Freddie
Horizon	10	10	20	20
Guarantee cost ($ billions)	16.54	19.30	38.25	32.32
Premium rate (bp)	23.62	13.30	29.23	25.23
Implied equity value ($ billions)	51.80	47.37	58.96	51.90
Default prob. (risk-neutral)	.21	.19	.34	.34
Default prob. (actual)	.068	.053	.112	.090
Trigger	1.09	1.08	1.14	1.12

Note: 3 percent annual probability of 5 percent reduction in asset size.

table 6.6. The effect is to increase the probability of default and the value of the guarantee by $10 to $20 billion. Increasing the size of the jump to 10 percent increases the twenty-year cost for Fannie to $43.8 billion, but also increase the equity value to $65.8 billion, significantly higher than its observed value. It appears that plausible jump processes increase estimated cost, but not enough to reconcile options-based and spread-based cost estimates.

Options-based estimates of guarantee value are quite sensitive to the assumed initial value of assets. In the months prior to Fannie and Freddie being put into receivership, their stock prices fell substantially and the underlying asset value for each firm clearly declined as well. It is interesting to see how the inferred guarantee value changes when the underlying assets suffer a loss. To illustrate the sensitivity to changes in initial leverage ratios, table 6.7 reports on guarantee values as a function of the initial ratio of market liabilities to market assets, holding other parameters the same as in the base case. In this table we simply reduce assets, holding asset volatility constant, and examine the effect on the value of equity and the insurance value.[10]

The optionality inherent in being an equity holder can be seen by considering the change in equity value as a function of the decline in asset value. A 5 percent decline in the value of assets for Fannie is about $40 billion. The decline in imputed equity value is about half of that when assets decline by the first $40 billion, and less than a third of that amount when assets decline by an additional $40 billion. The increase in the guarantee cost for the two scenarios is substantial, at $15 billion and $37 billion. The physical default probability also increases at an increasing rate with a drop in asset values. Similar results, not reported here, are obtained for Freddie.

10. An alternative approach would be to use observed equity value and volatility during the summer of 2008. However, Fannie and Freddie were not typical defaulting companies, and there was great uncertainty about whether, when, and how the federal government would intervene. This uncertainty makes it problematic to interpret observed market volatility.

Table 6.7   2005 Guarantee value estimates, varying initial equity for Fannie

	Fannie	Fannie −5% assets	Fannie −10% assets
Horizon	20	20	20
Guarantee cost ($ billions)	35.49	50.84	72.50
Premium rate (bp)	27.01	44.64	80.81
Implied equity value ($ billions)	55.78	36.02	23.84
Default prob. (risk-neutral)	.34	.43	.56
Default prob. (actual)	.084	.175	.394

6.5   Conclusions

In this chapter we develop a valuation model for a firm that can continue to periodically issue insured debt that is a fixed percentage of the value of its operating (i.e., nonguarantee) assets as long as it remains solvent. We use the model to explore whether the presence of such a guarantee changes the relation between the equity value of the firm, and the value of operating assets. This is important because in derivative-based approaches to valuing debt guarantees, the unobservable value and volatility of assets is inferred from the observable value and volatility of equity. If the presence of the guarantee changes these relations (for instance, by affecting equity dynamics), the inferences could be biased.

The theoretical analysis reveals that in fact, the presence of the guarantee does not fundamentally change the relation between the volatility of levered equity and the underlying assets, leaving intact the standard equations underlying derivatives-based pricing. It does, however, create a wedge between the value of operating assets and the market value of debt and equity equal to the present value of the future stream of income generated by the guarantee. This affects the initial conditions for derivatives-based estimates. The analysis also reveals that the spread-based approach is upwardly biased when no correction is made for the lower predicted default rate for guaranteed firms that optimally default less often to preserve the value of future guarantees.

To provide estimates that take into account these adjustments and that also incorporate potentially important complications such as jumps in underlying asset value, time-varying volatility, and a more complicated default policy, we calibrate and simulate a computational version of the model. We find that an insurance premium of 20 to 30 bps on Fannie and Freddie debt would be fair compensation for the default risk assumed by the government in the benign economic environment of year-end 2005. However, when asset values decline by 10 percent, it causes the fair premium to more than double, all else equal. This highlights the sensitivity of guarantee values to changes in equity value in highly levered financial institutions, and also demonstrates the usefulness of these types of models in setting risk-based insurance premiums.

References

Ambrose, B., and A. Warga. 2002. Measuring potential GSE funding advantages. *Journal of Real Estate Finance and Economics* 25 (2/3): 129–50.

Carnell, R. S. 2005. Handling the failure of Fannie Mae and Freddie Mac. Conference on Receivership Powers, American Enterprise Institute, Discussion Draft.

Collin-Dufresne, P., and R. S. Goldstein. 2001. Do credit spreads reflect stationary leverage ratios? *Journal of Finance* 56 (5): 1929–57.

Congressional Budget Office (CBO). 2001. Federal subsidies and the housing GSEs. Available at: http://www.cbo.gov/doc.cfm?index=2841.

———. 2004. Updated estimates of the subsidies to the housing GSEs. Available at: http://www.cbo.gov/doc.cfm?index=5368.

———. 2008, Cost estimate for H.R. 3221, Housing and Economic Recovery Act of 2008, July 2008. Available at: http://www.cbo.gov/ftpdocs/95xx/doc9597/hr3221 .pdf.

Crosbie, P., and J. Bohn. 2003. Modeling default risk. Moody's KMV White Paper. Available at: http://www.moodyskmv.com/research/whitepaper/Modeling DefaultRisk.pdf.

Demsetz, R., M. Saidenberg, and P. Strahan. 1996. Banks with something to lose: The disciplinary role of franchise value. *Economic Policy Review* 2 (2): 1–14.

Feldman, R. 1999. Estimating and managing the federal subsidy of Fannie Mae and Freddie Mac: Is either task possible? *Journal of Public Budgeting, Accounting, and Financial Management* 11 (Spring): 81–116.

Frame, W. S., and L. J. White. 2005. Fussing and fuming over Fannie and Freddie: How much smoke, how much fire? *Journal of Economic Perspectives* 19 (2): 159–84.

Hubbard, R. G. 2004. The relative risk of Freddie and Fannie. *Fannie Mae Papers* 3 (3)

Jaffee, D. 2003. The interest rate risk of Fannie Mae and Freddie Mac. *Journal of Financial Services Research* 24 (1): 5–29.

Keeley, M. 1990. Deposit insurance, risk, and market power in banking. *American Economic Review* 80 (5): 1183–200.

Leland, H. E. 1994. Corporate debt value, bond covenants, and optimal capital structure. *Journal of Finance* 49 (4): 1213–52.

Lucas, D., and R. McDonald. 2006. An options-based approach to evaluating the risk of Fannie Mae and Freddie Mac. *Journal of Monetary Economics* 53 (1): 155–76.

Marcus, A., and I. Shaked. 1984. The valuation of FDIC deposit insurance using option-pricing estimates. *Journal of Money, Credit and Banking* 16 (4): 446–60.

Merton, R. C. 1974. On the pricing of corporate debt: The risk structure of interest rates. *Journal of Finance* 29 (2): 449–70.

———. 1976. Option pricing when underlying stock returns are discontinuous. *Journal of Financial Economics* 3 (1): 125–44.

———. 1977. An analytic derivation of the cost of loan guarantees and deposit insurance: An application of modern option pricing theory. *Journal of Banking and Finance* 1 (1): 3–11.

Naranjo, A., and A. Toevs. 2002. The effects of purchases of mortgages and securitization by government sponsored enterprises on mortgage yield spreads and volatility. *Journal of Real Estate Finance and Economics* 25 (September-December): 173–95.

Nothaft, F. E., J. E. Pearce, and S. Stevanovic. 2002. Debt spreads between GSEs and other corporations. *Journal of Real Estate Finance and Economics* 25 (September-December): 151–72.

Passmore, W. 2005. The GSE implicit subsidy and the value of government ambiguity. *Real Estate Economics* 33 (3): 465–86.

Seiler, R. S. 2003. Market discipline of Fannie Mae and Freddie Mac: How do share prices and debt yield spreads respond to new information? Office of Federal Housing Enterprise Oversight Working Paper no. 03-4.

Sharpe, W. F. 1976. Corporate pension funding policy. *Journal of Financial Economics* 3 (3): 183–93.

Stiglitz, J. E., J. M. Orszag, and P. Orszag. 2002, Implications of the New Fannie Mae and Freddie Mac risk-based capital standards. *Fannie Mae Papers* 1 (2): 1–10.

Comment   Alan J. Marcus

This chapter is a valuable contribution to the literature on the too-often unacknowledged growth in explicit and implicit government guarantee programs. While the Federal Government did not originally provide explicit "full faith and credit" backing of Fannie Mae and Freddie Mac debt, its implicit support was, as Lucas and McDonald (henceforth, LM) point out, widely acknowledged and visibly apparent in the yields at which the two firms were able to issue their bonds. More recently, of course, that guarantee became explicit.

Lucas and McDonald estimate the ex-ante present value in 2005 of the combined guarantee to the two firms at around $65 billion over twenty years. This is a considerable amount; moreover, as a mean, it is actually a conservative estimate of the government's potential exposure. A value-at-risk estimate focusing on bad- or worst-case scenarios obviously would be multiples of this value. When comparing this implicit guarantee with some of the others discussed in this volume, it is good to remember that the risks of some programs have been assessed by worst-case scenarios and others by midpoint estimates. By either standard, Freddie-Fannie guarantees must be ranked among the more important contingent government obligations, and a careful demonstration of this point is by itself an important contribution of the chapter.

Alan J. Marcus is professor of finance at the Carroll School of Management, Boston College.

An even more important contribution of the model is the capability it provides for sensitivity analysis. Lucas and McDonald build behavioral assumptions regarding funding and asset management policy into their model. Among the more interesting features of their model is the flexibility they allow for the response of asset volatility to financial distress, the bankruptcy trigger, and the response of liabilities to target leverage. They find that the value of the guarantee is quite sensitive to some of these parameters, particularly the ones that link asset volatility to the financial status of the firm. This sort of sensitivity analysis allows one to determine which sorts of behaviors provide the greatest potential for growth in government exposure and therefore to progress from passive risk measurement to active risk management.

Comparing the LM approach to other valuation studies based on yield spreads highlights its advantages and disadvantages. Valuation using yield spreads revalues outstanding debt using an estimate of the yield at which it would sell in the absence of the implied Federal guarantee. The predicted drop in the value of debt when it is priced at a nonguaranteed yield is the estimated value of the guarantee. The advantage of this approach compared to structural models like that of LM is that we can tie our valuation down to more or less observable market statistics—the yields at which government-sponsored enterprise (GSE) debt actually sells and the yields at which otherwise comparable corporate debt sells. Passmore (2005) estimated that the implied federal guarantee reduced Freddie and Fannie debt yields by about 40 basis points, corresponding to a guarantee value of around $150 billion. This approach to valuing the impact of the guarantee is far simpler than the option-pricing approach used in LM. But that relative simplicity comes at a high price, since it is essentially a point estimate, and sheds limited light on the exposure of potential losses to changes in underlying economic conditions.

Lucas and McDonald's more structural option-pricing model forces them to take a stand on harder issues. For example, they need to specify jump and diffusion parameters, decide how to model the bankruptcy trigger, and how to model firm behavior if it enters financial distress. Any of these parameters are hard to estimate and inevitably are subject to second-guessing and imprecision. But there is an advantage to this approach as well, for to truly understand the risk and the value of the government's exposure we *need* to take a stand on these issues. If we learned anything from the Federal Savings and Loan Insurance Corporation (FSLIC) debacle it is that sensitivity analysis is crucial, and that value is highly subject to behavioral assumptions, and in particular, to moral hazard.

While these valuation approaches differ considerably, it would have been nice if LM's base-case estimates (about $65 billion) had turned out closer to those derived from yield spreads (about $150 billion in Passmore's study).

Lucas and McDonald note that part of this difference may be related to a feature that can only be captured in a multiperiod model such as theirs. In their model, a firm with a government guarantee may optimally choose not to default in some states that an uninsured firm would declare bankruptcy. The insured firm is less apt to default because it has an incentive to preserve the value of the government's future guarantees. This policy makes the value of the next-period guarantee to the firm greater than the cost to the government.

In any case, these differences may be less extreme than they appear. Lucas and McDonald note that their guarantee value translates to a yield spread of about 20 to 30 basis points, compared to 40 basis points in Passmore. Part of the difference seems to be due to Passmore's higher growth assumptions. More importantly, part of the yield spread may reflect the special status and the higher liquidity of GSE debt rather than default risk. Moreover, Passmore notes that the yield spreads as well as other determinants of guarantee value vary over time and that his estimates vary considerably across parameter combinations, so perhaps these differences are within shouting distance.[1] Nevertheless, even most of the LM sensitivity-analysis estimates are lower than those derived from than the seemingly simpler yield-spread approach, so it may be worth considering whether there is some reason that the option pricing method seems to result in lower valuations.

Of course in a mechanical sense, LM could always find parameters for which their valuation would match almost any other estimate, for example, by increasing volatility inputs, jump risk, funding policy, or the sensitivity of asset volatility to financial distress. But their parameter choices do not strike me as particularly conservative. In particular, the quadrupling of asset volatility in periods of financial distress (when assets fall below 1.01 times liabilities) seems sufficiently aggressive.

Another possibility worth some consideration is that the LM estimates of asset volatility may be low. All option pricing models are driven by asset volatility, which LM infer from the volatility of equity. But neither Fannie nor Freddie have been particularly transparent. Lucas and McDonald note that little information was available on their interest-rate hedging activities or efficacy. The firms released "fair value balance sheets" accounting for the market value of their extensive derivatives positions only quarterly (Freddie) or annually (Fannie), and even then, outside observers had to rely on their

1. Passmore obtains his estimate through a "simulation analysis" in which several inputs to the valuation formula such as growth rates, yield spreads, equity risk premia, and so on are allowed to take on multiple values. Therefore, he allows for a range of estimates. Note, however, that his simulation is of a very different nature than that conducted in LM, which employs Monte Carlo analysis driven by stochastic evolution in asset value. Passmore's approach does not specify a stochastic process for asset returns, and therefore does not answer questions about the sensitivity of guarantee value to changes in parameters such as asset volatility, nor does it provide a probability distribution of potential losses.

valuations, without any meaningful guidance as to their methodologies. This would be hard enough if one could have trusted their commitment to meaningful disclosure, but both firms had very troubling histories of earnings management, particularly earnings smoothing, which at the least, cast doubt on any such commitment.

What if opacity and aggressive earnings-smoothing practices significantly reduced firm-specific information? Specifically, what if lack of transparency meant that the market had only limited information about these firms? If so, stock price volatility may have reflected the value impact of *revealed* information, but not the full volatility of actual performance, most of which was not publicly observable. Morck, Yeung, and Yu (2000) note that opacity can lead to a reduction in the firm-specific component of returns. Jin and Myers (2006) extend this empirically, and further show that opacity is associated with crashes.[2] Either implication—higher volatility or crash risk—would increase LM estimates if opacity is an issue for the GSEs.

Can we test this hypothesis? Freddie Mac actually provides us with an interesting experiment. Before 1993, it was effectively a pure pass-through firm. Figure 6C.1 shows that in this period it held only one mortgage in portfolio for every ten mortgages that were securitized and passed through. In contrast, even in the pre-1993 period, Fannie maintained a large portfolio of retained mortgages, financed by issuing debt. After 1993, however, Freddie's retained portfolio rapidly caught up to Fannie's. Before 1993, therefore, Freddie Mac should have exhibited a different risk profile than Fannie Mae, but not after.

To compare the stock market risk of the two firms, I estimated the following two-index regression for each firm. Each regression is estimated year-by-year using daily data. The coefficient on the Standard & Poor's (S&P) 500 measures broad stock market exposure while the coefficient on the return on the seven-year Treasury bond measures interest rate risk (which could result from imperfect hedging). Firm-specific risk is reflected in the regression residual, e, and more particularly, its standard error.

$$(1) \qquad R_i = a + b\,R_{S\&P} + c\,R_{7\text{-year T-bond}} + e.$$

Among the questions we can address with these regressions are the following:

- Do factor exposures (especially the T-bond betas) of Freddie (compared to those of Fannie) increase after 1993?
- Does Freddie's residual standard deviation (compared to Fannie's) change after 1993 when it becomes equally "opaque"?

2. In the Jin-Myers model, the firm may hide an accumulating barrage of negative information until it is no longer feasible to do so. At that point, all is revealed to the market at once, which results in a stock-price crash. This seems like a reasonable fear for Freddie and Fannie in light of their past accounting practices.

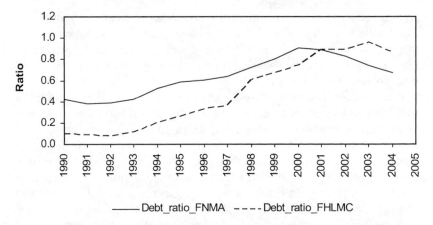

Fig. 6C.1   Ratio of debt outstanding to off balance sheet mortgages securitized and sold as mortgage-backed securities
Source: Data obtained from Lucas and McDonald (2006).

Figures 6C.2 and 6C.3 show the S&P 500 and T-bond betas for Fannie and Freddie. While there is considerable variation in annual values, the overlap in the values for the two firms is remarkable. There clearly is no break in the relationship between the two firms in 1993, or for that matter, at any other point in the sample. Figure 6C.4 shows the standard errors of the regressions for each firm in each year. Again, there is nothing that distinguishes one firm from the other. Given the almost identical values for both coefficients and the residual standard deviations, it is not surprising that plots (not presented here to save space) of R-squares or of correlation coefficients between raw returns and regression residuals are also effectively identical for both firms.

These figures are interesting mostly for what they do *not* show. Until 1993, Fannie and Freddie followed significantly different risk-management models. Freddie Mac bundled and sold virtually all mortgages as mortgage-backed securities, retaining only credit risk in return for a guarantee fee. In contrast, Fannie Mae held a considerable fraction of mortgages in portfolio, thereby adding interest rate risk from imperfect hedging strategies into the mix. Despite this, the stock return behavior of the two firms as presented in figures 6C.2 through 6C.4 are virtually identical in both the pre- and post-1993 periods.

One might conclude from these figures that the market simply disregarded the fact that Fannie had to be riskier in the earlier period. Perhaps in the absence of daily information about the efficacy of the hedging program, there was no news to which Fannie's stock price might react. There would then be little else to differentiate the performance of the firms. If so, the nearly identical regression results in the two periods is consistent with opacity and stock

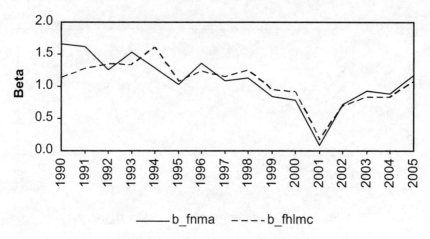

Fig. 6C.2   Coefficient on S&P 500 return in the following regression: $R_i = a + b\,R_{S\&P} + c\,R_{7\text{-year T-bond}} + e$
Note: Regression estimated year-by-year using daily return data.

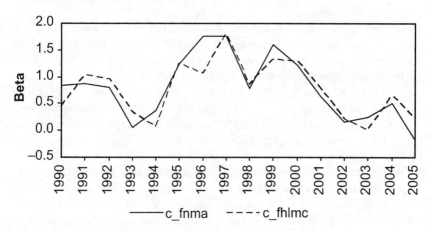

Fig. 6C.3   Coefficient on T-bond return in the following regression: $R_i = a + b\,R_{S\&P} + c\,R_{7\text{-year T-bond}} + e$
Note: Regression estimated year-by-year using daily return data.

price volatility that does not reflect all potential risks. This would be bad news, for it would suggest that equity (and therefore asset) volatility for the purpose of the LM valuation exercise should be greater than that obtained from stock price returns or short-term implied volatilities.

On the other hand, the residual standard errors in figure 6C.4 do not seem abnormally low compared to typical firms, nor did Freddie's fall after 1993 when it adopted an arguably less transparent business model. Under the common interpretation that residual returns proxy for firm-specific information, there is no support for opacity there. The likely impact of opacity is not

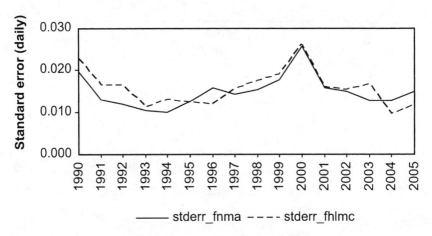

Fig. 6C.4   Standard deviation of residual return in the following regression: $R_i = a + b\,R_{S\&P} + c\,R_{7\text{-year T-bond}} + e$

Note: Regression estimated year-by-year using daily return data.

easily resolvable, but might at least suggest that the LM valuation numbers be taken as conservative. This interpretation also is consistent with the fact that they are somewhat lower than Passmore's midrange estimates.

In the end, however, this may not be the most important question. As noted previously, risk management is as important as risk measurement; to my mind, the true value of the LM model is as a tool for sensitivity analysis. One needs a structural model like theirs to see where the government's exposures lie, and particularly, what factors may drive potentially rapid changes in that exposure.

While it is not the focus of their chapter, their model does offer the opportunity to think about an interesting question: what would happen to the value of the guarantee if Freddie and Fannie were forced to follow Freddie's portfolio strategy of pre-1993? There is no inherent reason that either firm needs to hold significant amounts of mortgages in portfolio, or that doing so strengthens its competitive position. Freddie held few mortgages in portfolio until 1993, and its market share actually *declined* slightly after 1994 when it adopted Fannie's portfolio model.

In a real sense, both firms have acted as a bundle of two distinct business lines: one is plain-vanilla securitization, but the other is as an implicit hedge fund in which mortgages are held in portfolio and hedged with positions in callable bonds and derivatives. While there may be good reasons for the government to support the first activity in the interest of potential spillovers to mortgage rates and the housing market, there is no reason to subsidize the second. Certainly, a limit on portfolio size would be the easiest way to limit and manage the government's exposure to interest rate risk (but not credit risk, since that attaches to securitized as well as held mortgages). Since there seems to be little economic rationale for the portfolio activities, the only cost to imposing such limits would most likely be to the shareholders, who would forfeit the value of much of their unpaid-for subsidy.

References

Jin, L., and S. C. Myers. 2006. R^2 Around the World. *Journal of Financial Economics* 79 (2): 257–92.

Lucas, D., and R. McDonald. 2006. An options-based approach to evaluating the risk of Fannie Mae and Freddie Mac. *Journal of Monetary Economics* 53 (1): 155–76.

Morck, R., B. Yeung, and W. Yu. 2000. The information content of stock markets: Why do emerging markets have synchronous stock price movements? *Journal of Financial Economics* 58 (1): 215–60.

Passmore, W. 2005. The GSE implicit subsidy and the value of government ambiguity. *Real Estate Economics* 33 (3): 465–86.

Guaranteed versus Direct Lending
The Case of Student Loans

Deborah Lucas and Damien Moore

7.1 Introduction

The federal government makes low-cost financing for higher education widely available through its fast-growing student loan programs. The existence of two competing government programs—the Federal Family Educational Loan Program (guaranteed program) and the Federal Direct Loan Program (direct program)—provides a unique opportunity to compare the cost to the government of direct federal lending versus loan guarantees.

Both the direct and guaranteed student loan program offer their borrowers very similar loan products and terms, but the programs differ significantly from the perspective of other key stakeholders, including educational institutions, commercial lenders, and state guarantee agencies. The programs also have widely divergent budget costs: The Fiscal Year (FY) 2007 budget records a 2 percent subsidy rate on direct loans, versus a subsidy rate of 10 percent for the guaranteed program.

In this study, we propose and implement a methodology to provide a comprehensive cost estimate for the two programs in market value terms, and analyze the sources of the differential. There are several reasons for emphasizing market values. Arguably, they are the best estimate of the cost of federal obligations from the perspective of taxpayers. Increasingly,

Deborah Lucas is the former Donald C. Clark HSBC Professor of Consumer Finance, Kellogg School of Management, Northwestern University, and is currently Associate Director of Financial Analysis at the CBO and a research associate of the National Bureau of Economic Research. Damien Moore is an analyst in the Financial Markets Unit of the CBO.

We thank Marvin Phaup and Janice Eberly for many helpful comments and suggestions. The views expressed are not necessarily those of the Congressional Budget Office. Lucas gratefully acknowledges the support of the Searle Foundation.

federal and local government agencies incorporate market valuation principles in cost-benefit analyses (e.g., Gramlich 1990). Further, almost all noncredit transactions—including grants, purchases of goods, and the direct provision of services—appear in the budget at market prices (Lucas and Phaup, chapter 3 in this volume). In the context of improving access to higher education, outright grants are the main alternative to subsidized loans. The omission of certain costs for loans and loan guarantees understates their true cost to taxpayers, and artificially favors expanding the student loan programs over funding for grants.

Obtaining market value estimates allows us to address the question of how much of the difference in reported subsidy rates can be attributed to real cost differences between the programs, and how much is due to idiosyncrasies in the rules for budgeting federal credit. To preview the main results, we find that budget costs for both programs are well below their market value. This is mostly attributable to budget rules that require discounting expected net cash flows at Treasury rates. Understatement of the market cost of capital also accounts for why some direct loans appear to make money for the government, despite the favorable terms offered to borrowers. Administrative costs are accounted for inconsistently across programs, with some costs of the direct program not incorporated into the subsidy rate.

Even after adjusting for the market cost of capital, asymmetric treatment of administrative costs, and other inconsistencies in how the programs are budgeted for, the guaranteed program appears to be fundamentally more expensive than the direct program. Adjusting for the cost of risk has little effect on the differential, since the government bears most of the credit risk in either case. The differential can be attributed primarily to the fact that guaranteed lenders are paid more than is required to induce them to lend at statutory terms. The excess payments appear to be partially absorbed in competition for borrowers, which occurs through various discounts, marketing activities, and higher service levels and subsidies to educational institutions. To the extent that the market is not perfectly competitive, guaranteed lenders presumably are able to retain some of the surplus. The direct program also has a real cost advantage. As well as lower administrative costs, the direct program has the advantage of raising funds via the Treasury rather than through private financial institutions. The size of the Treasury's apparent advantage, and whether it should be considered a real cost saving, is also discussed.

In light of its cost disadvantage, a natural question is whether the guaranteed program provides offsetting benefits. In principal, private intermediaries can add value; for instance, through better screening or monitoring of borrowers. Student loans, however, have categorical entitlement and an almost full credit guarantee, making the value added by private intermediation less obvious. Beyond loan administration, the guaranteed program channels money and services to students, schools, and guarantee agencies, but these transfers might be better targeted and controlled if they were separated from the lending function.

The rest of the chapter is organized as follows. Section 7.2 provides an overview of federal student loan programs: their size, product offerings, the roles of various stakeholders, and their market structure. Section 7.3 describes how student loans and loan guarantees are budgeted for; how these rules lead to budget estimates that are inconsistent with market valuation; and the decomposition of costs in the budget. In section 7.4 we discuss the private student market and the information it provides on the market cost of capital and the composition of administrative costs. In section 7.5 we turn to the central problem of estimating the market cost of the direct and guaranteed loan programs. The resulting market value estimates are presented and subjected to sensitivity analysis. Section 7.6 assesses cost from the perspective of guaranteed lenders. Section 7.7 concludes with a discussion of some of the broader policy questions raised by the analysis, and of the implications of the recent financial crisis for the student loan market.

7.2   Overview

The Department of Education (ED) oversees two competing student loan programs: the Federal Family Education Loan (FFEL, or guaranteed) program, and the William D. Ford Federal Direct Loan (direct loan) program. In the guaranteed program, which dates back to the mid-1960s, the government guarantees loans originated by private lenders against losses from default and makes supplemental payments to lenders. In the direct program, which began operation much more recently in 1994, the government directly lends to qualifying students.

7.2.1   Program Size

The federal student loan program is one of the largest credit programs operated by the US government. Table 7.1 shows the rapid growth in total federally-backed student loans outstanding, which in 2005 totaled over $380 billion. Statistics compiled by the Department of Education indicate that in the same year, about 6.8 million students, and 750,000 parents of students, borrowed $56 billion in new federally-backed loans. The guaranteed program was responsible for 77 percent of this new loan volume. Another 2.5 million borrowers took advantage of the option to convert their outstanding Stafford loans into more favorable consolidation loans, resulting in $69.6 billion of new consolidation loans.

7.2.2   Product Offerings and Loan Terms

Both the direct and guaranteed programs offer three basic types of loans: Stafford Loans, Parent Loans to Undergraduate Students (PLUS), and

Table 7.1   Federal student loans outstanding, 1998–2005

	1998	1999	2000	2001	2002	2003	2004	2005
FFEL								
Unconsolidated (Stafford and PLUS)	74,727	92,760	106,220	122,423	129,757	130,455	142,405	148,391
Consolidated	9,675	20,008	27,891	32,384	49,434	79,017	100,176	138,457
Subtotal	84,402	112,768	134,111	154,807	179,191	209,472	242,581	286,848
Direct								
Unconsolidated (Stafford and PLUS)	26,937	33,763	43,091	47,958	50,264	51,013	52,090	47,679
Consolidated	4,733	12,067	14,622	22,526	29,807	33,507	37,155	47,027
Subtotal	31,670	45,830	57,713	70,484	80,071	84,520	89,245	94,706
Total	116,072	158,598	191,824	225,291	259,262	293,992	331,826	381,554

Source: OMB, as reported in the budget appendix.

Consolidation loans. We restrict the analysis to Stafford and Consolidation loans, since these comprise the vast majority of loans in both programs.

The terms on all loans are set by statute under the Higher Education Act. From the perspective of students, the terms on Stafford and Consolidation loans are virtually identical under both the direct and guaranteed programs. Government payments to and from guaranteed lenders are also set by statute, and differ across loan types.

Stafford

These ten- to thirty-year loans are available to students enrolled in eligible educational institutions, which includes most US colleges and universities but not trade or for-profit schools. Between 1998 and July 2006, these loans carried a floating rate that reset annually, based on the three-month Treasury rate plus a fixed spread. Since July 2006, Stafford loans carry a fixed 6.8 percent per annum interest rate, with flexible repayment plans that begin upon completion or dropping out of a course of study.[1] Borrowers in the guaranteed program are assessed a onetime 2 percent origination fee, although this may be paid by the lender.[2] Borrowers pay a further 1 percent guarantee fee at origination that accrues to guaranty agencies in the guaranteed program. In the direct program borrowers are charged 3 percent upfront, although they can receive a 1.5 percent rebate for an on-time first payment.[3]

Although all Stafford loans carry below-market rates, the loans are further classified as "subsidized" or "unsubsidized." The federal government pays all of the accrued interest on subsidized Stafford loans while a borrower

1. From July 2008, the rate on new loans is scheduled to decline in gradual increments until it reaches 3.4 percent in July 2011 before reverting to 6.8 percent in July 2012, at which time the Higher Education Act comes up for reauthorization. The analysis here is based on the rules in effect from August 2006 to June 2007.
2. Under current law, the origination fee phases out over the next several years.
3. Historically, the guarantee fee has also been waived, but this is no longer the case.

is in school, grace period, or deferment, whereas interest accrues on unsubsidized loans. Eligibility for subsidized loans is based on income.

On Stafford loans, guaranteed lenders receive special allowance payments (SAP) from the government that provide net cash flows (including payments from students) equal to the three-month commercial paper rate plus a fixed spread. The spread is 1.74 percent while students are in school and 2.34 percent when loans are in repayment. The spread is primarily compensation for administrative costs rather than risk, since lenders also are reimbursed for 97 to 99 percent of principal and accrued interest on loans that default, and the commercial paper (CP) rate is approximately the cost of capital for federally guaranteed loans (see section 7.4.1, subsection "Capital Cost for Guaranteed Loans"). Net payments to lenders are reduced by a onetime, 50 basis point origination fee assessed on lenders.[4] Guaranty agencies receive 40 basis points (bps) of this origination fee, reducing the net federal cash inflow to 10 basis points.

Consolidation

Borrowers with one or more Stafford loans may replace them with a single Consolidation loan any time after completing their course of study. Consolidation loans offer a new repayment plan and a fixed interest rate equal to the weighted average of interest rates on the underlying Stafford loans rounded up to the nearest eighth of a percentage point. Thus, the portion of post-July 2006 Stafford loans that are consolidated will carry a rate slightly above 6.8 percent. Consolidation loans now offer a similar set of flexible repayment terms as do Stafford loans, but in the past also provided additional repayment extension options.

Guaranteed lenders receive lower compensation from the government for Consolidation than for Stafford loans. For Consolidation loans, the spread over the three-month commercial paper rate, net of fees, is 1.59 percent. In addition, they pay a further origination fee of 50 bps, of which 40 bps goes to the guaranty agencies. Despite generating less income than Stafford loans, the net return on the loans is generally positive, and competition to offer these loans until recently has been brisk. However, it appears that guaranteed lenders avoid consolidating distressed loans, since a disproportionate share of distressed loans is consolidated into the direct loan program.

7.2.3   Stakeholders

Students and parents of students pursuing post-secondary degrees are direct beneficiaries of these programs, which lower the cost and increase the availability of funding for higher education. Unsubsidized Stafford loans are not means-tested, and borrowing limits are tied to educational expenses, which are higher at private and four-year institutions. Hence, students from

4. This fee will increase to 1 percentage point beginning October 2007.

middle- and upper-income-class families receive a large share of total program benefits. From an economic perspective, loan assistance can be welfare improving when imperfections in private credit markets limit access to education, or when education has significant positive externalities.[5] A caveat is that some students may take on an excessive amount of debt to pay for degrees that add little to their earning potential.

Educational institutions also depend on federal student loan programs for financial support. Without assistance, many students would be unable or unwilling to pay the high tuition charges at many schools.[6] To a lesser extent, schools benefit directly if they elect to participate in the guaranteed loan program. Guaranteed lenders offer schools various types of support in exchange for featuring their loans, including educational grants and administrative, educational, and systems support to financial aid offices. In "school as lender" programs, where the educational institution itself takes on the origination role, the school retains the excess of government payments over its cost of extending credit.

The guaranteed loan industry—lenders, servicers, and guarantee agencies—also have a large stake in the program. Providing financing for guaranteed student loans has been a profitable line of business for guaranteed lenders, although competition in the industry has intensified over time. Although there are more than 3,500 for-profit and not-for-profit lenders, the market is dominated by a few large for-profit players, including the leading commercial banks and Sallie Mae. Sallie Mae, by far the largest guaranteed lender, began as a government-sponsored enterprise but now is fully privatized.

State and private nonprofit guaranty agencies administer the federal guarantee and provide services to schools and lenders. As of 2006, there were thirty-five active guaranty agencies, some operating in multiple states. Each guaranty agency maintains an account in federal trust, which is used to pay out claims from lenders. Those funds are replenished by the federal government. Guaranty agencies also receive federal funds for performing collection activities, historically as high as 25 percent of the recovered amounts (even if the amount was recovered through federal loan consolidation). The agencies may use their share of collections to fund scholarships, education outreach programs, and default aversion activities.

7.2.4   Market Structure

To evaluate the costs associated with lending and the likely disposition of the rents created when government payments exceed the cost of guaranteed

---

5. Several studies question the effectiveness of such policies; for example, De Fraja (2002), Dynarski (2002), Edlin (1993), Hanushek (1998), and Keane (2002). Gale (1991) points out that many federal credit programs probably have a small real effect on the allocation of credit, in many cases simply crowding out private borrowing and lending.

6. Some have argued that the generous borrowing limits in the federal student loan program have accommodated the growth in college tuition, which has exceeded the growth of the overall economy.

lending, it is necessary to understand how the market for student loans is organized and the extent to which it is competitive.

Schools have a choice of whether to participate in the direct or guaranteed loan program, and all of its students must borrow through that program. Simultaneous participation in both programs is not permitted, but a school can elect to switch programs and some choose to do so.[7] Competition for volume between the two programs therefore centers on school administrators, particularly financial aid officers. Recall that both programs offer students nearly identical loan terms, so differentiation occurs primarily along other dimensions. The direct program offers greater administrative simplicity, which initially attracted many schools to the program. Guaranteed lenders responded by offering schools and borrowers improved service and other inducements, and since the late 1990s the guaranteed program has slowly regained market share (see figure 7.1).

Competition also takes place at the school level between guaranteed lenders. Although there are thousands of lenders potentially competing for borrowers' business, at the individual institutions competition is much more limited. The financial aid office serves as a gatekeeper, counseling students who seek advice, and only including a limited number of lenders on its "preferred lender list."[8] Most students have little financial experience and rely on the advice of the school, although direct-to-student marketing of loan products has become more common, and some students venture beyond the preferred lender list.

The market for consolidation loans is more competitive because borrowers are free to choose between the direct program and any guaranteed lender. In recent years, very favorable terms on consolidation loans led to high rates of consolidation and the entry of competitive new entrants into the consolidation business. Under the new fixed rate regime, consolidation is less advantageous to students, and since it is also financially disadvantageous to Stafford lenders, its prevalence has been declining.

We conclude that because of the active competition between guaranteed lenders to capture volume, it is likely that all but the most efficient lenders retain little in the way of abnormal profits. The gatekeeper role of schools further suggests that they are in a position to capture a large portion of rents, but those may be passed through to students through scholarships, expanded program offerings, or other means. The common practice of lenders paying all or part of the origination fee for students and offering benefits like discounts for on-time payments is direct evidence that some of the rent

7. A single university may have some schools participating in the direct program and others using the guaranteed program.

8. Northwestern University provides a fairly typical example. It includes five major lenders on its preferred list for undergraduate students. It does not officially rank them, but Citibank holds the coveted first position on the (nonalphabetical) list. The preferred lender lists for its various graduate and professional schools are shorter. The business, law, and medical schools offer only three options, with the first one being Northwestern University itself. Only two lenders are recommended to students pursuing part-time MBAs.

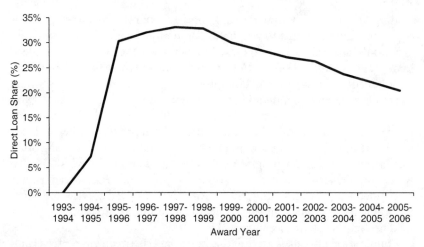

Fig. 7.1   The direct program share of new federal student(?) loan volume
Source: The Department of Education.

goes directly to students. Some rents, however, are absorbed by marketing costs and inducements to schools and financial aid officers that seem unlikely to provide much benefit to students.

7.3   Budget Estimates

Most analyses of the cost difference between the direct and guaranteed loan programs rely on budget estimates prepared by the Congressional Budget Office (CBO) and the Office of Management and Budget (OMB). Although the underlying premise of this study is that market value estimates offer a more accurate representation of cost than do budget estimates, the budget provides a useful and more familiar starting point for evaluating program cost. In this section we describe the rules governing budgeting for credit, noting where they deviate from market valuation principles. We also discuss what budget estimates reveal about the breakdown of cost for the two programs, and how those comparisons can be misleading.

7.3.1   Budgeting for Federal Student Loan Programs

Before 1990, credit, like most other government programs, was accounted for on a cash basis. Under cash basis accounting, new direct loan programs have a very high up-front cost since the loan principal is recorded as a cash outflow. In contrast, loan guarantees initially can appear to make money, since fees are paid up-front but the cash flows associated with defaults may not materialize for many years. The Federal Credit Reform Act of 1990 (FCRA) made the treatment of direct and guaranteed loans more symmetric by effectively putting credit on an accrual basis, with cost measured as a net discounted value of expected current and future cash flows associated with the current year commitment.

Federal budget rules have had a significant effect on the structure and evolution of the federal student loan programs. Most notably, the direct student loan program appears to have been made feasible from a budgetary perspective by FCRA. Proposed on several occasions in the late 1980s, direct lending's high initial cash cost was a decisive obstacle. The direct loan program was enacted in 1993, shortly after the FCRA went into effect.

7.3.2 Budget Cost versus Market Cost

Before turning to the budget estimates, it is important to understand in general terms why those numbers are systematically lower than the market value estimates of cost presented later on. The main reason for the downward bias is that FCRA mandates using maturity-matched Treasury rates without risk adjustment for discounting. This practice makes both direct and guaranteed loans appear less costly to the government than when discounting at market rates.

The omission of certain administrative costs further lowers budget estimates relative to comprehensive market value estimates. In addition, administrative costs are accounted for inconsistently across the two programs. Most administrative costs associated with guaranteed loans are included in the reported subsidy rate. By contrast, administrative costs in the direct program are accounted for separately and on a cash basis, and so are not included in subsidy estimates.[9]

A discrepancy between budget and market cost also arises from CBO's budgetary treatment of floating rate loans.[10] The CBO interprets FCRA as requiring the use of final maturity-matched Treasury rates for discounting, whereas market valuations reflect the shorter effective maturity of floating rate loans, which equals the time to the next rate reset. Because of the term premium in long-term rates, this tends to bias down federal estimates of floating rate direct loan value relative to their market value. Although the switch to fixed rates for new student loans after June 2006 reduces this distortion prospectively, federal payments to guaranteed lenders still depend

---

9. Administrative costs for most federal loan programs are accounted for separately on a cash basis, and hence do not appear in subsidy rates.

10. This misvaluation has potential real effects. For instance, it prompted the Department of Education to propose a sale of direct loans in 2003. The loans had a higher market than budget value because the relatively high level of long-term rates caused the government to discount future guaranteed cash flows at a higher than market rate. The plan was to sell the loans, apply some of the proceeds to paying off Treasury debt, and to use the net gain to provide additional assistance to students. In fact, the sale would have entailed additional administrative costs without generating any real savings; the loans could not have been sold for more than a fair price. The OMB treats floating rates as short-term rates, so this problem is not reflected in the President's Budget.

on short-term interest rates and this convention will tend to bias down that component of cost in CBO estimates.

7.3.3   Budget Cost Decomposition

The Credit Supplement to the Budget, prepared by OMB, provides a breakdown of subsidy cost across four cost components—defaults, interest, fees and other—for four loan categories (Stafford Subsidized, Stafford Unsubsidized, PLUS, and Consolidated). Table 7.2 reproduces some of this data from the 2007 Credit Supplement. The total subsidy rate is the discounted value of projected net losses divided by the underlying loan principal at origination.

Both the direct and guarantee programs report small but similar subsidy cost components for defaults. The last two columns of table 7.2 break out cumulative lifetime default rates and recovery rates. Recovery rate estimates in excess of 100 percent are attributable to OMB's reporting convention rather than to exceptional performance: recovery amounts are not discounted and not all collection costs are deducted. After discounting and adjusting for collection costs, we estimate that the federal recovery rate averaged about 50 percent, in line with experience in the private student loan market. We also cannot reconcile the low reported default rates with our calculation of default rates from historical data from the Department of Education, which are described in section 7.5.

Default rates are for the most part similar in the two programs, reflecting similarities in the borrower populations. The exception is for consolidation loans, which experience much higher default rates in the direct program. As noted earlier, the higher default rate may be explained by the reluctance of guaranteed lenders to consolidate loans on the brink of default, and the fact that the direct program must consolidate the loans of qualified borrowers that wish to consolidate but have been turned down by guaranteed lenders.

For the remaining components of subsidy cost, the breakdown is markedly different across the direct and guaranteed programs. The biggest difference is that the direct program reports large interest income, whereas the guaranteed program reports large interest costs. This occurs in part because OMB defines the "interest" component of cost very differently across programs. In the direct program, the government reports net interest income as the present value of any interest paid by borrowers in excess of the Treasury rate, which it takes as the government's cost of capital. Because the borrower interest rate exceeds the Treasury rate, this item reduces the reported subsidy cost. In contrast, the interest component in the guaranteed program represents the present value of the net payments made to guaranteed lenders, which is an outflow. Although classified as interest, these payments are more accurately described as covering administrative and other costs, since borrowers' payments generally cover lenders' cost of funds. Hence

Table 7.2   Composition of subsidy costs

| | Subsidy rate | Composition of subsidy | | | | Default rate | Recovery rate |
		Defaults (net of recovery)	Interest	Fees	All other		
Ford Direct Loan Program							
Weighted average of total obligations	2.05	1.31	−2.66	−1.67	5.07	14.00	118.29
Subsidized Stafford	9.83	0.67	6.44	−3.00	5.72	12.04	118.93
Unsubsidized Stafford	−8.28	0.82	−12.59	−3.00	6.49	12.09	116.57
PLUS	−6.37	0.89	−11.97	−4.00	8.71	5.50	101.51
Consolidation	4.37	1.92	−0.99	n.a.	3.44	17.20	119.56
Family Federal Education Loan Program							
Weighted average of total obligations	9.87	0.89	11.12	−5.54	3.40	12.04	117.65
Subsidized Stafford	17.78	0.86	17.62	−3.25	2.55	12.04	118.99
Unsubsidized Stafford	1.12	0.96	0.79	−3.25	2.62	11.15	116.27
PLUS	−0.01	0.88	−1.73	−3.25	4.09	5.38	101.08
Consolidated	12.20	0.88	15.46	−8.26	4.12	13.27	118.64

Source: Federal Credit Supplement 2006.
Note: n.a. = not applicable.

the reported "interest costs" cannot be meaningfully compared without adjustments.

Administrative costs in the direct program that are borne directly by the federal government are excluded from subsidy estimates, and do not appear in table 7.2. Costs that entail payments to third parties for tasks such as collecting on loans do appear, and are recorded in the category "other." In the guaranteed program, the corresponding costs are accounted for as part of "interest," as just discussed.

Fees levied on borrowers, guaranteed lenders, and guaranty agencies reduce subsidy costs. Only borrower fees affect the direct loan program, and they make a negative contribution to the subsidy rate. For the guaranteed program, these fees also include the upfront application fee on Stafford and PLUS loans in both programs, as well as the 1.05 percent per annum consolidation fee paid by guaranteed lenders to the federal government. Logically it makes more sense to think of lender fees as reducing the net administrative payments from the government to guaranteed lenders. To facilitate comparison, a more parallel treatment of administrative costs is presented in section 7.5.

7.4   Inferring Economic Costs and Cost Differentials

Estimating market cost requires a comprehensive measure of the cash flows associated with each program, and also a measure of the cost of capital. We impute the market risk premium on student loans from pricing in the private student loan market, and also use lender data to infer some components of administrative cost.

Private lenders primarily serve students who have exceeded federal lending limits.[11] The main players in the private loan market are also the largest guaranteed lenders—Sallie Mae and major national and regional commercial banks. Economies of scale in marketing, systems administration, and funding, and the experience gained from guaranteed lending, give these institutions a competitive advantage over other potential entrants. Although students can obtain private loans on their own, as with guaranteed lending, students often rely on the financial aid office for recommendations, which as for federal loans tends to limit direct competition between lenders for individual students.

The private loan market provides data that is useful in estimating inputs into the market value of government loans and loan guarantees. Some differences in the borrower populations and loan characteristics, however,

11. Limits are currently set at a cumulative amount of $23,000 for undergraduates and a $65,500 combined limit for undergraduate and graduate. There are also various annual limits on federal borrowing.

suggest some caution. We discuss these differences and their implications for imputed capital and administrative costs.

7.4.1   Cost of Capital

We consider two distinct aspects of the cost of capital. First we estimate the discount rate for cash flows associated with uninsured student loans, which is a critical input for the total cost calculations. We also estimate the differential between the cost to guaranteed lenders of funding guaranteed student loans in the capital markets, and the government's cost of raising funds through the Treasury. The latter is informative because it may be a source of higher real costs for guaranteed lending, and because it affects the minimum compensation required by guaranteed lenders.

Finding the Risk-Adjusted Discount Rate

The starting point for our analysis of the cost of capital for federal student loans is the typical interest rates charged by lenders on private student loans in 2006. Rates ranged from LIBOR+2 to LIBOR+7 percent (LIBOR stands for London Interbank Offered Rate). The rate offered varies by credit score and educational institution, but LIBOR+4 percent was typical. Assuming a 30 bps spread between one-year LIBOR and one-year Treasury, the interest rate spread over one-year Treasury is on average about 4.3 percent.

What we mean by "the market cost of capital" is the discount rate that a fully private entity would use to value a claim on the net cash flows received by the government. The present value calculations can then be interpreted as what it would cost, on a per loan basis, to induce a competitive private entity to run each program. Since not all of the cash flows associated with the two programs have identical exposure to student loan risk, we adjust the risk premium to correspond to the risk of the various major components of cash flow, as described in more detail in section 7.5.3 and appendix B.

To derive the market cost of capital we adjust the rate charged to students for a variety of factors.[12] The 4.3 percent spread charged to students over Treasury rates has several components: it includes a risk premium that arises from the systematic risk in loan losses; administrative costs not covered by fees; expected losses from default; taxes; and a liquidity premium.[13] For our purposes, the market cost of capital is taken to include

---

12. Ideally, cost of capital estimates would be based on secondary market interest rates, which do not bundle financing costs with transaction costs. Unfortunately, data on whole loan secondary market transactions are not available.

13. The term "liquidity premium" is generally used to describe the component of credit spreads over Treasury rates not easily explained by other factors. The liquidity premium is thought to arise either from perceived risks that are not evident in historical data, or from the possibility that an absence of market participants could make it difficult to sell the security at fair value in the future.

the risk premium for systematic risk, the tax spread, and the liquidity premium. Default losses and administrative costs are excluded from the capital cost because they are explicitly accounted for in the derivation of expected cash flows.

The market cost of capital is identified by starting with the average 4.3 percent spread over Treasury, and subtracting estimates of administrative costs and expected default losses. As discussed below, administrative costs borne directly by guaranteed lenders, expressed as an annual cost rate, are on order of 97 bps. We add to this 15 bps to account for the higher costs of private over guaranteed loans. This leaves 3.18 percent for a risk premium, expected default losses, taxes, and a residual liquidity premium. We estimate the annual default loss rate from federal student loan data to be .75 percent per annum (see section 7.5), and assume it is slightly lower than default losses on private loans, which we take to be 1 percent. This leaves a 2.18 percent spread—the market cost of capital—that is attributable to the market risk premium, liquidity, and taxes. It is not possible to identify the size of the separate components, but we use this market premium in the base case cost analysis in the next section.

An alternative approach would be to approximate private lenders' cost of capital by looking at the weighted average cost of debt and equity capital for publicly-traded firms in this business. This turns out to be impractical for several reasons. First, there are few publicly-traded companies whose primary business is making and funding private student loans, as most of the big public lenders are divisions of major banks and do not report separately. The few public companies that specialize in private loans have been in business for a fairly short time, and given the volatility of returns, estimates based on a short history entail a high degree of uncertainty. Further, private lenders tend to manage risk through various contractual arrangements—for instance, through securitization structures and purchased credit guarantees—so their cost of capital does not accurately reflect whole-loan risk.

Capital Cost for Guaranteed Loans

The cost of capital for guaranteed lenders is lower than for private lenders because of the government guarantee. Nevertheless, their capital cost appears to exceed that of the Treasury. Here we consider the determinants of their borrowing costs.

Guaranteed lenders routinely obtain funding by securitizing parcels of previously originated federal loans and selling these asset-backed securities to investors, at a weighted average rate slightly over LIBOR.[14] This indicates

14. The LIBOR is a market interest rate frequently used on interbank loans between high-quality commercial banks. The default risk on LIBOR is thought to be small, but positive. Typically, LIBOR is 20 to 30 bps over the corresponding Treasury rate, but the spread varies over time.

that private investors do not view guaranteed loans as perfect substitutes for Treasury securities, despite the 97 to 99 percent federal credit guarantee.[15] In addition, lenders bear underwriting, Securities and Exchange Commission (SEC) filing, and other administrative fees that add to the total cost of capital for guaranteed loans. In comparison with the cost of Treasury funding for direct loans, it appears that even the largest guaranteed lenders typically pay 25 to 35 basis points more than the government to borrow.

There are a number of factors that may account for the premium over Treasury rates paid by guaranteed lenders. One is that a guaranteed loan is not truly risk-free—as well as the residual 1 to 3 percent retained default risk, lenders who fail to administer loans according to ED policy and regulations may have the guarantee voided for those loans. The exemption of Treasury interest from state and local taxes also lowers Treasury rates relative to LIBOR. Further, securitized student loans are less liquid than Treasury securities. The prepayment and extension options create uncertainty that increases investors' required return, as evidenced by higher spreads on the tranches of securitizations that absorb these risks.

Whether or not this higher funding cost is indicative of a real cost advantage of the government is debatable. Clearly, out-of-pocket funding costs are lower for the government, but the benefit may come at a commensurate cost to other stakeholders. For instance, the exemption from state and local taxes is a benefit to the federal government that is offset by the cost to local governments. The liquidity advantage may arise from the government's special legal status and ability to impose taxes, which lowers government expenditures at a hidden cost to taxpayers. We do not attempt to resolve the question of to what extent the cost advantage is real, but as a point of comparison we estimate what a 30 basis point per annum funding advantage is worth over the life of a loan.

7.4.2   Administrative Costs

Differences in administrative expenses on guaranteed loans and direct loans are an important driver of the economic cost differential between programs. Here we show that while many costs are similar in both programs, there are some additional costs associated with guaranteed lending that appear to make it fundamentally more expensive.

Administrative functions associated with all credit provision include origination, servicing, collection, and general overhead. Guaranteed lenders also consider the fees paid to the government to be administrative costs. From a programmatic perspective, however, lender fees affect the net cash flows from the government; they are not a program cost. The task of identifying administrative costs and allocating them across these activities is

---

15. This discussion is based on securitizations of floating rate loans, and prospectus data from Sallie Mae on recent issues.

complicated by limitations on data availability, but financial reports from ED and information from some guaranteed lenders provide the basis for our inferences.

Most lenders that originate private loans are also in the guaranteed loan business, and administrative costs appear similar for private and guaranteed loans (some minor caveats are discussed later). Financial statements from one such dual lender provides some data on administrative costs. The reports break noninterest expense into various categories. Some costs, such as servicing, apply to a portion of the outstanding loan portfolio in repayment, while other costs are incurred for origination activity, but do not apply to the outstanding portfolio. Although these financial reports do not allocate costs by activity, the reported numbers can be used to make some rough imputations.[16] We attribute 80 percent of personnel, consulting, and occupancy expenses to origination, 100 percent of promotional expenses to origination, and 50 percent of computer and other expenses to origination. Total origination expenses, divided by total volume of Stafford and private originations, is .95 percent. Representing this as an annual rate spread based on a ten-year amortizing loan implies an origination cost rate of 22 bps. The remaining noninterest expenses, divided by the portfolio of loans in repayment, yields an annual cost of 45 basis points. Thus, the dual lender directly bears an amortized cost of 67 basis points excluding collection costs, which we account for separately in default losses. Beyond this, the onetime origination fee paid to the government, debt issuance costs, spread over LIBOR on debt issued, and miscellaneous other expenses are estimated to add .3 percent to annual costs. Finally, we add an additional 10 bps for costs incurred by ED for administration of the guaranteed program, yielding a total administrative cost rate of 107 bps for guaranteed loans.

We want to emphasize that this estimate must be interpreted with caution. First, efficiency may vary considerably across lenders and there is likely to be considerable variation in administrative costs. Further, these costs reflect the current regulatory and organizational structure of the student loan market. Guaranteed lender origination costs include expenditures for the higher service levels and marketing expenses that arise from competition for borrowers and excess payments from the government that fund these practices. A different delivery system or lower federal payments to lenders would presumably reduce certain administrative expenditures.

The administrative costs for the direct program appear to be significantly lower than for guaranteed lenders, even taking into account costs that do not appear as part of the reported subsidy rate. An annual appropriation to the Department of Education covers the administrative costs of the direct pro-

16. Simply dividing total noninterest expense over the loan portfolio would be misleading because for a growing company not at a steady state, a disproportionate share of the total administrative cost is for current originations.

gram, although some of these costs are attributable to administering both the direct and guaranteed programs. This appropriation was approximately $800 million in 2006. At that time, the outstanding direct program portfolio was approximately $100 billion and the guaranteed portfolio approximately $300 billion.[17] In verbal disclosures, the Department reported allocating approximately $200 million of the appropriation to direct program servicing contracts, $30 million to direct program origination contracts, and $200 million to direct and guaranteed program recovery contracts (the latter is included in our estimate of default losses in the federal programs and subtracted here to avoid double-counting). We assume the remaining unallocated $370 million is attributable to servicing and origination functions of the direct and guaranteed programs in proportion to the size of each program. These amounts yield an estimate of amortized direct program origination and servicing cost of 32 basis points.

Taken together, these calculations suggest that the administrative costs of the direct program are about 75 bps per annum lower than on guaranteed loans. Again, this estimate must be interpreted with caution as it is based on incomplete data and simple approximations. Nevertheless, it suggests that real administrative cost savings could be achieved by restructuring or phasing out the guaranteed program.

7.4.3   Accounting for Government/Private Differences

Differences in borrower populations, loan terms, and administrative costs between government and private loans could bias inferences drawn from private market rates and administrative data. Those differences, and their likely effect on the estimates, are briefly discussed here.

Borrower Defaults

The federal programs serve a much broader population of students than do private lenders, suggesting that their risk profiles could differ. Since private loans appeal to students who have hit federal borrowing limits, they select for students at high-cost undergraduate institutions and professional students in medicine, law, and business.

Several factors suggest that federal borrowers are likely poorer average credit risks. Federal borrowers' eligibility does not depend on a credit score, whereas private lenders use credit scores to discriminate between borrowers, refusing credit entirely below some cutoff. Private lenders also can avoid originating loans at schools where graduates' employment prospects are weak. A partially offsetting factor is that private lenders extend credit to students who already have high federal loan balances and who start work with much higher levels of total indebtedness.

---

17. We assume the federal program is closer to a steady state, so dividing total costs by total loans is a reasonable approximation of annual costs.

Despite having quite different borrower populations, federal and the limited private statistics we have access to show quite similar losses from default (net of recoveries and collection costs). The composition of default losses, however, is quite different for the two types of borrowers. Default rates in the federal programs are approximately 1.8 percent of outstanding principal per annum, whereas they are only 1 percent per annum for private loans, supporting the idea that the private borrower population is less risky. The lower default rates in the private program, however, are offset by lower recovery rates. This is presumably because private lenders do not have access to federal collection remedies such as the Treasury offset program and administrative wage garnishment. To the extent that the lower private default rate implies lower market risk, the cost of capital inferred from that market is conservative when applied to riskier federal loans. As described in section 7.5, we estimate expected default rates on federal loans from extensive data on federal loans, so the cash flow estimates do not rely on private loan performance data.

Loan Terms and Fees

As well as bearing higher interest rates, private loan terms tend to be less favorable than on Stafford loans. Private loans cannot be consolidated at below-market rates, repayment options are more limited, and lenders may be less generous with forbearance. There are no grace or deferment periods, and unlike federal loans, death or disability does not trigger forgiveness. Private loans do offer loan maturities of up to twenty years, and the mechanisms to collect on defaulted loans are weaker than for the government. As on guaranteed loans (but not direct loans), lenders often offer incentives for on-time and electronic payments, and so forth. Among these nonrate differences, the consolidation option historically has been the biggest advantage of the federal programs. In Lucas and Moore (2007), we estimate that in every year from 2001 to 2005 the consolidation option has added more than 2 percent to the market value subsidy rate on new loans,[18] but with the switch to fixed rates, this will have less effect on relative value going forward.

Student fees appear to be somewhat higher on federal loans. Competitive pressures have reduced or eliminated origination fees on private loans, the result being that administrative costs are covered by higher rate spreads. Similarly, most guaranteed lenders pay the federal origination fee on behalf of borrowers. On direct loans, however, borrowers are still required to pay 1.5 percent up-front and the entire fee if they fail to make a timely first payment.

We make no quantitative adjustment for government/private differentials in loan terms or fees. To the extent that the more generous terms on gov-

18. With the switch to fixed rates, the consolidation option will have less value going forward, but the prepayment option will have more value.

ernment loans entail higher systematic risk (for instance, by increasing the duration of the average loan), estimates of the cost of capital based on private market rates are conservative.

Administrative Costs

Loan servicing is a competitive industry, and it is safe to assume that servicing costs are similar for government, guaranteed, and private lenders. Loan collection services can also be obtained at competitive prices, although guaranty agencies are paid a statutory amount that appears to exceed their cost of providing services, as discussed earlier. We assume similar collection costs for private and direct loans, and adjust for the subsidy component of payments to guarantee agencies in the guaranteed program. Some costs, however, are likely to be higher on private loans. Origination requires paying for credit scores (including those paid for students who ultimately borrow elsewhere or do not qualify). Private loans may also involve higher contracting costs (e.g., legal expenses) than do government loans. Finally, the purely administrative costs associated with loan financing are lower for the government. Securitizations of private and guaranteed loans involve fees to investment bankers and to rating agencies that presumably exceed Treasury's administrative costs. We assume that 15 bps of the private loan cost rate can be attributed to these additional costs.

7.5   Estimating Federal Program Costs

Estimating a comprehensive measure of cost involves projecting the distribution of future cash flows to and from the government over the life of a loan or guarantee obligation, and discounting at risk-adjusted rates. We start by modeling the cash flows associated with the underlying loans, taking into account program rules,[19] borrower behavior, and the various options affecting payment patterns. These cash flows, in combination with rules for payments between guaranteed lenders and the government, also determine the cash flows associated with guaranteed loans.

A subsample of student records from the Department of Education's National Student Loan Database System (NSLDS), described in appendix A, provides information on historical borrower payment patterns, which is used to parameterize the model. In particular, we derive new estimates of default and recovery, which are critical inputs. We use a sample from the database drawn in January 2006, which contained historical information on loans and borrowers dating back to 1980, although we used the older data only where absolutely necessary. The sample comprises over ten million loan records and one million borrowers.

19. Estimates are based on rules in effect for the 2006 to 2007 program year. Recent legislative changes alter these parameters for loans originated in 2008 and thereafter.

We then use Monte Carlo simulation to project future cash flows that depend on a model of stochastic interest rates and borrower behavior. Discounting projected net cash flows at the risk-adjusted rates (derived as previously described and in appendix B) yields cost estimates for both programs. A rougher but simpler estimate based on the difference between private and government student loan rates is shown to produce comparable results.

7.5.1   Cash Flows

On direct loans, there is an initial outflow of principal when the borrower takes a new loan, less fees paid by the borrower. Subsequently, net inflows of repaid principal and interest flow to the government over time, including amounts recovered from default less any recovery costs. The government also incurs ongoing administrative costs, which we apportion to individual loans on a per annum basis.

In the guaranteed program, government cash flows include net transfers to and from guaranteed lenders (some through guaranty agencies) on each outstanding loan, equal to the difference between the borrower's interest payment and the three-month commercial paper rate plus a spread. This is referred to as a Special Allowance Payment, or SAP. The spread is equal to 1.74 percent per annum for Stafford loans when the borrower is in school, 2.34 percent for Stafford loans when the borrower is in repayment, and 2.64 percent (less the 1.05 percent per annum lender consolidation fee) for consolidation loans. The government also makes guarantee payments to lenders for claims on defaulted loans, and pays "retention" fees to guaranty agencies in proportion to their recoveries on defaulted loans.

In both programs, the task of estimating cash flows is complicated by the many options available to students to defer and extend loan payments or to prepay, and also by default behavior. We now turn to the calibration of these behavioral assumptions, which is based on program rules and observed behavior in the NSLDS.

Effective Maturity and Repayment Status

Time to repayment varies widely, from less than a year to over thirty years. Borrowers may prepay their federal loans without penalty, and some borrowers repay rapidly. For example, approximately 8 percent of originated loans close in less than five years, and approximately 60 percent within fifteen years (see figure 7.2).[20]

There are also various options that extend the repayment period. Borrowers with high balances have standard options to extend Stafford loans beyond the basic ten-year maturity.[21] The right to consolidate Stafford loans

20. These estimates treat loan consolidations as an extension of the original loan rather than a new loan. Stafford loan lifetimes would otherwise appear to be much shorter than this.

21. Stafford borrowers with a balance of $30,000 or more from a single lender (whether a single guaranteed lender, or a loan from the direct program) may choose an extended repay-

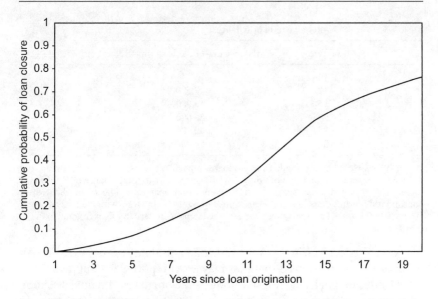

Fig. 7.2   Distribution of loan lifetimes
Source: Estimates from 2006 sample of the National Student Loan Database.

allows borrowers to extend the term of their original loans, as well as to convert floating rate loans to a fixed rate.[22] For some borrowers, consolidation allows them to extend for up to thirty years. Eligibility for term extension depends on the size of the consolidated loan, as shown in table 7.3.

While in school and for a few months after graduating, borrowers do not need to begin repayment. During this grace period, the federal government pays the interest for subsidized loans, whereas interest accrues on unsubsidized loans. Periods of grace necessarily raise the market-based subsidy cost even for unsubsidized loans, since the interest rate that accrues is typically lower than the market cost of capital. Over 95 percent of loans by originated value are in an in-school or grace period in the year of origination, but less than 10 percent of loans are in a grace period four years after origination. The average time in school is approximately 2.5 years (excluding time in loan deferral for subsequent schooling, discussed next).

Borrowers are also entitled to lengthy payment deferral in times of financial hardship or, for Stafford borrowers, to pursue further studies. Stafford

---

ment plan of up to twenty-five years. Income contingent and graduated repayment plans are also available.

22. The OMB treats consolidation loans as new loans rather than the extension of existing loans. This leads to a higher reported loan volume, but a lower subsidy cost per Stafford loan than reported in this chapter, as we treat consolidation as an extension of existing loans. This treatment makes it easier to interpret default and recovery experience, and also ensures that the subsidy cost includes the value of the option to consolidate.

Table 7.3   **Allowable term by balance**

Term	Balance must be at least (in US $)
10 years	—
12	7,500
15	10,000
20	20,000
25	40,000
30	60,000

Notes: Allowable term for extended and graduated repayment plans in the direct program and for newly consolidated loans in both programs. Balance refers to total balance of loans in the direct program for direct program extensions and total balance of loans consolidated for consolidation term extension. In the guaranteed program, borrowers with balances of more than $30,000 can elect a twenty-five-year extended repayment term on their original loans.

loans are also forgiven in the event of death or disability of the borrower. An effect of these provisions is that they may lower reported default rates. Periods of in-school deferment last as long as the borrower remains in school, whereas borrowers experiencing financial hardship may elect a three-year payment deferment or payment forbearance period (the former is available only under more restrictive conditions). Analysis of loans in the NSLDS suggests that borrowers enter deferment or forbearance at a rate of approximately 6 percent per annum for a typical term of three years.

The distribution of loan maturities and repayment behavior used to calibrate the model are based on NSLDS data. The effect of these repayment options is shown in figure 7.3, which breaks down outstanding loan principal by loan status in January 2006 for both the direct and guaranteed program. Overall, only about half of the loans are in repayment, while grace, deferral, forbearance, and default account for the remainder.

The future distribution of loan lifetimes may be more drawn out than indicated by historical data, since the closure rates at long horizons are based on loans taken out when the federal loan program offered less favorable terms to borrowers than currently or in the recent past. Nevertheless, the stochastic repayment behavior in the model is based on historical experience.

Default and Recovery

Borrower default is an ongoing concern in both the direct and guaranteed lending programs, despite the strong loan enforcement mechanisms that the government has at its disposal.[23] Before direct lending, the guaranteed lending program reported very high default rates. In response, Congress made a number of changes to the Higher Education Act. Chief among them was the use of cohort default rates as a performance measure and as a criterion

23. Student loans, both federal and private, are not dismissed in bankruptcy. The government can collect on defaulted loans through the Treasury Offset Program.

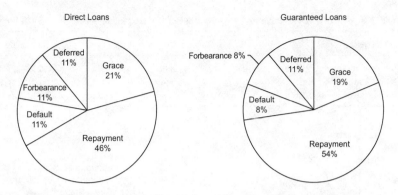

Fig. 7.3   Status of direct and guaranteed loan portfolio, January 2006

for schools to retain access to federal student loans and grant funding. Since the adoption of these measures, new default claims in both the direct and guaranteed lending programs have more than halved.

The strength of the US economy contributed to generally falling default rates over the period 1990 to 2005. The increased use of deferment, forbearance, and consolidation may also have contributed to lower default rates, although offering more generous terms to students is costly when it delays an inevitable default or makes recovery more difficult. Table 7.4 reports default claims as a percent of outstanding balances for 1990, 1996, and 2005.

Figure 7.4 shows the average default rate of loans issued between 1996 and 2006 by years since entering repayment for guaranteed Stafford, guaranteed consolidation, direct Stafford, and direct consolidation loans. Average default rates are around 1.8 percent per annum. Stafford loans experience higher levels shortly after entering repayment, which may in part reflect the cumulative effect of in-school grace periods (since a borrower cannot default while he or she remains in school even though adverse circumstances may arise that impair a borrower's current and future ability to repay their loans). Consolidated direct loans report higher default rates than consolidated Stafford loans because the Education Department frequently consolidates borrowers close to default. Data confirms that borrowers that consolidate defaulted loans are more likely to default on their consolidation loans than other borrowers. We attribute the cost of default to the program in which the loans were first originated rather than the program that consolidated them.

The OMB reports recovery rates on student loans that far exceed those on other forms of unsecured consumer credit, but as discussed in section 7.3.3, their measure neglects collection costs and time value. Relying instead on NSLDS data, we find that individual loans exhibit significant variability in recoveries, with some defaulted loans resolved quickly and others remaining uncollected for more than ten years. The typical pattern suggests that

Table 7.4	Default claims as a percentage of the outstanding federal loan portfolio		
Budget year	1990	1996	2005
Outstanding loan portfolio ($million)	49,890	57,557	242,581
Default claims ($million)	2,384	1,428	3,818
Percentage of loans in default	4.8	2.5	1.6

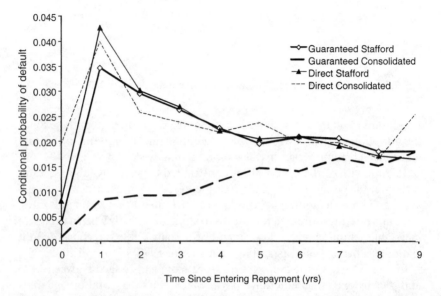

Fig. 7.4   Default rates (weighted by loan value) by years since entering repayment

collection rates diminish over time. Applying a risk-adjusted discount rate (equal to the average interest rate over the data period plus our assumed 2.18 percent risk premium) and subtracting a program-specific recovery cost suggests a recovery rate of around 60 percent of the defaulted principal on direct loans and a slightly lower rate on guaranteed loans because of higher recovery costs.[24] Combining this with the annual default rate of 1.8 percent per annum implies losses from default equal to .75 percent of principal outstanding per annum, which is the basis for our estimates.

7.5.2   Risk-Adjusting Discount Rates

A major goal of this analysis is to understand the effect of market risk on estimated program costs. As described in section 7.4.1, an analysis of the

24. The ED indicates collection costs on direct loans of about 16 percent. Statutory collection costs are higher on guaranteed loans, as guaranty agencies retain 23 percent of recoveries on Stafford loans, 18.5 percent for loan rehabilitation, and 10 percent on loans cured by consolidation.

private student loan market suggests an estimate of the credit risk premium for student loans is 2.18 percent. The 2.18 percent premium is used in the base case estimates, but the sensitivity analysis reports results for lower and higher risk premiums.

The cost of capital is also affected by the term premium: the difference between long-term and short-term Treasury rates. The valuation model incorporates the term premium in the interest rate model, but for simplicity and because there does not appear to be a strong empirical correlation between them, we treat the risk that generates the term premium as independent from the risk driving credit spreads.

To the extent that program cash flows are proportional to loan cash flows, one can simply apply the risk-adjusted discount rate for student loans to other program cash flows. The risk-adjusted discount rate is a maturity-matched interest rate from the interest rate model plus a credit risk premium. Applying this discount rate to all cash flows is a reasonable approximation for the direct program, assuming that administrative costs are proportional to loan cash flows.

Correctly discounting risky cash flows in the guaranteed program is more complicated because the various components of guaranteed cash flows have different exposures to market risk. With a 100 percent credit guarantee, the federal government's cash flows are equivalent to directly lending to the student but financing the loan by borrowing from the private sector instead of from the Treasury, and contracting with guaranteed lenders for origination, servicing, and part of collection (we call these equivalent credit arrangements *implied loans*).[25] The cash flows from the implied student loan have interest rate risk, since they are made at a fixed rate that is unrelated to market interest rates. They also have credit risk. Implied student loan cash flows are discounted at the same rate as cash flows in the direct program. In contrast the implied loan made by guaranteed lenders to the federal government is largely unaffected by default risk. Specifically, the guaranteed lender is assured of receiving full repayment of principal and interest (at a floating rate), so there is a component of cash flow that is virtually free of default and interest rate risk. At the same time, there is the risk that default, prepayment, or consolidation will terminate or reduce the stream of lender payments (i.e., the SAP), which introduces an element of market risk to the administrative cost reimbursements.

To incorporate the effect of these risks on the value of direct and guaranteed loans, we graft a simple two-state model of default onto a stochastic interest rate model to provide state-dependent discount rates (or

25. This implicitly treats borrower incentives offered by lenders, retention allowances to guaranty agencies, and the various onetime fees between lenders and the government as part of the contractual services purchased by the government.

state prices). Each state of the model corresponds to an interest rate and a borrower default state (i.e., whether default has occurred or not), allowing us to specify cash flows in each of those states and discount them accordingly. The appropriate discount rates differential between default and nondefault states is inferred from the spread between risky and risk-free loans (and justified by a no-arbitrage argument). Appendix B explains the interest rate and risk-adjustment models in detail.

7.5.3   Simulations

Subsidy value is estimated using Monte Carlo simulation. Each month a random draw from a normal distribution determines the innovation in the short-term interest rate, and the corresponding term structure of interest rates is derived from the Cox Ingersoll Ross (CIR) model (see Lucas and Moore [2007] for a complete description of the interest rate model and the parameters used in estimation, and also Jagannathan, Kaplin, and Sun [2003]). Variation in interest rates affects the discount rate and guaranteed lender payments.

Monthly loan repayment cash flows depend on various borrower behaviors: whether the borrower is in school; the borrower's repayment plan; consolidation; default, recovery, prepayment; and an administrative charge. Appendix B contains a description of how we simulate the cash flows that depend on stochastic borrower behavior. It also describes the aggregation of cash flows across representative loan groupings.

Base Case Assumptions

The cash flow model is calibrated under the following base case assumptions:

Borrower interest rates: From June 2006 onwards, borrowers will pay a fixed rate of 6.8 percent per annum on all new Stafford loans. When those loans are subsequently consolidated, the interest charged on that portion of the consolidation loan that comes from post-2006 Stafford loans will be at a 6.8 percent rate (plus up to 0.075 percent after rounding).

Repayment horizons: A typical loan repays over a twenty-year term, but any individual loan can be repaid over shorter or longer horizons. The probability of slower repayment is positively correlated with the borrower's balance. For borrowers entering repayment, approximately one-third of all loan value is in each of three balance categories, and, respectively 15, 40, and 60 percent of borrowers in each category take up the maximum term extension option.

Default losses: The value of default losses each year is equal to .75 percent of outstanding balances in the direct program and .82 percent in the guaranteed program. The guaranteed program losses are assumed to be higher because the federal government pays more to guaranty agencies for their collections from defaulted borrowers than they do to private contactors in the direct program.

Noncollection-related federal administrative expenses: The federal government incurs direct administrative expenses for both programs. These costs are not included in official budget subsidy estimates, but they are included in the more comprehensive estimates here. Each year, we assume the department directly spends 0.32 percent of outstanding principal administering the direct program (excluding collections costs accounted for in default losses) and 0.1 percent administering the guaranteed program. The administrative costs borne by guaranteed lenders in the guaranteed program do not directly affect subsidy rates.

Guaranteed lender payments: The federal government pays guaranteed lenders a spread above the quarterly reset three-month commercial paper rate, which is simulated using the CIR model. The spread paid to lenders varies with the type of loan and its payment status as described earlier, and terminates upon default.

Loan origination and guarantee fee receipts: The government charges borrowers 3 percent in origination and guarantee fees in both programs. In the direct program, this reduces the subsidy cost by about 2.2 percent, since .8 percent is returned to students as a borrower benefit.[26] In the guaranteed program, 1 percent of this is transferred to guaranty agencies. Finally, guaranteed lenders pay a 0.50 percent fee, but guaranty agencies receive four-fifths of it.

Adjustments for Federal revenue effects: The companies that serve the direct and guaranteed programs pay federal corporate income taxes. To the extent that incremental taxable income is generated because of the federal student loan program, the corporate income taxes paid should be taken into account in calculating the net federal outlay. However, current budget practice does not recognize income tax receipts in subsidy estimates, implicitly assuming no net change in private economic activity arises from federal actions. A recent study by Price Waterhouse Coopers (PWC 2005) estimated that the guaranteed lending program generates corporate income tax with a present value of 1.5 cents per dollar of loans originated, which translates to an approximate per annum tax receipt of 20 basis points per dollar outstanding. The direct program also generates corporate income taxes from information technology (IT), servicing, and collections contracts with private companies, but PWC did not estimate those revenues. We assume this generates no more than 5 basis points of

---

26. The ED has the option to reduce the cost to 1.5 percent for borrowers who enter repayment on time. The ED estimates that approximately 50 percent of borrowers receive this benefit.

tax revenue, leaving a 15 basis point per annum tax differential between the direct and guaranteed programs. To what extent a tax offset should be reflected in budget estimates remains a controversial issue. In our base case subsidy estimates and consistent current budget practice, we ignore the differential tax effect, but we do account for it in the sensitivity analysis.

7.5.4   Subsidy Estimates

Table 7.5 presents subsidy estimates for newly originated loans in academic year 2006 (July 1, 2006 to June 30, 2007) under the base case assumptions outlined previously. The overall subsidy rate for each program is computed by averaging over representative groupings of loans by subsidized status and outstanding balance. Two striking findings emerge. First, the market subsidy rates are considerably higher than those reported in the budget—20.1 percent for the direct program and 31.3 percent for the guaranteed program. Second, the market cost differential between the direct and guaranteed program is similar to the budget estimate, even after adjusting for omitted administrative costs in the direct program.

To understand these findings, it is instructive to break down the costs of each program into their major component parts. As shown in table 7.6, the difference between the loan amount and the present value of student loan repayments accounts for the biggest cost for both programs at approximately 20 percent of the loan amount. The higher federal servicing and origination expenses under the direct program are more than offset by the value of federal payments to guaranteed lenders, and this difference accounts for most of the overall difference in subsidy rates between the two programs.

Within each program, subsidy rates vary with whether loans are "subsidized," and with the availability of longer loan terms (table 7.5). Costs are

Table 7.5   **Base case market-based subsidy estimates for new Stafford loans originated in award year 2006**

	Direct	Guaranteed	Difference
Unsubsidized loans			
Up to 10-year term	11.7	22.0	10.3
Up to 20-year term	13.5	25.3	11.8
Up to 30-year term	14.7	27.1	12.4
Weighted average subsidy of unsubsidized loans	17.5	27.6	10.1
Subsidized loans			
Up to 10-year term	25.4	34.3	8.9
Up to 20-year term	27.0	37.0	10.1
Up to 30-year term	28.6	39.2	10.6
Weighted average subsidy of subsidized loans	30.4	39.0	8.6
Program average	20.1	31.3	11.2

Table 7.6   **Components of subsidy rate**

	Direct	Guaranteed
Loan disbursement	100.0	100.0
Present value of loan repayment (after collection)	−79.8	−79.8
Borrower origination fees	−3.0	−3.0
Net present value of representative loan	17.1	17.1
plus		
Federal servicing and origination expenses	2.1	0.8
Direct program origination fee reduction	0.8	n.a.
Lender origination fees	n.a.	−0.7
Lender share of guaranteed loan losses	n.a.	−0.2
Lender special allowance payments	n.a.	13.2
Guaranty agency origination and excess collection fees	n.a.	1.1
Subsidy rate	20.1	31.3

higher for subsidized than for unsubsidized loans by the present value of in-grace and in-deferment interest paid by borrowers with unsubsidized loans that is not paid by borrowers with subsidized loans. A typical subsidized borrower spends around three years in grace and deferment, and avoids paying the 6.8 percent interest rate during these periods. This increases the subsidy to the student by about 12 percent of the loan amount.

Subsidy rates increase with loan maturity. Allowing borrowers to extend a ten-year Stafford year loan to twenty years raises the subsidy rate by about 3 percent. This takes into account that many borrowers fail to take advantage of term extension options and frequently pay their loans off early, so potentially the extension cost could be even higher if borrower behavior changes.

7.5.5   Sensitivity Analysis

Borrower Behavior and Economic Conditions

Aggregate subsidy estimates under alternative assumptions about model parameters are shown in table 7.7. Subsidy estimates are quite sensitive to the assumed risk premium. Assuming a 1 percent higher (lower) risk premium than in the base case raises (lowers) subsidy rates by 7 percent. For the direct program, this is most easily understood as a higher discount rate, reducing the value of future repayments. On the guaranteed loans, the effect of market risk is to raise the present value of guarantee payments made on defaulted loans. By contrast, the credit risk premium has a small effect on the present value of net income payments to guaranteed lenders. The effective duration of the loans also affects value, with loan extension generally increasing cost. This can be attributed to the below-market interest rate charged to borrowers. Table 7.6 reports subsidy costs with 25 percent faster and slower loan repayment rates, which serve to lengthen or shorten the average loan term by approximately four years. The increase (decrease) raises (lowers)

Table 7.7   **Parameter sensitivity of subsidy rates**

	Direct	Guaranteed	Difference
Base case subsidy rate	20.1	31.3	11.2
Varying credit risk and credit risk premium			
High credit risk premium (3.58% p.a.)	26.2	36.2	10.0
Low credit risk premium (1.58% p.a.)	12.6	25.3	12.7
No credit risk premium	1.1	16.5	15.4
Speed of repayment			
25% faster than base case	17.3	27.1	9.8
25% slower than base case	22.3	34.6	12.3
Not sensitive to interest rates	19.8	31.0	11.2
Other			
No treasury financing advantage in direct program	21.9	31.3	9.4
Longer Stafford repayments/reduced consolidation	20.3	31.5	11.2

Note: p.a. = per annum.

subsidy costs by about 2 percent. The final experiment assumes that with the less favorable conditions for consolidation going forward, more loans will be extended in the Stafford program rather than being consolidated. This scenario raises the subsidy rate in the guaranteed program because of the higher lender payments on Stafford loans.

Looking to the future, subsidy rates for new loans may be considerably different from the estimates for 2006 reported in table 7.5. The most obvious cause of future variation in new loan subsidy rates is changes in interest rate conditions. This is because borrower interest rates are fixed at 6.8 percent per annum for all new Stafford loans, whereas the government's opportunity cost moves with prevailing interest rates. Figures 7.5 and 7.6 show simulated average, tenth, and ninetieth percentiles of the subsidy estimates for, respectively, the direct and guaranteed programs over each of the next ten years. To make these forecasts, we use the interest rate model combined with current yield curve information to provide simulated paths of future interest rates to determine starting conditions for each year. We assume loan cash flow performance is consistent with the assumptions of the base case (but appropriate to interest rate conditions). As the horizon lengthens, the course of future interest rates becomes more uncertain so the band of subsidy values widens in both programs.

Finally, we consider a set of parameters that are more favorable to guaranteed lending. We credit the guaranteed program with 15 bps per annum for tax revenues, and allocate a higher portion of administrative costs incurred by the Department of Education to direct lending.[27]

27. In this scenario, 90 percent of the $360 billion in unallocated costs is assumed to be for the direct loan program, whereas in the base case it is allocated proportionally to loan volume. This reduces the administrative cost advantage in the direct program from 75 basis points to 45 basis points.

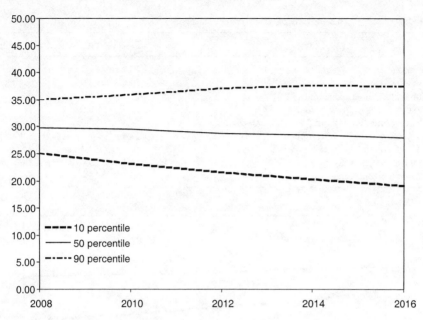

Fig. 7.5   Distribution of future subsidy rates given interest rate uncertainty in the direct lending program

All other assumptions are as in the base case. The result is a narrowing of the subsidy rate difference of the two programs from 11.2 percent to 8.0 percent.

Policy Alternatives

The model is also useful for examining the effect of various policy alternatives on subsidy costs. One option is to lower the guaranteed lender payments to bring the guaranteed subsidy closer to the direct loan subsidy rate, and to reduce the excess of payments over basic administrative costs. The first two rows of table 7.8 report the predicted subsidy estimates after lowering lenders' payments by 0.5 percent and 1.0 percent per annum, respectively. The effect of the 1.0 percent reduction is to bring the subsidy in the guaranteed program to within 5 percent of the direct program. The calculations in the next section suggest, however, that a reduction of this magnitude might make guaranteed lending unprofitable for many lenders. The 0.5 percent reduction still leaves a cost differential of 9.1 percent between the programs. The cuts in lender payments enacted in 2007 are at the lower end of this range, suggesting a lower but still significant cost differential for loans originated after September 2007.

Another set of alternatives relate to whether the interest rate paid by borrowers is fixed or floating. Switching from variable to fixed interest rates on Stafford loans has increased the subsidy cost for 2006 by approximately

Table 7.8   **Subsidy rates under alternative policies**

	Direct	Guaranteed	Difference
Base case	20.1	31.3	11.2
Cut annual lender payments by 0.5%	20.8	28.0	7.7
Cut annual lender payments by 1.0%	20.9	25.2	4.8
Floating rates as under 1998–2006 law	19.4	30.6	11.2
Floating rates but without floor on Lender's Special Allowance	19.4	30.0	10.6
3.4% rate on loans—without behavioral response	37.4	47.2	9.8
3.4% rate on loans—with behavioral response	40.5	50.3	9.8
90% federal guarantee	20.1	28.7	8.6
75% federal guarantee	20.1	25.4	5.3

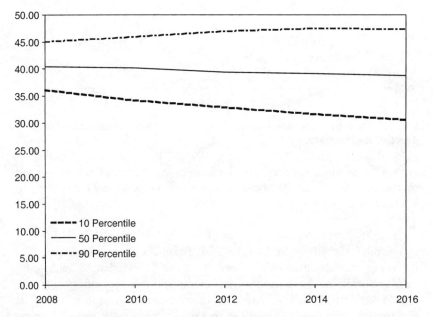

Fig. 7.6   Distribution of future subsidy rates given interest rate uncertainty in the guaranteed lending program

2 percent, in part because the opportunity cost of a fixed rate loan is higher than for variable rate loans (because the term premium is positive), and in part because our long-term interest rate projection implies the variable rate will average more than 6.8 percent. The switch to fixed rates also exposes the government to interest rate risk. If market interest rates continue to increase, subsidy costs on loans originated after 2006 could be significantly higher than they would be under the variable rate policy.

Changing the level of rates charged to students also obviously affects cost.

Recent legislation will gradually reduce the rate on loans to undergraduate students until it is 3.4 percent in 2011. All else equal, this increases the subsidy rate by approximately 16 percentage points. In fact, the subsidy cost likely will increase by more than this since the lower rate provides incentive for borrowers to reduce prepayment rates, and to switch to longer term repayment plans.[28]

7.6   Decomposition of Guaranteed Lender Costs

The analysis thus far has focused on government costs. Here we look at costs from the perspective of a guaranteed lender. This decomposition is useful in considering how much government payments to lenders could be reduced without causing many lenders to exit the market, and also for quantifying the extent to which guaranteed lending is fundamentally more expensive.

Our decomposition of guaranteed lender costs relies on section 7.4 calculations of administrative and capital costs. As mentioned earlier, these estimates are based on limited data and the costs of individual lenders may vary considerably. Recall that lenders are guaranteed of receiving the three-month commercial paper rate plus a spread that averages about 2.28 percent on Stafford loans, and 1.59 percent on Consolidation loans. Estimated lender origination, servicing, and other expenses are .97 percent. Subtracting this from the guaranteed payment rate leaves a margin of 1.31 percent (2.28 – .97) on Stafford loans and .62 on Consolidation loans (1.59 – .97). The 2007 legislative cuts to lender payments absorb less than half of this margin on Stafford loans, but almost all of it on Consolidation loans. These calculations may explain the subsequent exit of many lenders from the consolidation business in recent years, and that some borrower benefits have been reduced or eliminated.

The amount by which guaranteed lending as it is currently structured is fundamentally more expensive than direct lending can be estimated by comparing the administrative expenses and funding costs of the programs. Our estimates suggest that on the high end, this disadvantage is 105 bps per annum—based on a 75 basis point administrative cost disadvantage relative to the direct program, and a 30 bp funding disadvantage relative to Treasury. Capitalizing the resulting annual cost differential of 105 basis points over the life of a typical loan yields a present value cost advantage equal to 5.34 percent of loan principal.

---

28. The availability of such low cost credit could lead to abnormally high lending volumes, which would increase the total dollar subsidy. Moreover, the subsidy will increase on a per loan basis if borrowers choose to prepay their loans less frequently. We estimated the latter effect using the historic response of borrower prepayment to the level of interest rates for fixed rate consolidation loans and found that accounting for reduced prepayment in high interest rate environments increases the subsidy by approximately 3 percent.

7.7   Conclusions

In this chapter we have developed a model that provides comprehensive estimates of the federal cost of providing student loans, which takes into account the effect of borrower behavior, economic conditions, and program rules. We find that the cost of both the direct and guaranteed student loan programs is significantly understated in the federal budget, primarily because the budget neglects the full cost of capital, but also because of the way administrative costs are accounted for. This is important because it suggests that the relatively rapid growth of federal funding for student loans relative to outright grants may have been influenced by misleading estimates of loan cost.

Our second major finding is that even after adjusting for the cost of capital and administrative costs that are omitted in the budget, the direct program is considerably less costly to the government than is the guaranteed program. It appears that the higher cost of the guaranteed program arises primarily from the statutory payments to guaranteed lenders that exceed their cost of offering loans. Even if payments to lenders were cut to the minimum required to induce participation, the guaranteed program appears to be fundamentally more expensive due to a market structure that entails higher administrative and capital costs.

Despite its higher cost and recent concerns about certain lending practices, the guaranteed program has survived periodic attempts to supplant it with direct lending. History shows that the political fortunes of the two programs have shifted over time, but that cost has yet to be a decisive factor.[29] The 2007 legislation that cuts payments to guaranteed lenders and creates new advantages for the direct program will reduce future cost differences, and will likely increase direct lending volume at the expense of guaranteed lenders. However, the changes were for the most part incremental: they do not address the factors that make guaranteed lending fundamentally more expensive, and lenders still receive fixed compensation rather than a competitively determined payment.[30] The question of how these costs could be more effectively controlled is an important one that we leave for future analyses.

The financial crisis that began in late 2008 placed unprecedented stresses on the guaranteed student loan program. Despite the government guarantee, the securitization market for student loans collapsed and rate spreads ballooned. To ensure continuity in funding for students, the Department of Education stepped in and purchased new originations from guaranteed lenders financed by Treasury. It has also prompted stronger calls for scaling back the role of guaranteed lending.

29. The New America Foundation (2009) provides a lively description of the history of the competing programs.

30. A provision that introduces an auction for some PLUS loans does take a step toward creating such a mechanism.

Appendix A
Description of NSLDS Data

The Department of Education administers the National Student Loan Database System (NSLDS), a record-keeping system that tracks the status of individual loans and borrowers. The Congressional Budget Office receives an annual subsample of loan and borrower records each January, which it uses to make cost estimates. The database comprises multiple linked files containing current and historical information about borrowers and their loans. The files used to produce market-based subsidy estimates in this chapter are as follows.

Loan file: The file comprises one record per loan on the type of loan (direct or guaranteed, consolidated or original), the date the loan was taken, the amount disbursed, the principal outstanding at the time the sample was drawn, the current status of the loan, and the academic level of the student when the loan was taken. Each loan record also contains a unique identifier for the borrower, school, and guaranty agency associated with the loan, making aggregation of loans by borrower possible. The file contains 5.42m loan records for 1.30m distinct borrowers, spanning the period from 1985 to 2006.

Loan status history file: The file contains a sequence of records with dates and codes for each loan's status changes. A status change occurs for various reasons including: entering repayment, default, deferment, forbearance, consolidation, and payment in full. The historical timing of status changes provides a basis for estimating the probability that new loans transition through the various statuses over their lifetime. The file contains 25.60 million records for 5.42 million distinct loans.

IRS and guaranty agency collections files: These files track the timing and amount collected by the IRS, guaranty agencies, the Department of Education, and their contracted agents from borrowers with guaranteed loans in default. No recovery information is available on direct program loans in default. The files contain the amount collected and date of collection for each defaulted loan. The amounts recovered by issuing the borrower with a consolidation loan are not recorded as a dollar amount so the value must be imputed. Collection amounts are combined with historical loan status changes of defaulted loans in the loan status history file to compute a recovery rate on defaulted guaranteed loans, which we assume is very similar to that in the direct program. The IRS offset file contains 340,000 loans on 156,000 loans. The combined guaranty agency and departmental collection file contains 4.05 million records on 355,000 distinct borrowers.

Several features limit the usefulness of this data set for estimating loan cash flows over time. Except for the collections on defaulted loans, the CBO sample of NSLDS loans does not contain a record of borrower payments over time. Similarly, when the sample is drawn each January, only the current level of outstanding principal is recorded. Another problem is that repayment plans are not reported, making it difficult to infer loan lifetimes and to distinguish on-time repayment from prepayment.

Appendix B
Modeling Assumptions[31]

Cash Flows

Loans originate at time 0, begin repayment at time T^R, and have a maturity of T^M so the loan is repaid in $T^R + T^M$ months. Variable T^M depends on whether the consolidation option is exercised or, in the counterfactual case, the loan term is extended. The original maturity of Stafford loans is ten years. See later in this appendix a description of the stochastic rules governing consolidation and extension.

Interest accrues on outstanding principal every month, except for Subsidized loans when the borrower is in school, deferment, or default. The borrower interest rate in period t, denoted $R_{S,t}^j$, is either 0 percent, 6.8 percent, or 6.875 percent, depending on the type and status of the loan.[32]

The variable P_t^j denotes the evolution of principal (prior to default) over time in each simulation j. Given an initial principal of $P_0^j = P_0$, principal evolves according to:

$$(1) \qquad P_{t+1}^j = P_t^j[1 + r_{S,t}^j] - A_{t+1}^j$$

where

$$(2) \qquad r_{S,t}^j = (1 + R_{S,t}^j)^{1/12} - 1$$

is the monthly compounding student rate. The prescribed monthly payment, A_t^j, depends on the loan's status, and is based on amortizing the principal at the current interest rate over the remaining life of the loan:

$$(3) \qquad A_{t+1}^j = \begin{cases} \dfrac{P_t^j r_{S,t}^j}{1 - (1 + r_{S,t}^j)^{-k}}, & t \geq T^R \\ 0, & t < T^R. \end{cases}$$

31. This appendix uses some of the text, figures, and equations in appendix 2 of Lucas and Moore (2007).
32. The numerical implementation of the model is flexible enough to accommodate floating interest rates tied to particular rates on the yield curve.

Borrowers may pay more or less than this prescribed amount due to default, prepayment, consolidation, deferment, and forbearance. Because we do not have reliable data on actual payments, we assume that borrowers make the prescribed payment unless they default on their loans, prepay their loans in their entirety, defer, or receive forbearance on their loans. In the direct program, the government's cash flows on performing loans are the student loan payments less an administrative charge:

(4) $$A_t^j - fP_t^j,$$

where f is the proportional administrative fee. The fee is 0.50 percent per annum in the benchmark calibration, reflecting typical servicing and other administrative costs of the direct program. In default, the government recovers in proportion to the present value of remaining payments.

In the guaranteed lending program, the government cash flows are the quarterly payments to lenders—the SAP less any consolidation fee paid by lenders to the government—while the loan is in good standing, and the lump sum payment of outstanding principal and accrued interest in the event of default. We ignore administrative costs since they are largely borne by the guaranteed lender.

The quarterly SAP is the difference between the student rate and the three-month commercial paper rate plus a spread, but has a floor of zero. We assume the annualized three-month commercial paper rate, R_C, tracks the t-bill rate with a 20 basis point spread:

(5) $$R_{C,t}^j = \exp\left[4y^j\left(3k, 3k + \frac{3}{12}\right)\right] + .002 - 1, \forall t = 1, 2, \ldots, T.$$

Absent default, the government cash flow in each month is the SAP less any consolidation fee paid from lenders to the government (1.05 percent of principal). The net guarantee payment to the government is

(6) $$G_t^j = \begin{cases} \dfrac{-P_{3k}^j[R_{C,3k}^j + 1.74\% - R_{S,3k}^j]}{4}, & 3k < T^R \text{ and } 3k < T^C \, \forall k = 0, 1, 2, \ldots \\[2ex] \dfrac{-P_{3k}^j[R_{C,3k}^j + 2.34\% - R_{S,3k}^j]}{4}, & 3k \geq T^R \text{ and } 3k < t^C \, \forall k = 0, 1, 2, \ldots \\[2ex] \dfrac{-P_{3k}^j([R_{C,3k}^j + 2.64\% - R_{S,3k}^j] - 1.05\%)}{4}, & 3k \geq t^C \, \forall k = 0, 1, 2, \ldots \\[2ex] 0, & \textit{otherwise.} \end{cases}$$

In default, the government pays the outstanding principal, P_t^j, to the lender, assumes the loan, and recovers in proportion to the present value of the remaining outstanding payments. The default and recovery rates used in the calibration are described in a later section of this appendix.

Stochastic Rules Governing Borrower Behavior

Borrowers make a variety of decisions that can dramatically shorten or lengthen the life of their loans, and correspondingly raise or lower their monthly payments. Borrowers do not enter repayment until six months after completing their course of study so loans taken early in the borrower's degree will have longer periods of nonrepayment than loans taken later. Some students shorten or extend the duration of their studies, which adds an uncertain element to the time until a borrower begins repayment. Upon entering repayment, borrowers typically enter a standard ten-year repayment plan but borrowers with larger balances can choose a longer repayment plan of twenty-five years or consolidate their loans into a new loan with terms as long as thirty years. Some borrowers that have left school but take further studies are entitled to payment deferment and borrowers experiencing financial hardship are entitled to loan forbearance. We model the take up of these options using a sample of loans from the NSLDS (as described in appendix A).

In estimating the time before entering repayment, we abstract from the uncertainty and simply assume that all loans experience in-school plus grace period of two years.[33] On the other hand, we assume loan consolidation and loan prepayment behavior are random and sensitive to prevailing interest rates. Prepayment and consolidation may also be related to default rates but, for simplicity, we ignore this. Default rates are discussed in the next section of this appendix.

We posit a rule for the intensity of consolidation for a given loan that is consistent with the Probit model described in appendix A. Specifically, consolidation is decreasing in the student interest rate and decreasing in the time since repayment begins. We assume borrowers consolidate loans during the grace period consistent with the rule for consolidation at other times, but cannot consolidate at all while they are in school.[34] Thus, the annualized probability of consolidation, $q_{C,t}$, at month t is

$$(7) \qquad q_{C,t}^{j} = \begin{cases} 0, & t < T^R - 6 \\ \Phi\left(\beta_1 + \beta_2 \max\left(\dfrac{t - T^R}{12}\right), 0\right), & t \geq T^R, \end{cases}$$

where Φ is the cumulative standard normal distribution function and β_1 and β_2 are loan-type specific parameters, based on probit estimates reported in Lucas and Moore (2007). Table 7A.1 summarizes these parameters for loan type.

Forbearance and deferment rates are likely to exhibit correlation with

33. Averaging the subsidy costs over a distribution of repayment start dates yields similar results when the mean of the distribution is the same as the fixed repayment rate used.

34. For the 2006 academic year, borrowers were allowed to consolidate during their in-school period.

Table 7A.1   **Parameters determining the annual frequency of consolidation**

Maximum eligible consolidation loan term (loan type)	Model coefficient estimates		Proportion of loans consolidating over 10 years
	β_1	β_2	
10 years	−1.94	−0.03	0.16
20 years	−0.6	−0.09	0.55
30 years	−0.43	−0.16	0.51

both interest rates and borrower default rates, as well as the borrowers' cumulative loan balance. For simplicity, we ignore these correlations and just assume that each year a loan has a 6 percent chance of entering deferment or forbearance for a fixed duration of three years. By assumption, each loan enters deferment or forbearance at most one time, which results in a cumulative ten year rate of deferment and forbearance of approximately 0.55 in base case calibrations. During this period borrowers do not make payments, hence $A_t = 0$ for each period t.

Adjusting Discount Rates for Default Risk

Under the CIR model, the risk-neutral monthly compounded discount rate, d_t, for default free but possibly interest rate contingent monthly cash flows is

$$(8) \qquad d_t = \frac{1}{p(t, t + 1/12)} - 1 \ \forall t = 0, 1, 2, \dots .$$

In both the direct and guaranteed lending programs, the underlying payments between parties are contingent on default. We assume that default occurs with probability q in each month until the borrower completely repays the loan and that default risk is orthogonal to interest rate risk. To establish a simple no-arbitrage pricing mechanism for interest rate and default sensitive cash flows, we suppose there is a pair of simple one-period securities traded in every period. The first is risk free, offering a certain payoff of one dollar in one period's time. The second is a risky claim that pays one dollar if the borrower does not default and α if the borrower does default. The fair price of the default free claim along a particular interest rate simulation path is:[35]

$$(9) \qquad \frac{1}{1 + d_t}.$$

With a constant monthly risk premium of π and a default probability of q, the fair price of the risky claim is:[36]

---

35. We omit the subscript j in the remainder of this appendix.
36. The probability of default and the risk premium can be time varying, but this is suppressed for simplicity.

(10)
$$\frac{1 - q(1 - \alpha)}{(1 + d_t)(1 + \pi)}.$$

More conveniently, we can define state price deflators to value cash flows in $t + 1$ paid if the borrower defaults:

(11)
$$\frac{h}{1 + d_t}$$

and if the borrower does not default:

(12)
$$\frac{1 - h}{1 + d_t},$$

where h is the risk-neutral probability of default:

(13)
$$h = \frac{\pi + q(1 - \alpha)}{(1 + \pi)(1 - \alpha)}.$$

Calibrating State Prices for Default Contingent Prices

Data from the NDSL suggests a cumulative default rate of 15 percent over the life of a typical Stafford loan. Default rates vary over the life of a loan, with the rate decreasing as the loan ages. Abstracting from the time pattern, an annual default rate of 2 percent is consistent with this cumulative experience. Hence, the quarterly default rate, q, is set to .25 percent. Estimates from the NSLDS suggest a recovery rate on defaulted loans in the range of 40 to 60 percent. We assume the midpoint of 50 percent in the computation of subsidy cost for the two programs.

Present Value of Program Cash Flows

For a given sequence of interest rates, the transition of a loan through defaulting and nondefaulting states can be represented as a binomial tree. Figure 7A.1, panel A, shows borrower payments on a direct loan in a two-period binomial tree. The tree tracks the status of the loan over time, with discrete intervals of time indicated on the horizontal axis. From a given node, each upward move indicates the borrower does not default in the subsequent period, and each downward move corresponds to a borrower default. To ensure a stationary representation, rather than terminate the loan after default, we assume that the borrower and lender agree to a new loan with payments reduced to fraction α of the originally prescribed payments (reflecting failed collections and collection costs).[37] That is, the lender recovers a lump sum proportional to the present value of remaining payments. Cash flows in each state can be priced back to the previous period by using the default and nondefault state prices in equations (26) and (27) and

---

37. This makes it possible to calibrate the risk premium using the observed loan spread above the risk free rate(s) and the recovery adjusted default rate $q\,(1 - \alpha)$ as in equation (30).

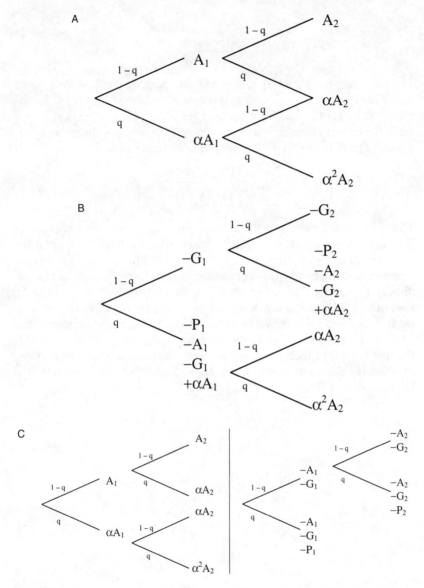

Fig. 7A.1   Binomial representation for the cash flows of a two-period student loan for a given simulation of interest rates

to earlier periods by applying (26) and (27) recursively. The present value of loan cash flows is then:

(14)
$$\sum_{t=0}^{\infty} \frac{A_t}{\left(\prod_{k=0}^{t-1}(1 + d_k)\right)(1 + s)^t},$$

where

(15)
$$s = \frac{1 + \pi}{1 - q(1 - \alpha)} - 1.$$

The variable s has an interpretation as the monthly credit spread, which depends on the rate of default (q), the rate of recovery (α), and the risk premium for credit risk (π). Assuming the administrative fee is paid only while the loan is not in default (only along the uppermost branches of the binomial tree), the present value of administrative fees is:

(16)
$$\sum_{t=0}^{\infty} \frac{(1 - h)^t f P_t^j}{\left(\prod_{k=0}^{t-1}(1 + d_k)\right)}.$$

Thus, the present value of a direct loan is the difference between equation (14) and (16). The cash flows for the guarantee also have a binomial tree representation, as shown in panel B of figure 7A.1 for the two-period case. These cash flows can be decomposed into two simpler binomial trees, as displayed in panel C of figure 7A.1. The first is just the binomial tree for the student loan and the second is a residual that captures the net payments to lenders as described in section 7.5.3. Those lender payments have only two nonzero branches in each period because the loan is assumed to become federal property following default. Valuing the two components of using the risk-neutral discount rates and probabilities of default gives the following present value of cash flows:

(17)
$$\sum_{t=0}^{\infty} \frac{A_t}{\left(\prod_{k=0}^{t-1}(1 + d_k)\right)(1 + s)^t}$$
$$- \sum_{t=0}^{\infty} \frac{(1 - h)^t (G_t + A_t)}{\left(\prod_{k=0}^{t-1}(1 + d_k)\right)}$$
$$- \sum_{t=0}^{\infty} \frac{(1 - h)^{t-1} h(P_t + G_t + A_t)}{\left(\prod_{k=0}^{t-1}(1 + d_k)\right)}.$$

References

Center on Federal Financial Institutions (COFFI) 2005. Student loans: A budget primer. Available at: http://www.coffi.org/pubs/Student%20Loans%20A%20 Budget%20Primer%20v2.pdf.
Congressional Budget Office (CBO). 2005. Estimating the value of subsidies for federal loans and loan guarantees. Washington, DC: CBO.

De Fraja, G. 2002. The design of optimal education policies. *The Review of Economic Studies* 69 (2): 437–66.

Dynarski, S. 2002. The behavioral and distributional implications of aid for college. *The American Economic Review* 92 (2): 279–85.

Edlin, A. S. 1993. Is college financial aid equitable and efficient? *The Journal of Economic Perspectives* 7 (2): 143–58.

Gramlich, E. 1990. *A guide to cost-benefit analysis.* Englewood Cliffs, NJ: Prentice-Hall.

Lucas, D., and D. Moore. 2007. The student loan consolidation option. Congressional Budget Office Working Paper no. 2007-05, Washington, DC.

Hanushek, E. A. 1989. Expenditures, efficiency, and equity in education: The Federal government's role. *The American Economic Review* 79 (2): 46–51.

Jagannathan, R., A. Kaplin, and S. G. Sun. 2003. An evaluation of multi-factor CIR models using LIBOR, swap rates, and cap and swaption prices. *Journal of Econometrics* 116 (1–2): 113–46.

Keane, M. P. 2002. Financial aid, borrowing constraints, and college attendance: Evidence from structural estimates. *The American Economic Review* 92 (2): 293–97.

New American Foundation. 2009. History of guaranteed (a.k.a. Federal Family Education Loans) and Direct Student Loans. Available at: http://www.newamerica.net/programs/education_policy/student_loan_watch/history.

Price Waterhouse Coopers. 2005. The limitations of budget score-keeping in comparing the federal student loan programs. Available at: http://www.studentloanfacts.org/resources/.

Comment   Janice C. Eberly

This chapter brings rigorous quantitative evaluation to an important policy topic, and hence it is hard to quarrel with either the motivation or the execution. Student lending is important both as a Federal budget item and as a component of household balance sheets (as I argue later). Moreover, student loans are an instrument of access to higher education. Largely as a result of these programs, some prominent researchers argue that financing should no longer be considered a barrier to college enrollment (Carneiro and Heckman 2005). Nonetheless, policymakers should remain vigilant about the cost and efficiency of the programs that provide this access.

The chapter makes three contributions. First, it provides a primer on student lending programs, which are large and ubiquitous in higher education in the United States. Second, the chapter makes an important technical contribution by calculating the cost of student loans in the main federal programs. This is a substantial undertaking because of the complexity

Janice C. Eberly is the John L. and Helen Kellogg Professor of Finance at the J. L. Kellogg School of Management, and a research associate of the National Bureau of Economic Research.

and opaque measurement of these programs. Finally, the chapter explores policy implications by comparing the direct lending and guaranteed loan programs. The former provides financing for student loans directly from the government, while the guaranteed or Federal Family Education Loan Program (FFELP) provides a federal guarantee to loans originated and held privately.

My comments focus on three issues raised by the chapter. First, why are student loans an important segment to understand? Student loans represent a large and growing segment of household debt. This category of household liabilities is relatively new, at least in its current form, but composes more than 40 percent of household debt for young households (age of household head less than thirty-five). Second, because of the structure of federal loan programs, valuing the outstanding liabilities is not easy. The valuation project undertaken by this chapter is challenging, but important and useful to understand the nature of the instruments held by the federal government, as well as liabilities incurred by students. Finally, there are policy implications for education finance, which is largely a government-owned or sponsored activity. The chapter suggests that direct lending is substantially cheaper to the government than the guaranteed loan program through private financial institutions. Recent legislation has tended to move in the direction suggested by the chapter, in cutting the subsidy payments to the institutions that originate and distribute the guaranteed loans.

The Importance of Student Loans

Student loan programs loom large for both borrowers and lenders. From the government's point of view, the annual cash commitment is large, as is the liability that the government takes on by either holding or guaranteeing the loans. Quantifying the size of this liability is also one of the goals of this chapter. Similarly, the amount of debt taken on by student borrowers is substantial. Student loan debt is becoming a visible presence in household balance sheets.

Debbie and Damien's chapter describes the quantity of debt from the government's and lenders' perspective, which was $380 billion in 2005. Here I focus on the student level. The average federal student loan debt among 2004 graduating seniors is $19,202 (Stafford and Perkins loans); adding in parent loans (PLUS) takes the total to $21,814. For graduate and professional students, the debt level doubles, on average (see table 7C.1).

Looking at student lending in the context of household balance sheets, it is helpful to first start with total household debt, using data from the Survey of Consumer Finances. Median total household debt has almost doubled from $22,000 to $38,000 from 1989 to 2004 (in real 2004 dollars). Generally, however, this debt is concentrated among households headed by

Table 7C.1   2004 education debt

Graduate and professional degree programs	Graduate education debt		All education debt (Grad and Undergrad)	
	Percent borrowing	Cumulative debt (US $)	Percent borrowing	Cumulative debt (US $)
Total	60.1	37,067	70.1	42,406
Master's degree	58.4	26,895	69.3	32,858
Doctoral degree	51.0	49,007	58.3	53,405
Professional degree	86.5	82,688	88.4	93,134
MBA	53.0	35,525	63.6	41,687
MSW	76.5	27,136	81.0	37,029
PhD	40.0	36,917	46.8	41,540
EdD	53.4	49,050	65.7	47,725
Law (LLB or JD)	87.7	70,933	89.7	80,754
Medicine	95.0	113,661	95.0	125,819

Source: Department of Education.

forty- to fifty-year-olds, and is in the form of collateralized mortgage debt. Education debt is not broadly held, though the share of households with holdings has risen from nine percent to 14 percent from 1989 to 2004, and both the median level of education debt and the mean have doubled; the mean has risen from $8,000 to $16,000 per household. However, these aggregate values mask the concentration of debt among younger households, who have experienced the run-up in student lending. Among households under age thirty-five, almost 30 percent have student loans (see figure 7C.1). Among these households, the median level of education debt is $9,000, which is more than 40 percent of their total debt (the median level of total debt is $22,000).

The data also indicate that education debt is concentrated among the lowest wealth households. Keep in mind that student loans are not means-tested and are unsecured debt. If the investment in education pays off, then this is not necessarily bad—presumably, higher education generally leads to higher future income. There is strong evidence of the return to education in the large literature documenting the education skill premium.

It is more difficult to document how well students understand the obligations they assume when they take on an education loan. The terms are often far from transparent, and may include conditions that depend on the student's payment history. Moreover, student loans are not discharged in bankruptcy, and it is very difficult to default on student loan debt. Consider the following exchange on a student loan question-and-answer website (the following adapted from www.WikiAnswers.com). Question: "How long before outstanding student loans are forgiven?" Answer: "It doesn't matter

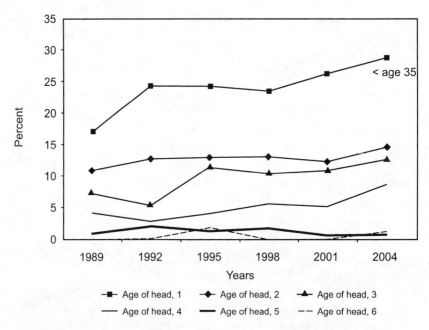

Fig. 7C.1   2004 percent of families with education debt, by age of head of household
Source: Survey of Consumer Finances.

how long you had the loan, you have to pay it back unless you are disabled, a teacher in low-income schools, part of the peace corps, or the school forged your signature." In fact, the Department of Education regularly garnishes the wages and tax refunds of borrowers who fail to make their payments on federal loans. Garnishment is limited to 15 percent of disposable income, and continues until the debt is fully repaid.

A Sketch of Student Lending Programs: Direct and Guaranteed

The Federal government currently offers two parallel systems for students to finance higher education. In both cases, the Government sets the terms of the student loan (interest rate, maturity, deferment options, etc.), so the terms of the two government programs are broadly the same from a borrower's viewpoint. The administration and financing of the two loan programs, however, are quite different.

In the direct lending program, the government makes the loan directly to the student and services the loan through a third-party servicer.

In the guaranteed lending program a "bank" or other financial institution originates and services the loan to the student. The government pays the bank a floating rate plus a premium, to compensate the lender for the cost of funds, plus the preferential loan terms of student loans and for administrative costs. The government compensates the lender 97 percent of principal if the student defaults.[1]

The Stafford loan is one of the largest guaranteed student loan programs. Congress sets the interest rate, pegged to a floating rate until 2006, now fixed. The "first hundred hours" legislation in 2007 halved this rate. The loans have a basic maturity of ten years, but this can be extended to up to thirty years under various programs. Stafford loans can either be "subsidized" loans or "unsubsidized." The government pays the interest accumulation on a subsidized loan while the student is in school or defers payment. The subsidy is need-based and borrowing is capped at $23,000 for undergraduates, and $65,500 for graduate students. The student pays all the interest on an unsubsidized loan, and the total borrowing is capped at $23,000 for undergraduates and $138,500 for graduate students (total, including any undergraduate borrowing).

Because the total cost of education can easily exceed the caps on Stafford loans, Congress has also created the "PLUS" loan, or Parent Loan. This program allows parents to borrow on behalf of undergraduate dependents. The interest rate is fixed at 8.5 percent, and the maturity varies from ten to thirty years. The PLUS program was recently extended to graduate education. Prior to this extension, adult graduate and professional students typically turned to the private loan market to finance their educations in excess of the caps on Federal Stafford loans. The introduction of the PLUS loan for graduate and professional students greatly reduced demand for these private loans.

The private loan program is the final source of education debt financing. There is no government guarantee, but the loans are not dismissed in bankruptcy (as of 2005). These loans are privately offered by financial institutions in a very competitive market. Because there is no federal back up, these loans provide a market benchmark against which to compare the federal programs. This is a key component of the analysis of the government programs, since the private market provides an estimate of the market interest rate for student loans.

Comparing Private versus Federal Loans: How Big is the Subsidy and Who Gets It?

The presence of these three loan programs—direct lending, guaranteed loans, and private loans—allows a three-way comparison of private versus the two government loan programs. In particular, using the private loans as a benchmark, Debbie and Damien estimate how heavily subsidized the federal loans are. Moreover, they can then compare the subsidies and costs embedded in the two federal loans and compare their costs to the

---

1. This amount can vary depending on the servicer, and at times was as high as 99 percent. New legislation retained the 97 percent guarantee.

government. Specifically, the government pays nothing for private loans. For direct loans it pays the difference between the market interest rate and the interest rate that the student pays, plus any subsidized interest, plus its own administrative costs. For guaranteed loans, the government pays the principal if the loan defaults, plus payments to the originators to compensate them for the subsidized interest rate, as well as their administrative costs.

The approach in the chapter compares government cash outflows to the cash inflows in each of the Federal programs, taking present values using the appropriate cost of capital. A direct loan has the simplest cash flows: the Federal government disburses the loan and incurs administrative servicing costs, eventually receiving loan payments back, subject to deferrals, consolidation, early repayment, or default. The present value of the cash inflows (repayments) minus the cash outflow (the initial loan amount) gives the cost of the loan. Since the loans are offered at a below-market interest rate, this calculation is usually equal to a negative number, giving the present value of the subsidy to the student borrower.

The cash flows made by the government to support guaranteed loans are trickier. In this case the "bank" obtains financing privately and disburses it to the student. The bank incurs marketing and administrative costs, services the loan (or obtains a third party to do so), and receives repayments, subject to deferrals, consolidation, early repayment, or default. Government payments are made to the bank to defray its administrative costs and the subsidized interest rate, and the government also makes the guarantee payment in the case of student default. (Banks also make some payments back to the government, but we will focus on the net payment from the government to the bank.)

From the results in the chapter's table 7.5, consider a typical $25,000 debt with a twenty-year term: it costs the government $3,375 (13.5 percent) unsubsidized in direct lending and $6,325 in the guaranteed program. If subsidized, these numbers jump to $6,750 and $9,250, respectively. First, note that even the unsubsidized loan is subsidized; the government pays 13.5 percent of the cost of the loan. If we assume that the $3,375 cost in the direct lending program represents the cost of the preferential borrowing rate, plus reasonable administrative costs, then the student's cost is $3,375 lower than it would be for a similar private loan. The cost to the government to make the same loan through the guaranteed loan program is almost twice as high—$6,328—and the student receives fundamentally the same product.

The obvious question to ask then is what happens to the additional $2,953, or 12 percentage points, in costs paid by the government to financial institutions to make guaranteed loans? Financial institutions may have higher costs than the direct lending program (due to a higher cost of capital or operational inefficiencies, for example). Originating and distributing federal student loans is a very competitive business, so it is likely (as Debbie and Damien argue) that any excess payments to lenders are dissipated through competition. The extra cost could be spent on marketing, or in "sweeteners" to students that improve the borrowing terms; say, through a discounted interest rate for on-time payments or electronic withdrawals. This decomposition does not affect the subsidy to guaranteed lending, but it does change how one thinks about the incidence of costs. If the extra cost for guaranteed lending is due to higher financing/operating costs or marketing expenses, there is little payoff to the government of using guaranteed lending. If, on the other hand, the payments go to improved terms for borrowers, then the additional government cost is passed along to student borrowers. In this case, the guaranteed loan program is more expensive to the government, but the student borrowers receive a better loan.

Policy Implications and Responses

To the extent that the guaranteed program is more expensive to the government than direct lending, without passing through the benefits to students, the guaranteed program is simply more costly to the government without benefitting students. Not surprisingly, the program has been under increased scrutiny. The most recent reauthorization of the Higher Education Act in 2007 improved loan terms to students by halving the interest rate, and also cut payments to lenders. The former, as indicated in Debbie and Damien's table 7.8, dramatically increases the subsidy to students—by a factor of 2 even under direct lending. The reduction in payments to financial institutions has caused a large number of lenders to cease participation in the guaranteed lending program, leading to a substantial shift to direct lending.

These changes may indicate a change in the federal lending model, eliminating the dual approach, in which direct and guaranteed lending programs coexist, and instead moving toward a model in which all student loan financing is provided by the federal government. Even under direct lending, servicing is generally privately provided through third-party servicing contracts with the government. Origination could also follow a contracting model, where financial institutions originate loans and sell them to the government (as has occurred with the disruption in financial markets in 2008). This model preserves some of the potential benefits of competition in origination and servicing, while eliminating what Debbie and Damien identify as wasteful subsidies in the guaranteed lending program.

Reference

Carneiro, P., and J. J. Heckman. 2005. Human Capital Policy. in *Inequality in America: What role for human capital policies?,* ed. J. J. Heckman and A. B. Krueger, 77–240. Cambridge, MA: MIT Press.

Market Valuation of Accrued Social Security Benefits

John Geanakoplos and Stephen P. Zeldes

8.1 Introduction

One measure of the health of the Social Security system is the difference between the present value of Social Security benefits accrued to date and the market value of the Social Security trust fund. This measure, referred to as the *maximum transition cost,* is comparable to the one used to gauge the fundedness of private defined benefit pension plans and provides an estimate of the cost of switching from a primarily pay-as-you-go Social Security system to a fully-funded one.

How should present values be computed for this calculation in light of future uncertainties? We argue that it is important to use market value. Since claims on accrued benefits are not currently traded in financial markets, however, we cannot directly observe a market value. In this chapter, we therefore use a model to estimate what the market price for these claims would be if they were traded.

In valuing such claims, the key issue is properly adjusting for risk. We

John Geanakoplos is the James Tobin Professor of Economics at Yale University and an external professor of the Santa Fe Institute. Stephen P. Zeldes is the Benjamin Rosen Professor of Economics and Finance at Columbia University and a research associate of the National Bureau of Economic Research.

We thank Ryan Chahrour, Ben Marx, Theodore Papageorgiou, and Sami Ragab for research assistance, and Mark Broadie, Deborah Lucas, Kent Smetters, and seminar participants at the Conference on Measuring and Managing Federal Financial Risk (Kellogg School of Management, February 2007) and at Columbia University for helpful comments and suggestions. This research was supported by the US Social Security Administration (SSA) through grant #10-P-98363-1-04 to the National Bureau of Economic Research as part of the SSA Retirement Research Consortium. The findings and conclusions expressed are solely those of the authors and do not represent the views of SSA, any agency of the Federal Government, or the NBER.

contend that the traditional actuarial approach—the approach currently used by the Social Security Administration (SSA) in generating its most widely cited numbers—does not adjust appropriately for aggregate risk in future financial flows. In particular, the SSA methodology computes the expected value of aggregate cash flows for each future date and then discounts these at a riskless rate of interest. Instead, we treat aggregate Social Security payments as dividends on a risky asset, and ask what that asset would be worth if it were traded in financial markets. We call the resulting estimate the *market value* of Social Security obligations. Effectively, market valuation incorporates a risk premium that reflects the market risk of the cash flows being discounted. If benefits are risky and this risk is priced by the market, then market value will differ from actuarial estimates.

Why do we believe that market value is the relevant measure of financial status? Let us begin with a simple example. Suppose that a worker's Social Security benefits were always equal to the dividends of one share of a particular stock. It would be sensible to quote the value of those benefits at the market price of the stock. That would, for example, allow the worker to compare the size of his private portfolio, which might hold shares of the same stock, and his Social Security portfolio of benefits. Similarly for the Social Security system as a whole, if all the promised benefits together were identical to 20 percent of the combined European stock market, then one-fifth of European stocks' market capitalization would be a useful guide to understanding the cost of transitioning to a fully funded Social Security system. The market value can also be seen as the amount that the government would need to pay participants in the financial market to accept its obligations or liabilities.

Under the current methodology, however, the SSA would likely report much larger numbers for this worker's promised benefits, because the SSA numbers would ignore the riskiness of the dividends. Historically, total stock returns have been much higher than the riskless rate. This suggests that stock dividends are indeed subject to the kind of uncertainty that leads cash flows to be more heavily discounted by the market. Of course theory, beginning with the capital asset pricing model, also suggests that stock dividends should be discounted by more than the riskless rate.

This example, linking stock market risk to risk in Social Security benefits, is not as far-fetched as it might appear. Benefits are by no means risk free. The US Social Security system is "wage-indexed"; that is, future benefits are tied directly to the economywide average wage index around the year of the worker's statutory retirement age. (We discuss the precise formula later.) We argue that wages and stock prices are linked in the long run, effectively linking Social Security benefits to the performance of the stock market.

Theoretically, a long-run relationship between wages and stocks is natural. If we believe that fifty years from now American businesses will be failing and paying small dividends, we should expect wages to be low by then as well. Over the long term, countries with high business profits per capita have also paid high wages. Empirically, Benzoni, Collin-Dufresne, and Goldstein (2007) find evidence of cointegration between stocks and wages over a long sample of US data (1927 to 2004), despite the well-known difficulties of identifying such relationships in finite samples. We believe there is already strong evidence for the wage-stock link; our chapter suggests one more reason why studying this relationship further is important.

Real wages and stock market returns do not seem to be contemporaneously correlated, as Goetzmann (2008) and others have pointed out. But it is crucial to realize that a lack of short-run correlation does not imply the absence of a long-run correlation. Consider a simple thought experiment. Suppose that wages (W) and dividends (D) always moved one for one in a geometric random walk, and that at every period investors could forecast dividends one period in advance with certainty, but had no information about the more distant future. Assuming a constant risk-free interest rate and pricing kernel, the price of the stock would then be $P_t = \varphi D_{t+1}$ for some constant φ. Stock market returns $(P_{t+1} + D_{t+1})/P_t = D_{t+2}/D_{t+1} + 1/\varphi$ would be independent of contemporaneous wage growth $W_{t+1}/W_t = D_{t+1}/D_t$, but in the long run stock levels and wage levels would be nearly perfectly correlated.

To take another example, suppose, following Benzoni, Collin-Dufresne, and Goldstein (2007), that dividends follow a geometric random walk and that wages also follow a geometric random walk with an independent fluctuation, but with a drift that depends on the ratio of current dividends to current wages. Once again we would find almost no short-run correlation between wage growth and stock returns, but it is easy to see that a sustained period of high stock dividends and high stock returns would likely foreshadow a period of high wage growth.

In what follows, we assume that wages and dividends follow this process, so that there is a positive long-run correlation between average labor earnings and the stock market. We then use derivative pricing methods standard in the finance literature to compute the market price of individual claims on future benefits, which depend on age and macro state variables. Finally, we aggregate the market value of benefits across all cohorts to arrive at an overall value of accrued benefits and of the maximum transition cost.[1]

We find that the market value of accrued Social Security benefits is substantially less than the "actuarial" value, and that the difference is especially large for younger cohorts. Overall, the market value of accrued benefits is only four-fifths of that implied by the actuarial approach. Ignoring retirees

---

1. In this chapter, we focus on the maximum transition cost measure of financial status. In ongoing work (Geanakoplos and Zeldes, 2009b) we examine alternative open and closed group measures that incorporate future taxes and future accruals.

(for whom the valuations are the same), market value is only 70 percent as large as that implied by the actuarial approach. This implies that the market value of Social Security's unfunded obligations, as measured by the maximum transition cost measure, is significantly less than the actuarial value commonly presented by the SSA.

This difference by itself might change the public's view of the transition cost of the system, and is therefore reason enough to pursue a measure of market value. Recent suggestions by the Federal Accounting Standards Advisory Board to include Social Security obligations on the US balance sheet make the question of their value especially pertinent.

One logical consequence of our approach is that large decreases in the stock market, such as we saw in 2007 and 2008, should significantly decrease the market value of accrued Social Security benefits. The SSA, by contrast, does not seem to have moved its calculations by much.

In work done after the original version of this chapter was written, Blocker, Kotlikoff, and Ross (2008) also attempt a market valuation of outstanding Social Security obligations. They argue for risk adjustments due to (a) the correlation between wage growth and returns on traded assets and (b) the inflation insurance provided by consumer price index (CPI)-indexed benefits. They empirically estimate the correlations between wage growth and traded assets, and they conclude that the market value of Social Security obligations is *greater* than the actuarial value. In contrast, we reach the opposite conclusion, namely that the market value is *less* than the actuarial value.

One reason for this disparity is that in addition to adjusting for risk, Blocker, Kotlikoff, and Ross also change the risk-free rate of interest to what they argue is a more reasonable value. Based on the term structure for Treasury Inflation Protected Securities (TIPS), Blocker, Kotlikoff, and Ross assume a risk-free rate between 1.5 percent and 2 percent, while the SSA projections assume a rate of 2.9 percent for nearly the entire horizon of its projections. To the extent that the SSA uses too high a risk-free rate, SSA will underestimate the present value of accrued benefits, but this would be felt even if Social Security benefits were not at all risky (and thus required no risk adjustment). Blocker, Kotlikoff, and Ross do not disentangle the effects of the adjustment for risk and the change in the risk-free rate, but it appears to us that their choice of a lower risk-free rate is the primary factor driving their results.

It is difficult to ascertain from the Blocker, Kotlikoff, and Ross paper the size or even the direction of the two true risk adjustments that they make. Regarding risk adjustment for wages (see point [a] previously), Blocker and colleagues focus on short-run correlations of wages and stocks; they estimate the correlation using at most a one-period lag and find it to be small. We argue that even though the short-run correlation is close to zero, the long-run correlation is large and positive, which implies that risk adjustment should be large and should *decrease* the market value today of a claim on future economywide wages.

Regarding the risk adjustment to the value of the inflation-indexed annuity as of the retirement date (see point [b] previously), we agree that some adjustment for inflation insurance may be appropriate (as reflected in the difference between the real return on nominal bonds and the real return on indexed bonds). However, this inflation risk premium is likely much smaller than the 90 to 140 basis point spread used by Blocker, Kotlikoff, and Ross. We assume this premium is zero in our analysis.[2]

Our chapter is structured as follows. In section 8.2, we describe why we think that market value is the most appropriate measure for estimating Social Security obligations. Section 8.3 describes how our previous work can be used to frame accrued benefits in terms of units of a potentially tradable financial security (a Personal Annuitized Average Wage [PAAW]). Section 8.4 shows how to price this security, incorporating the market price of risk. In section 8.5, we estimate the quantity of PAAWs outstanding by cohort, and in section 8.6 we combine the information in 8.4 and 8.5 to arrive at an estimate of the market value of accrued Social Security benefits. In section 8.7, we consider the robustness of our results to changes in the parameter that determines the strength of the wage-stock link. Section 8.8 concludes.

8.2   The Importance of Market Valuation

Market valuation answers the question: "what payment would financial markets require for taking on the responsibility of paying Social Security benefits?" A market price for Social Security obligations would also provide important information to households, governments, private pension plans, other market participants, and administrators of Social Security. In fact, the 2007 Social Security Technical Panel on Assumptions and Methods (Technical Panel 2007) cited an earlier version of our chapter and recommended that the Trustees of Social Security consider adopting risk-adjusted discount rates.

Finding the market value of Social Security liabilities also implies the ability to hedge them, since valuation and hedging are dual computations. If the Social Security trust fund were someday permitted to diversify out of government bonds, this would provide a valuable guide to determining the optimal portfolio allocation.

It is worth noting that the measure we compute ignores the general equilibrium effects of selling the full quantity of the asset; bringing all Social Security obligations to market at once could well change how the market

---

2. Note that the measure of financial status that Blocker, Kotlikoff, and Ross (2008) examine (a closed group measure that includes future taxes and future accrued benefits of current workers) differs somewhat from ours, but this cannot explain the difference in results.

values these and other assets. In this respect, our measure is no different than "market capitalization" in the stock market, or measures of aggregate holdings in real estate.

A market price for Social Security obligations will be especially important for improving government accounting. In its annual Financial Report, the US government produces a balance sheet that summarizes the assets and liabilities of the Federal Government. One controversial aspect of the balance sheet is how to account for social insurance programs. In 2006, the Federal Accounting Standards Advisory Board (FASAB) published a preliminary statement on new standards for social insurance accounting (FASAB 2006). The document described two views. The Primary View, held by the majority of the board, would recognize every accrued benefit as a liability of the system.[3] Under this view, liabilities should be based on expected benefits "attributable" to earnings to date, using current benefit formulas. In contrast, the Alternative View advocates continuing the current practice of acknowledging only those benefits that are "due and payable" at the time of valuation. Essentially, under the alternative view only current-period benefits not yet paid to beneficiaries (an amount close to zero) would be counted as a liability.

Supporters of the Primary View argue that recognizing the new liability is most consistent with the principle of accounting based on accrual, as opposed to cash flows, and best captures the economic costs incurred by social insurance programs each year. Supporters of the Alternative View argue that given political and economic uncertainty regarding Social Security, such obligations are neither legally guaranteed nor reliably estimable. They also worry that, because of the large size of the obligation, incorporating it as a liability may make other important spending choices appear inconsequential.

In a November 2008 update of the statement (FASAB 2008), FASAB proposed a compromise between these views: accrued benefit "obligations" are to be provided in a note on the federal financial statements, and another measure referred to as the closed group measure (equal to the accrued obligations to date plus future taxes and future accruals of *current* participants) is to be reported as a separate line just below the balance sheet. If the compromise prevails, measures of Social Security's future obligations will gain prominence in government financial statements, but no new *liabilities* will be recognized on the balance sheet at this time.

Whether or not one wishes to characterize future benefit obligations as "liabilities," correctly computing their value is essential. It is widely agreed that some measure of the present value of future cash flows should be

3. Accrued benefits would be those earned by fully-insured participants (e.g., Social Security participants who have achieved forty-quarters of covered earnings, the minimum to receive benefits) based on their earnings histories to date.

reported, even if not on the balance sheet. Proper valuation of these risky flows will be essential to the new guidelines' efficacy in accurately portraying the financial status of the Social Security program.

For individuals, a market price for cohort benefits would provide information about the market value of their own benefits, helping them with financial planning decisions regarding saving and asset allocation. A true market price would allow individual households to consider Social Security benefits as any other asset in their portfolio. The cohort-specific estimates in this chapter give some idea of the value of new benefit accruals and how they compare with tax contributions. Workers could compute, for example, a market-based "money's worth" measure such as the ratio of the present value (PV) of benefits to the PV of contributions (for a further description of money's worth measures, see Geanakoplos, Mitchell, and Zeldes [1999]). A market value for benefits would also likely make it more difficult for the government to take them away, enhancing property rights.

Finally, if markets for bonds indexed to Social Security obligations actually develop in the future, buyers and sellers of these new securities would be forced to make the same kind of computations we propose here. If the private sector were permitted to issue these securities, the government could purchase them from the private sector in order to cover a portion of the benefit obligations accrued each year.

8.3   Translating Accrued Benefits into Units of Marketable New Securities (PAAWs)

Under current Social Security rules, workers and employers together contribute 12.4 percent of "covered earnings" (i.e., all labor income up to the earnings cap, equal to \$102,000 in 2008). Upon retirement, workers receive benefits that are linked to their earnings history, and in a particular way, to average earnings in the economy. For each year in the worker's history, earnings are divided by the average economywide wage index from that year, and then multiplied by the average economywide wage index in the computation year (typically age sixty).[4] Since a worker's benefits depend crucially on average wages in the computation year, they are subject to a type of aggregate risk. In this chapter, we price this risk.

The maximum transition cost is reported annually in a recurring note from the Office of the Actuary (Wade, Schultz, and Goss 2008), and is intended to represent the present value of benefits accrued by current and past workers, net of current trust fund assets. Estimating this measure requires establishing what it means for benefits to be accrued. By definition, accrued benefits

---

4. In Geanakoplos and Zeldes (2008), we assumed all wages were indexed to age sixty-five wages. Under SSA rules, however, wages after age sixty-two are included at their nominal levels in the formula while wages from earlier years are indexed to economy average wages in the individual's sixtieth year. Thus, aggregate wage risk in a cohort is resolved after year sixty.

can rise, but never fall. In Geanakoplos and Zeldes (2009a), we show that there are many feasible accrual rules and describe two natural rules in detail. For simplicity, we focus here on one of these, "the straight-line" accrual rule, in which accrued benefits to date are defined by setting future wages equal to the worker's average wage to date and prorating the resulting benefits by a scale factor related to years of work.[5] This is a relatively conservative accrual rule (in the sense of delaying accrual) and thus tends to decrease the accruals of younger cohorts. Since these are the cohorts for whom the risk adjustment is important, this accrual rule tends to decrease the magnitude of the overall risk adjustment. We show that, even with this accrual rule, the risk adjustment is quite significant.

In Geanakoplos and Zeldes (2009a), we described how to create a system of personal accounts that achieves many of the core goals of supporters of the current system, including risk-sharing and redistribution. We called these "Progressive Personal Accounts." One step in that process was to show that a personal account system could be structured to exactly reproduce the benefits promised under the current system. This involved the creation of a new financial security, which we named a Personal Annuitized Average Wage security, or PAAW for short. Whether or not Progressive Personal Accounts are adopted, this equivalence means that establishing a price for this theoretical security is sufficient for pricing existing Social Security obligations.

We define a PAAW as a security that pays its owner one inflation-corrected dollar for every year of his life after the year (t_R) in which he hits the statutory retirement age (R), multiplied by the economywide average wage (W_{tc}) in the computation year (t_c) that he hits age sixty. The PAAWs are tied to specific individuals, indexed by i, through their mortality, the wage index in their cohort's computation year, W_{tc}, and the year of the first payout on their security (t_R). In this chapter, we assume all workers retire at sixty-five, fixing the relationship between t_c and t_R. In this context, the notation PAAW(i, t_R) identifies the relevant information for any PAAW.

Each additional dollar that an individual earns generates additional

5. Specifically, we compute average relative earnings over all years the worker has earnings, up to thirty-five years. If the worker has earnings from more than thirty-five years, we take the average over the thirty-five highest earning years. Average relative earnings are then entered into the current Primary Insurance Amount (PIA) formula, and the result is prorated by min{1,(work years/35)}. For example, if a worker has worked for twenty-five years (equal to 5/7 of thirty-five years), we average the relative earnings from just these twenty-five years (effectively setting future wages equal to this average), compute the resulting number of PAAWs using the PIA formula, and then multiply the result by 5/7. Note that this is not identical to the SSA procedure for calculating accruals for their Maximum Transition Cost measure (they average the best 4/5 of earnings years and scale PIA by (age-22)/40), but the two procedures give similar results. An alternative accrual method, also described in Geanakoplos and Zeldes (2009a), is one we call the "fastest" accrual method, which sets future wages to zero and does not prorate, giving more rapid accruals by adjusting for age before the (progressive) calculation of PIA rather than after. (This is termed "fastest" because no other possibilities exist that have faster accumulation and also satisfy the constraint that accrued benefits will not fall even if future earnings are all zero.) See Jackson (2004) for a further discussion of accrual accounting.

accrued benefits or PAAWs. At any point in time t, an individual's accrued benefits can be summarized completely by the number of PAAWs owned. The present value of accrued benefits is therefore equal to the quantity of accrued PAAWs (known at time t) multiplied by the present value of a PAAW(i, t_R).

The PAAW valuations should differ for individuals in the same age cohort with different mortality probabilities. For example, the longer life expectancies of women means their PAAWs would be more valuable, if they were traded separately. We assume that all members of a birth cohort have the same age profile of survival probabilities.[6] In the following sections, we examine how to price PAAWs for each cohort, and we then estimate the quantity of PAAWs outstanding and the market value of these PAAWS for each cohort.

8.4   The Price of a PAAW

In Geanakoplos and Zeldes (2009a), we argued that if the Social Security system either required workers to sell a small fraction of their PAAWs or issued extra PAAWS, these securities could be pooled together and sold to financial markets. In this section, we estimate what the market price of these pooled PAAWs would be if they were traded in financial markets. To do so, we develop a valuation model that links the risk in PAAWs to the risk in an asset that is already priced, namely stocks. We compare this value with the value generated from the same model, but ignoring the adjustment for risk. We refer to these respectively as the "market" (or "risk-adjusted") and "actuarial" (or "unadjusted") values.[7]

8.4.1   Methodology

The PAAW payouts are tied to average economywide wages in a specific year in the future. They are therefore tied to the macroeconomy and potentially to the stock market. Lucas and Zeldes (2006) show how to value defined benefit (DB) pension liabilities when payouts are tied to future wages of the individual. We apply that approach here, modifying it to take into account the specifics of Social Security benefit rules. One important difference between the two applications is that under private DB pensions, the accrued benefit obligation (ABO) depends only on past labor earnings (and thus requires no risk adjustment), while the projected benefit obligation (PBO) depends on future labor earnings. Due to the wage indexing of Social Security, even the ABO measure of Social Security depends on

6. To the extent that there is a correlation between life expectancy and number of accrued PAAWs, we will underestimate the value of each cohort's accrued PAAWs.

7. A comparison of the risk-adjusted and actuarial values could be used to back out an estimate of the appropriate risk-adjusted discount rate. We pursue this in Geanakoplos and Zeldes (2009b).

future (economywide) labor earnings, and therefore even the ABO measure of Social Security requires an adjustment for salary risk.

The cash flow stream on a PAAW(i, t_R) depends on the economywide average earnings index W_{tc} at time t_c, the life span of individual i, and the year of retirement t_R. In particular, an individual's retirement benefits are an annuity proportional to the average wage in his sixtieth year. If we define a wage bond as a security that pays an amount equal to the average wage in some future year, then we can decompose the problem of pricing a PAAW into the problem of pricing the wage bond (which requires a model of wage growth), and pricing the annuity (which we assume is independent of wage growth). We proceed in this manner, first pricing the wage bond, then combining our result with a standard valuation for the cohort-specific annuity.

The key issue for pricing the wage bond is the correlation, at different horizons, between aggregate wages and dividends, and thus the value of the stock market. To model this relationship, we use a simplified, discrete-time version of the model used in Benzoni, Collin-Dufresne, and Goldstein (2007). We model the relationship between real variables and assume that inflation does not affect the relationship between real wages and real dividends. We begin with a stationary geometric random walk process for log real dividends (d):

$$(1) \qquad d_{t+h} - d_t = h\left(g_d - \frac{\sigma_d^2}{2}\right) + \sigma_d \sqrt{h} z_{d,t+h}.$$

The dividend growth shock, $z_{d,t+h}$, is assumed to be standard normal.[8]

Benzoni and colleagues assume a stationary pricing kernel with a constant price of risk, λ. This implies a constant price-dividend ratio, and therefore a constant dividend yield, δ.[9] Because the stock price is proportional to current period dividends, it too will follow a geometric random walk with the growth in the stock price exactly equal to the growth in dividends. The total real stock return (r^s) thus equals the dividend yield *plus* the growth in real dividends:

$$(2) \qquad r^s_{t+h} = h\delta + (d_{t+h} - d_t) = h\left(g_d + \delta - \frac{\sigma_d^2}{2}\right) + \sigma_d \sqrt{h} z_{d,t+h}.$$

---

8. Equation (1) therefore implies a representation of dividend levels with log-normal shocks and expected growth in the level of dividends equal to g_d.

9. We can see this from the present value relationship,

$$P_0 = E\sum_{t=0}^{\infty} (1 + r + \lambda\sigma_d)^{-t} D_t = D_0 \sum_{t=0}^{\infty} (1 + r + \lambda\sigma_d)^{-t} (1 + g_d)^t.$$

Computing the sum, we have

$$\frac{P_0}{D_0} = \frac{1}{1 - (1 + g_d)/(1 + r + \lambda\sigma_d)} \approx \frac{1}{r + \lambda\sigma_d - g_d}.$$

In continuous time, the last statement is an exact equality.

Note that equation (2) implies the counterfactual result that stock returns and dividend growth have the same volatility.

Next, we describe the process for log real wages (w_t), in which log wage growth is a function of (a) a deterministic wage growth, or "drift", parameter; (b) the current-period deviation from the long-term average wage-dividend ratio; and (c) an independent and identically distributed (i.i.d.) wage growth shock:

$$(3) \quad w_{t+h} - w_t = h\left(g_w - \frac{\sigma_w^2}{2}\right) - h\kappa(w_t - d_t - \overline{wd}) + \sigma_w \sqrt{h}z_{w,t+h}.$$

In this model, wage growth tends to correct deviations in the wage-dividend ratio from its long term level, $\overline{wd}$. The parameter κ determines the rate at which the wage-dividend ratio "error corrects."

As a baseline calibration, we choose parameters that are consistent with the 2008 Trustees Report intermediate cost assumptions. As discussed before, Blocker, Kotlikoff, and Ross argue that this is not the most reasonable parameterization. In order to emphasize the role of *risk-correction,* however, we believe this is the best starting point. Accordingly, the real risk-free rate, r, is set to 2.9 percent and average real wage growth, g_w, to 1.1 percent. In addition, we choose the dividend yield, δ, in order to match the empirical equity premium, which we estimate to be 5.1 percent annually over the period from 1959 through the first half of 2008 and we set g_d to 1.1 percent (equal to g_w).[10] Note that this implies a counterfactually large dividend yield, δ, of 6.9 percent = 5.1 percent – 1.1 percent + 2.9 percent. Finally, we set σ_d (the standard deviation of stock returns and dividend growth), equal to 12 percent, based on the volatility of real stock returns in our sample.[11]

From the perspective of this chapter, the most important parameter calibration is our choice of κ. Benzoni, Collin-Dufresne, and Goldstein (2007) estimate κ to be between .05 and .2, and take 0.15 as their baseline value, which we follow in this chapter. We also examine the robustness of our results to different values of κ.

Following Lucas and Zeldes (2006), we assume that all risk not captured by the relationship between wages and stocks would be priced by the market at zero, and we use risk-neutral Monte Carlo derivative pricing techniques (as in Cox, Ross, and Rubenstein 1979) to price a wage bond as a derivative

10. Our estimate of the equity premium is equal to the (arithmetic) average of the monthly return on the S&P 500 index minus the average interest rate on three-month T-bills.

11. Benzoni, Collin-Dufresne, and Goldstein (2007) assume an equity premium of 6 percent and use the parameter configuration $g_d = 1.8$ percent, $r = 1$ percent, and $\sigma_d = 16$ percent. We have selected g_d and r to best match the assumptions underlying the SSA actuarial estimates, even though these choices may be controversial. Because of Jensen's terms in the wage process, however, $E(W(t+n)/W(t))^\wedge(1/n)$ is increasing over time. Thus, although we match the actuarial projection of wage growth year-over-year, cumulative wage growth increases to an annualized rate of 1.6 percent at the forty-year horizon. In levels, expected wages are about 20 percent higher at this horizon than they are under the SSA expected growth assumptions.

on the stock market. This entails generating a set of hypothetical "risk-neutral" probabilities on the set of possible returns for stocks such that, under those probabilities, the expected return would equal the risk-free rate. In our simple model, this "risk-neutral" distribution for stock returns is normal with a mean equal to the risk-free rate and the standard deviation equal to its original empirical value.

We use Monte Carlo techniques to simulate stock returns and wages using the risk-neutral probabilities. We generate 200,000 replications of the wage and dividend process, each forty-five years in length, and take averages over the realizations. Our estimate of the "risk-adjusted" price of a year-t wage bond is equal to the average value of the simulated wage at year t, using risk-neutral probabilities, discounted at the risk-free rate.

We use the wage bond price to compute the current market value of a PAAW. A PAAW for this worker promises payments proportional to the age sixty average wage, starting in the retirement year, which we assume to be age sixty-five. To compute annuity prices, we use the cohort life tables from Bell and Miller (2002) and assume that all individuals of the same age face the same conditional survival probabilities[12] (i.e., that there is no heterogeneity or private information about these probabilities). We also assume that the market price of aggregate longevity risk and inflation risk are each zero.

As a concrete example of how we compute PAAW prices, consider the cohort of age fifty, which reaches age sixty in 2015, ten years from our valuation date. We compute the market (risk-adjusted) value in 2005 of the 2015 wage bond to be 0.658 current wage units. The age sixty value of a one dollar perpetual real annuity starting at age sixty-five, valued using cohort-specific mortality and a risk-free rate, is $10.88. Finally, conditional on being fifty years old in 2005, there is a 92.3 percent chance of reaching age sixty, the year we value the annuity. Therefore, the 2005 market value of a PAAW for this cohort is $(10.88) \cdot (0.658) \cdot (0.923) = 6.60$ current wage units. Multiplying by the current value of the average wage gives the market value of a PAAW, measured in dollars.

8.4.2   Actuarial Value

The standard actuarial approach for computing present value makes no adjustment for risk; that is, it computes the expected value of the cash flows and discounts at the risk-free rate.[13] To estimate the "non-risk-adjusted" or actuarial price of a wage bond, we use the same model described before, but generate a set of wage and dividend realizations that are based on the true

12. For the calculations presented, we used the survival probabilities for males born in 1980. Using sex-specific survival probabilities increases our measure of accrued benefits by about 7 percent (since women typically live longer than men). The risk-adjustment, however, is only negligibly affected.

13. Note that if all individuals in the economy were risk-neutral, no adjustment for risk would be necessary, and the actuarial and market approaches would yield identical results.

probabilities, and then discount the average value of the simulated wage at the risk-free rate. We use the resulting wage bond price to compute the actuarial price of a PAAW. In the example above, the actuarial value in 2005 of a 2015 wage bond is 0.830 wage units (versus a market value of 0.658). The resulting actuarial value in 2005 of a 2015 PAAW is (10.88) × (0.830) × (0.923) = 8.34 current wage units (versus a market value of 6.60).

8.4.3   Results

Figure 8.1 compares the actuarial and market prices of the wage bonds. The risk adjustment causes the market price to be everywhere lower than the actuarial price. In addition, the difference grows over time, since wages further out are more risky and subject to a larger adjustment.[14]

Figure 8.2 compares the actuarial and market prices of PAAWs. Figure 8.3 shows the ratio of market (risk-corrected) to actuarial PAAW prices for each cohort. For cohorts that have already surpassed the computation age (sixty), the risk-adjustment has no impact on the valuation. This occurs because aggregate wages are the only source of priced risk in our model, and cohort benefits depend on aggregate wages in the year it turns sixty. For younger cohorts, however, there is a significant difference between the two methods. For cohorts under age forty, the market measure is less than half of the actuarial valuation. For the youngest cohorts we consider (age twenty in 2005), risk-adjusted accruals are worth less than 20 percent of their value under the standard approach.

8.5   The Quantity of PAAWs Outstanding

In this section, we estimate the stream of future benefits that have been accrued by each cohort based on contributions to date. As pointed out previously, these can be neatly described with a single summary statistic: the number of PAAWs accrued by the cohort.

To construct accrual, we use data from the Continuous Work History Sample (CWHS), a 1 percent sample of workers and beneficiaries.[15] The key feature of this data set, for our purposes, is that it includes individual-specific earnings histories.[16] We compute accrued benefits for both current

14. Both prices decrease with the horizon, reflecting the fact that the risk-free rate is greater than average wage growth. In addition, both prices are slightly less than one in the initial 2005 period due to our assumption that cash flows occur at the end of each period and are discounted back to the beginning of the period.

15. We are grateful to Jae Song and Wojciech Kopczuk for providing us with summary statistics from the CWHS.

16. Earnings occurring before 1951 are treated differently in this data set and are typically available only as single entry summing all earning from 1950 and earlier. We ignore these earnings entirely, meaning we slightly underestimate benefits for the oldest cohorts we consider. Because the benefit formula allows workers to exclude low earnings years, typically early years in a worker's history, our underestimate should be very small.

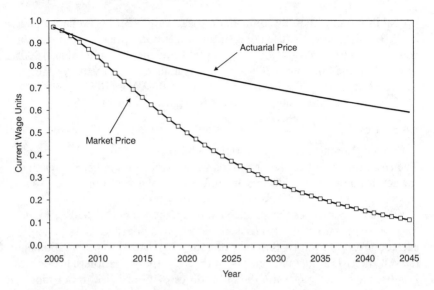

Fig. 8.1   Wage bond prices

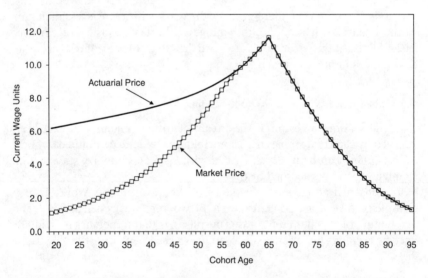

Fig. 8.2   Price-per-PAAW

and former workers (including retirees). For retirees this simply entails averaging the thirty-five years of highest relative earnings and entering this average into the Primary Insurance Amount (PIA) formula (redefined to be in units of future economywide wages). For workers who have not already retired, we use the straight-line accrual formula described before to compute PAAW accruals based on worker earnings histories to date. Because our data

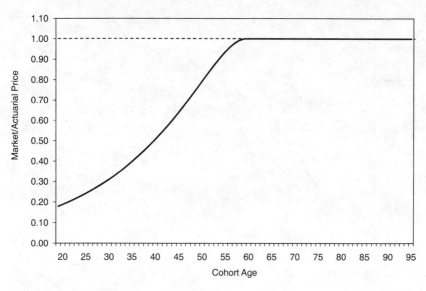

Fig. 8.3   PAAW price ratios

set has no information on spousal earnings or status, our results ignore any potential spousal or survivor benefits. The quantity of PAAWs accrued to date by a cohort is equal to the sum of the PAAWs accrued to date by all individuals in the cohort.

8.5.1   Estimates of PAAW Quantities by Cohort

Figure 8.4 shows our estimate of PAAWs earned through 2004 for cohorts born between 1910 and 1986 (ages nineteen through ninety-five in 2005). The hump shape in quantities reflects three key features of benefit accruals and Social Security demographics: (a) younger cohorts have shorter work histories and thus have accrued fewer benefits; (b) the middle-aged cohorts are large and have already accrued most of their benefits; and (c) older cohorts have fewer members because of mortality (for example, in 2005 there were 3.6 million living individuals aged fifty-five but only 2.3 million aged sixty-five and 1.7 million aged seventy-five).

8.6   The Market Value of Accrued Benefits

Once we have computed the price of a PAAW for each cohort and the quantity of PAAWs outstanding for each cohort, estimating the market value of accrued benefits simply involves multiplying the two and summing across cohorts. Figure 8.5 compares the risk-adjusted and the actuarial valuations by cohort. As with the wage bond prices in figure 8.1, the risk-adjustment reduces the value of the liability for all of the nonretired cohorts.

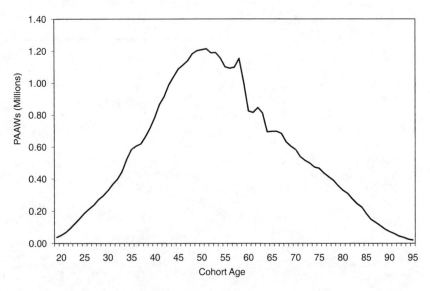

Fig. 8.4   Quantity of accrued PAAWs

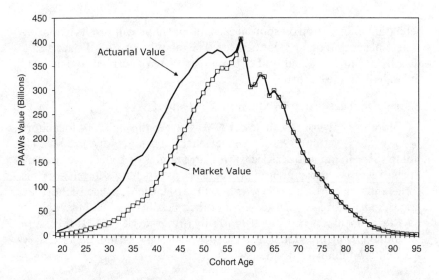

Fig. 8.5   Value of accrued PAAWs

Differences across cohorts of the adjustment suggest that risk-correction should be a key consideration in evaluating the "fairness" of proposals to reform Social Security.

Table 8.1 sums accrued benefits across cohorts for an estimate of the total value of accrued benefits. We present two estimates: an actuarial valuation and a risk-adjusted valuation. Our estimate of total accrued benefits, based on the actuarial valuation methodology, is just under $13 trillion. Adjusting

Table 8.1   **Present value of accrued Social Security benefits under alternative**
valuation methods

	Total value (billions)	Under 60	Over 60
Actuarial (unadjusted)	12,977	8,572	4,405
Market (risk-adjusted)	10,451	6,046	4,405
Market/actuarial	0.81	0.71	1.00

Note: 2006 Office of the Actuary (OACT) Actuarial Note estimate of Max. Trans. Cost + Jan
1st 2006 Trust Fund balance, adjusted to include "own-history" benefits only, equals 12.2 tril.

the Office of the Actuary's own 2005 estimate of accrued benefits for compa-
rability gives a value of $12.2 trillion.[17] Given our lack of information about
benefits other than basic retirement benefits paid to primary beneficiaries,
our estimate of accruals without risk adjustment comes remarkably close
to SSA figures.[18]

We estimate a market value for the same liability of $10.5 trillion, only 81
percent of the actuarial value.[19] This difference in valuation comes entirely
from the risk-correction; all other features of the pricing model are held

17. Our estimate from CWHS data includes only "own-history" accruals; that is, it excludes
spousal and survivor benefits. To obtain a comparable estimate from SSA publications we start
with the January 1, 2006 value of the Maximum Transition Cost of $15.8 trillion, which is the
present value of accruals less the amount of the Social Security Trust Fund (Wade, Schultz,
and Goss 2008). To this we add back the December 31, 2005 value of the OASDI Trust Fund
of $1.86 trillion (Social Security Administration 2008). We then multiply this sum by the per-
centage of benefits paid to retired workers based on their own earnings history, which was
roughly 70 percent in 2005 (Social Security Administration 2006). To make this adjustment,
we assume that the proportion of benefits going to disability and survivors is constant across
cohorts and over time. This implies that these programs represent a constant proportion of
accrued benefits as well.

18. In principle our actuarial estimate should exactly match the adjusted SSA figure.
Differences may arise for at least three reasons: (a) Our limited information does not allow us
to perfectly adjust SSA figures derived from micro models. To make this adjustment, we make
the simplifying assumption that the proportion of benefits going to spouses, survivors, and
disabled beneficiaries is constant across cohorts and over time. (b) The "straight-line" accrual
formula we use is slightly different than the one used by SSA to compute the maximum transition cost (MTC) measure, principally because SSA excludes some years of low earnings in
estimating PIA, even for workers who have yet to reach thirty-five years of earnings, while we
do not (see footnote 5). (c) Expected long-term growth in wages differs from SSA projections,
as described in footnote 11.

19. This differs from an earlier (2007) draft of this chapter for three reasons. First, in this
version we have linked retirement benefits to wages at age sixty (as opposed to age sixty-five in
the earlier draft), effectively removing five years of risk from every cohort. This is appropriate
because, as noted earlier, the age sixty wage index is used in computing benefits. Second, in
this version, we use the straight-line method of accrual, instead of the "fastest" method used
in the earlier draft. We choose this because it more closely matches the measure used by the
Office of the Actuary to compute the maximum transition cost estimates. It implies lower
current accruals for nonretired workers—those for whom the risk adjustment matters. Under
fastest accrual, the corresponding adjustment is 22 percent. Finally, in this draft we are using
revised estimates from the 2005 CWHS, whereas in the previous version we used two sources:
the 2004 CWHS and a set of OASDI benefit expenditure projections provided by the SSA
Office of the Actuary.

constant in generating the figures. This suggests that the standard approach of discounting expected future benefits by the risk-free rate is significantly overstating the size of accrued benefits. Appropriately correcting for risk to aggregate wage growth reduces our measure of Social Security benefits obligations by nearly 20 percent. Subtracting the end of 2005 value of the Old-Age and Survivors Insurance (OASI) trust fund (1.66 trillion) from both measures indicates that the market value estimate of the maximum transition cost measure of Social Security's financial status is only 78 percent as large as the actuarial value, suggesting a healthier system (in the sense of ease of transition to an alternative system) than found using traditional actuarial methods.

Table 8.1 also breaks down the liability for cohorts below age sixty, and those sixty and above. Age sixty is key because that is the year by which the wage risk to benefits is resolved. For the sixty and over group, the actuarial and risk-adjusted estimates are identical, and the aggregate numbers reflect this. When we examine the pre-sixty-year-old group alone, however, we see significantly larger differences between the actuarial and risk-adjusted estimates: correcting for risk reduces our measure of Social Security benefits obligations for those under sixty by nearly 30 percent.

8.7   Robustness

The parameter κ plays a key role in our analysis because it governs the strength of the link between wages and the stock market. Our baseline calibration follows Benzoni, Collin-Dufresne, and Goldstein (2007) in setting this parameter to .15. However, because of the difficulty in estimating such cointegrating relationships, it is informative to examine the sensitivity of our results to this parameter. To do this, we perform the same simulation with a high (.25) and a low (.05) value for κ. Figure 8.6 shows the ratio of the risk-adjusted price to the actuarial price for PAAWs under the alternative calibrations.

First, we find, not surprisingly, that the importance of risk correction varies directly with κ: higher κ implies that wage growth is more "exposed" to stock market risk and increases the size of the risk adjustment.

In addition, we see in figure 8.6 that the size of the risk correction varies in a nonlinear way with κ. For all cohorts, increasing κ from a low value of .05 to our baseline value of .15 has a large effect on the ratio of market to actuarial value, whereas further increasing κ from the baseline to a value of .25 has a much smaller effect.

Finally, the impact of varying κ differs across cohorts. Define the risk adjustment as the distance as measured down from the dashed line. The percentage change in this risk adjustment in response to changing κ is lower for the older cohorts than it is for the younger cohorts. Consider the fifty-year-old cohort as an example. The adjustment represents under 1 percent

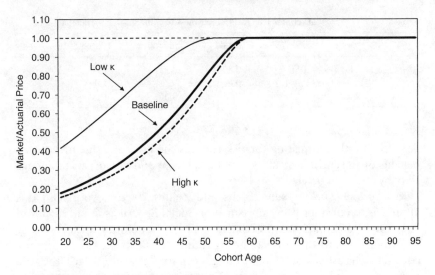

Fig. 8.6   PAAW price ratios: Robustness

of the actuarial value under the "low κ" parameterization, but 27 percent of the actuarial value under the "high κ" parameter choice. In contrast, for the twenty-year-old cohort, the adjustment is large even for low κ, and raising κ results in a much smaller percentage increase in the adjustment than it did for the fifty-year-old cohort. This pattern is natural; in our model, the long-run correlation between wages and the stock market is 1 for any κ greater than 0, even a small value. Thus, the risk adjustment for benefits far in the future will be (essentially) independent of the parameter κ. On the other hand, the shorter-run correlation between wages and the stock market is highly dependent on κ, so that the risk adjustment of the benefits of workers closer to retirement is much more sensitive to the value of κ.

Table 8.2 aggregates the results across cohorts and examines how they change as κ varies. Increasing κ from the baseline of .15 to .25 increases the risk correction by only 4 percentage points (from 19 percent to 23 percent). On the other hand, lowering κ from .15 to .05 decreases the risk adjustment by 8 percentage points (from 19 percent to 11 percent), a much larger amount. The risk adjustment remains important, however, even with this weak link between wages and stock prices.

8.8   Conclusions, Policy Implications, and Future Research

We have argued that market value is the appropriate way to measure both the assets and the liabilities of the Social Security system. Market value calculations adjust for risk and differ in important ways from the standard actuarial approach that discounts expected cash flows with a risk-free rate.

Table 8.2   Market/actuarial ratio: Robustness to cointegration parameter

	Total	Under 60	Over 60
Low ($\kappa = .05$)	0.89	0.83	1.00
Baseline ($\kappa = .15$)	0.81	0.71	1.00
High ($\kappa = .25$)	0.77	0.66	1.00

We estimate that adjusting for risk reduces the present value of accrued benefits of the entire system by about 20 percent and of workers under age sixty by about 30 percent.

In ongoing work (Geanakoplos and Zeldes 2009b), we extend this approach to consider other measures of Social Security's financial status, including open group measures that incorporate both future Social Security contributions and the corresponding future accruals. Because future tax contributions are proportional to wages (up to the earnings cap), they are subject to a similar risk correction. For the measure we study here, where only future benefit flows must be valued, the direction of the risk adjustment effect is unambiguous; Social Security obligations are worth less under market valuation. Once we consider adjusting both the assets (future taxes) and the liabilities of Social Security (including future accruals), the picture becomes significantly more complicated, and preliminary results suggest that the market value of open group measures shows a larger deficit than the actuarial value.

References

Bell, F. C., and M. L. Miller. 2002. Life tables for the United States Social Security Area 1900–2100. Social Security Administration, Actuarial Study no. 116.

Benzoni, L., P. Collin-Dufresne, and R. Goldstein. 2007. Portfolio choice over the life-cycle when the stock and labor markets are cointegrated. *Journal of Finance* 62 (5): 2123–67.

Blocker, A. W., L. J. Kotlikoff, and S. A. Ross. 2008. The true cost of Social Security. NBER Working Paper no. 14427. Cambridge, MA: National Bureau of Economic Research, October.

Cox, J. C., S. A. Ross, and M. Rubenstein. 1979. Option pricing: A simplified approach. *Journal of Financial Economics* 7 (September): 229–63.

Federal Accounting Standards Advisory Board. 2006. Accounting for Social Insurance, revised—Statement of Federal Financial Accounting Standards. Available at: http://www.fasab.gov/pdffiles/socialinsurance_pv.pdf, (October).

———. 2008. Accounting for Social Insurance, revised. Available at: http://www.fasab.gov/pdffiles/socialins_exposurefinal.pdf.

Geanakoplos, J., O. Mitchell, and S. P. Zeldes. 1999. Social Security money's worth. In *Prospects for Social Security reform,* ed. O. S. Mitchell, R. J. Meyers, and

H. Young, 79–151. Philadelphia: Pension Research Council, University of Pennsylvania Press.

Geanakoplos, J., and S. P. Zeldes. 2009a. Reforming Social Security with progressive personal accounts. In *Social Security policy in a changing environment,* ed. J. Brown, J. Liebman, and D. A. Wise, 73–128. Chicago: University of Chicago Press.

———. 2009b. The market value of Social Security. Columbia University Graduate School of Business. Unpublished Manuscript.

Goetzmann, W. N. 2008. More Social Security, not less. *Journal of Portfolio Management* 35 (1): 115–23.

Jackson, H. 2004. Accounting for Social Security and its reform. *Harvard Journal on Legislation* 41 (1): 59–159.

Lucas, D., and S. P. Zeldes. 2006. Valuing and hedging defined benefit pension obligations: The role of stocks revisited. Columbia University Graduate School of Business. Unpublished Manuscript, September.

Social Security Administration. 2006. *Annual statistical supplement to the Social Security bulletin,* Table 5.A1. Washington, DC: Office of Policy. Available at: http://www.socialsecurity.gov/policy/docs/statcomps/supplement/2006/5a.html.

———. 2008. *The 2008 annual report of the board of trustees of the Federal old-age and survivors insurance and federal Disability Insurance trust funds.* Table II.C.2. Washington, DC: Office of Policy. Available at: http://www.socialsecurity .gov/OACT/TR/TR08/trLOT.html.

Technical Panel. 2007. *Report on assumptions and methods.* Report to the Social Security Advisory Board, October. Available at: http://www.ssab.gov/documents/ 2007_TPAM_REPORT_FINAL_copy.PDF.

Wade, A., J. Schultz, and S. Goss. 2008. Unfunded obligation and transition cost for the OASDI program. Actuarial Note no. 2008.1. Social Security Administration, Office of the Chief Actuary, July.

Environment and Energy
Catastrophic Liabilities from Nuclear Power Plants

Geoffrey Heal and Howard Kunreuther

9.1 Introduction

Through a comprehensive system of preparedness, protection, response, and recovery administered by the Federal Emergency Management Agency (FEMA), the Federal Government has responsibility for reducing risks and aiding the recovery of natural disasters, acts of terrorism, and other man-made disasters. The manner in which public sector organizations manage the natural environment can affect the risks that government will ultimately face. Some possible liabilities of the Federal Government are associated with environmental risks, many of which are linked to climate change. For example, the potential for global warming depends on what we do with our energy systems. Moreover, the way the Federal Government manages many environmental processes can affect our vulnerability to a range of natural disasters, not just those associated with climate change.

One source of energy that is now being seriously considered for addressing the climate change issue is nuclear power. Since the accident at the Three Mile Island nuclear power plant in Middletown, Pennsylvania in March 1979, there has not been a single nuclear power plant constructed in the United States. However, James Rogers, CEO of Duke Energy, said in 2007 that nuclear power "is still the best way to produce electricity with zero greenhouse gases from the actual operation"—even compared with energy

Geoffrey Heal is the Paul Garret Professor of Public Policy and Corporate Responsibility at Columbia Business School. Howard Kunreuther is the Cecilia Yen Koo Professor of Decision Sciences and Public Policy and codirector of Risk Management and Decision Processes Center at the Wharton School, University of Pennsylvania.

We are grateful to Carol Heller, Debbie Lucas, Billy Pizer, and two referees for valuable comments on an earlier draft of the chapter. Financial support from the Wharton Risk Management and Decision Processes Center is gratefully acknowledged.

sources such as wind. The Congressional Budget Office (CBO) estimated in May 2008 that a carbon price of between $20 and $45 per ton—which many projections say is feasible—would make nuclear competitive with coal (Johnson 2008). We therefore include the risks associated with nuclear power in our analysis.

We begin with an overview of the economic value of environmental systems in mitigating natural disasters and then consider the role of the Federal Government in managing these hazards and the potential liabilities that they may incur should there be a catastrophic disaster. In the second part of the chapter we focus on nuclear power as a source of energy and ask whether the risks associated with this technology could be managed more efficiently by private insurance markets rather than through the current arrangements under the Price-Anderson (P-A) Act. As we demonstrate, the P-A Act imposes significant liabilities on the Federal Government should there be large-scale losses from a future accident at a nuclear power plant. To gain insights into an increased role for the private sector in managing this technology, programs by which other catastrophic risks are managed today are reviewed in the concluding portion of the chapter.

9.2   Natural Capital as an Asset

A nation's environmental assets are diverse and important. Environmental economists talk about natural capital on a par with physical, human, intellectual, and other forms of capital.[1] Environmental assets, like any other assets, provide a flow of services over time. Often they provide these services over very long periods of time, periods that are orders of magnitude greater than those relevant for most other forms of capital. If we value these assets at the present value of their services, then by applying conventional discount rates we lose most of the contributions that they make.

A good example is the New York City watershed, a collection of naturally-occurring ecosystems in the Catskills that cleanse and stabilize the flow of water to New York, and if not disturbed can continue to do so for centuries. Recently, the city spent over $1 billion restoring the ecological integrity of this watershed, in order to restore the city's water to earlier levels of purity. We can see this as an investment in natural capital, with the benefit being the flow of clean water and the avoidance of a complex and expensive filtration plant costing over $8 billion.[2] Although the Catskills watershed is an asset to New York City, which has invested extensively in it, the city does not own it. The watershed consists of land in the Catskills, most of which is privately owned either as farms or as homes. Today the city provides financial incen-

1. For a discussion see Barbier and Heal (2006) and the references there.
2. For more details see Heal (2000) and National Research Council (2004). For a detailed study of all aspects, economic and scientific, see also National Research Council (2000).

tives for people living and working in the watershed area to behave in ways that are consistent with the continued operation of the watershed, such as paying for farm fences to be set back from stream boundaries to keep animals well away from streams.

Natural resources such as oil, gas, coal, and various other mineral deposits are also a form of natural capital, and the values of these are often reflected in the valuations of their owners, usually corporations. It is generally recognized that one of the main determinants of the stock market value of an oil company is the value of its oil reserves.[3] An interesting point is that if a corporation depletes its oil reserves, then under US GAAP[4] and most equivalents, it must record this as depletion of assets in its financial statements. If, however, a nation depletes its reserves of oil or any other mineral resource, then the United Nations System of National Accounts does not require that it record a depletion charge against its income. If the national accounts of oil-producing countries were to record depletion charges, then their incomes would drop very significantly indeed.[5]

The climate system as well can also be viewed as an asset to the extent that it may induce individuals to reside in specific areas. Florida's climate goes a long way to explaining why people choose to live there, and some of the economic value that it generates is reflected in land values. Climate also plays an important role in determining agricultural productivity. The climate system is more than the temperature, though that is a central part of it: the humidity, precipitation, and wind patterns all impact on the economic value of specific areas.

Today, we are seeing that changes in the world's climate system, combined with increasing assets at risk, is threatening this value. For example, the population of Florida has increased significantly over the past fifty years: 2.8 million inhabitants in 1950, 6.8 million in 1970, 13 million in 1990, and a projected 19.3 million population in 2010 (almost a 600 percent increase since 1950) (Kunreuther and Michel-Kerjan 2007). The increase in the exposed property values in risk-prone areas due to a combination of pure inflation, speculation, and rises in the standard of living increase the chance of significant insured losses from future natural disasters. If Hurricane Andrew had occurred in 2002 rather than 1992, it would have inflicted twice the economic losses, due principally to increasing development and rising asset values in Miami-Dade County and adjoining coastal areas in Florida affected by the storm (Dlugolecki 2006).

Compounding this increase in exposure is a trend for tropical storms/hurricanes and typhoons to become more intense over time due to

---

3. See, for example, Miller and Upton (1985).
4. Generally Accepted Accounting Principles.
5. See Heal (2007) and references therein.

global warming. Emanuel (2005) introduces an index of potential destructiveness of hurricanes based on the total dissipation power over the lifetime of the storm. The index shows a large increase in power dissipation over the past thirty years and concludes that this increase may be due to the fact that storms have become more intense, on average, and/or have survived longer at high intensity. His study also shows that the annual average storm peak wind speed over the North Atlantic and eastern and western North Pacific has increased by 50 percent over the past thirty years. Recent work by the Intergovernmental Panel on Climate Change (IPCC 2007) indicates that one of the impacts of a change in climate will be an increase in weather extremes. We are likely to witness not only more intense storms, but also more intense heat waves and drought, and more intense flooding episodes as well. The impacts are predicted to be more important in many low- and middle-income countries (Africa, South America, Asia) than in the developed world.

9.3   Environmental Liabilities

What does this tell us about environmental liabilities? Certain categories are widely recognized, such as those generated by the Superfund legislation and liabilities associated with past pollution activities. In the case of Superfund there are open questions as to who is liable because of the complexities of joint liabilities. But in general, these are the responsibilities of the private sector not the Federal Government, with the exception of Department of Defense sites, whose clean-up costs have been estimated at over $30 billion.[6]

A more prominent source of liabilities of the Federal Government arises from changes in natural capital that lead to its ceasing to provide important services, often protective services. Much natural capital has the characteristics of public goods, so that the government is normally responsible for its maintenance. A timely example is the gradual destruction of the barrier islands in the Gulf of Mexico offshore from New Orleans. Historically, these islands protected New Orleans from storm surges, mitigating the impacts of the strongest storms. Their gradual disappearance contributed to the severity of the destruction wrought by Hurricane Katrina,[7] creating liabilities for the Federal Government through the designation of the region as a Presidentially-declared disaster area. Some estimates suggest that the total cost of Hurricane Katrina is in excess of $150 billion, with a significant part being the liability of the Federal Government (Kunreuther and Michel-Kerjan 2009). This is an environmental liability because it arose in part as a predictable consequence of the degra-

6. See the Congressional Budget Office (2005) report for more details.
7. See Bourne (2004).

dation of natural capital. The 2007 Stafford Act makes the Federal Government legally liable for damages of this sort, and politically it surely is: the public expects the Federal Government to step in and offer restitution in situations such as Katrina.

Hurricane Katrina is illustrative of a class of situations where the Federal Government may incur liabilities as a result of its failure to adequately manage environmental issues. In this case, a part of the cause of the disaster was undoubtedly the changes in the topography of the area around New Orleans as a result of dredging and canalization, and the removal of barrier islands, all of which can be considered degradation of natural capital or of environmental assets. The US Army Corps of Engineers, a Federal Agency, carried out many of these changes. In addition, some argue that climate change made a contribution to the severity of Katrina, and that the Federal Government, by failing to act on this issue contributed further to the severity of the problem (Emanuel 2008). The general point here is that to the extent that degradation of natural capital leads to increased severity and frequency of natural disasters, there is an increase in Federal liability, although this is hard to quantify. The natural disasters associated with the mismanagement of natural capital could include storms, wildfires, floods, and droughts, all of which can generate liabilities in the billions.

The bottom line is that natural capital is a hugely important asset, and its maintenance, normally being a Federal responsibility, can have huge impacts on Federal liabilities. These liabilities are hard to measure, but as the de facto insurer of last resort for catastrophes, it will often pick up the check.

9.4   Nuclear Liabilities

The current resurgence of interest in nuclear power owes a lot to concerns about the environmental impacts of fossil fuels. Nuclear power is largely carbon neutral and has no significant climate impact, but it does have other risks. A move to nuclear power is replacing one kind of environmental risk by another. The Federal Government accepted liability for the lion's share of the risks from a nuclear power plant catastrophe through the passage of the Price-Anderson (P-A) Act in 1957. Nuclear power stations have a rather unique environmental profile, in that when operating as planned they produce little if any environmental damage, emitting neither gases nor pollutants of any kind. There is, however, a small chance of a very serious accident, such as a core meltdown leading to damaging pollution, as in 1986 at the Chernobyl nuclear reactor in the Ukraine. In this case, clouds of radioactive waste floated over much of the Ukraine, Belarus, Eastern and Western Europe, and Scandinavia with fatalities estimated by international agencies to be about 9,000 individuals. Core meltdowns have also occurred twice in the United States, once at the Enrico Fermi reactor in Newport, Michigan, in 1966 and again at Three Mile Island in Middletown, Pennsylvania in 1979.

It is generally believed that little or no radiation was released in either of these cases (Lochbaum 2006).

In addition to the risk of a core meltdown, nuclear power stations pose problems associated with the disposal of their radioactive wastes. Over its operating life, a nuclear power station will produce many tons of highly radioactive long-lived waste, which pose a health hazard for many centuries. Since September 11, 2001, the wastes have been recognized as a possible ingredient for a dirty bomb used in a terrorist attack. The method for disposing of radioactive wastes from nuclear power stations is highly controversial, with no country having yet implemented a coherent long-term policy. In the United States, the proposed policy is that waste will be buried at the Yucca Mountain Repository in Nevada, but this has not been implemented. In the meantime, many hundreds of tons of highly radioactive waste sit in containment tanks at the sites of commercial nuclear power stations, often poorly guarded. Were some of this to fall into the wrong hands, the costs could be immense and would be the responsibility of the Federal Government: there is a Federal liability here.

A core meltdown is generally agreed to be the most serious accident that can occur to a nuclear power station. What is the risk of this event, and what are the possible consequences? In the United States, 104 commercial reactors have been built and operated. As noted, two reactors—Enrico Fermi and Three Mile Island—have experienced core meltdowns. In addition, according to data from the Nuclear Regulatory Commission (NRC), four have been closed in excess of one year for serious failures that if not corrected could have caused core meltdowns.[8] This means that six in 104 reactors have experienced meltdowns or near-meltdowns. Normally these data are not presented as X meltdowns or near-meltdowns in Y reactors, but rather as X meltdowns or near-meltdowns per Z reactor years, a numerically much smaller risk.

All the meltdowns and most of the near-meltdowns occurred in the 1960s and 1970s, which suggests that the risks are highest early in the life cycle of a reactor design. This would be reasonable, and consistent with the idea of a learning curve associated with the management of something as complex as a nuclear power station. This may be reassuring as far as the safety of existing reactors is concerned, but disturbing when one recognizes that the currently-proposed expansion of nuclear power would be through new and as-yet untried reactor designs that are focused on reducing the (very substantial) capital costs of nuclear power stations. The Federal Government has received or expects to receive applications to build thirty-four new nuclear reactors at twenty-three sites (Wald 2008). A new generation of reactors could take us back to the top of the learning curve and into an era of risk not experienced since the 1960s and 1970s.

8. Data from the US Nuclear Regulatory Commission is available in Lochbaum 2006.

What would be the costs of a core meltdown in which, as in the Chernobyl case, radiation was released from the containment vessel? There is no general theory for such an estimate, so we focus on a specific case, the case of Indian Point, a nuclear power station owned by Entergy Corporation and situated on the Hudson River twenty-four miles north of New York City. The huge population densities in the region make an accident here particularly threatening. Nuclear fallout from the plant could reach populated areas including New York City, northern New Jersey, and Fairfield County, Connecticut. A 1982 study by Sandia National Laboratories found that a core meltdown and radiological release at one of the two operating Indian Point reactors could cause 50,000 near-term deaths from acute radiation syndrome and 14,000 long-term deaths from cancer.[9] In addition to these horrifying health impacts, the release of a cloud of radioactivity over New York City could close the city down for business for a considerable period of time.

The financial costs of such an event are clearly stunning: 64,000 deaths valued at $6 million per person alone would imply a cost of $384 billion. By contrast, insured business losses and business interruptions from the September 11 terrorist attacks were valued at $32.5 billion (Kunreuther and Michel-Kerjan 2004). A disaster at Indian Point could possibly have a more disruptive effect on activity in the New York metropolitan area than the September 11 attacks, and for a much longer period of time. Business interruption losses in the range of $50 to 100 billion are possible, in addition to the costs associated with loss of life and damage to health. It is therefore reasonable to think that the direct and indirect costs of a nuclear accident could be in the hundreds of billions of dollars. Indeed, a worst-case scenario could lead to the closure of New York City for years, as happened at Chernobyl, which is still closed over twenty-two years after the meltdown, leading to almost unthinkable costs.

9.5   The Price-Anderson Act and Nuclear Accident Insurance[10]

The Price-Anderson (P-A) Act, originally enacted by Congress in 1957, limits the liability of the nuclear industry in the event of a nuclear accident in the United States. The Act was passed in order to encourage the construction of nuclear power plants in the United States. At the same time, P-A provides a ready source of funds to compensate potential accident victims that would otherwise not be available. The Act covers large power reactors, small research and test reactors, fuel reprocessing plants, and enrichment facilities for incidents that occur through plant

9. For more details see http://www.ucsusa.org/news/press_release/new-study-predicts-up-to-44000-prompt-fatalities-and-518000-longterm-deaths-from-indian-point-terror-attack.html.

10. For more details on nuclear accident insurance see Nuclear Energy Institute (2005).

operation as well as transportation and storage of nuclear fuel and radio-active wastes. The Act is seen as central to the commercial viability of nuclear power.

The P-A Act sets up two tiers of insurance. Each utility is required to maintain the maximum amount of coverage available from the private insurance industry—currently $300 million per site. This coverage is written for nuclear power plants in the United States by the American Nuclear Insurers, a joint underwriting association or "pool" of insurance companies. If claims following an accident exceed that primary layer of insurance, all nuclear operators are obligated to pay up to $100.59 million for each reactor they operate, payable at the rate of $10 million per reactor, per year. As of February 2005, the US public currently has more than $10 billion of insurance protection in the event of a nuclear reactor incident. More than $200 million has been paid in claims and costs of litigation since the Price-Anderson Act went into effect, all of it by the insurance pools. Of this amount, approximately $71 million has been paid in claims and costs of litigation related to the 1979 accident at Three Mile Island.

As part of the Energy Policy Act of 2005, signed into law by President George W. Bush on August 8, 2005, Price-Anderson was reauthorized for the next twenty years. This is the fifth time that Congress has reauthorized the Act since it was first passed in 1957 but it is the longest extension ever granted. High prices and dwindling supplies of fossil fuels have increased interest in nuclear energy, and the long extension of P-A may increase the feasibility of investment in nuclear power plants. Although, as noted before, no nuclear power plants have been built in the United States since the Three Mile Island accident in 1979, there are now nearly three dozen applications for new reactors.[11]

9.6   Are Nuclear Power Plant Accidents an Insurable Risk?

A principal reason for the passage of the P-A Act was to protect the utilities against the possibility of a catastrophic loss from a nuclear power plant accident. Private insurers were reluctant to provide this coverage because they were uncertain about the likelihood of a severe accident (e.g., a core meltdown) and the consequences of such a disaster. In other words, it was believed at the time that protection against nuclear accidents did not satisfy the conditions for insurability of a risk by the private sector. Is this indeed correct—is it really necessary that the government should assume the liabilities associated with the P-A Act, or could we, in fact, rely on the private sector to play this role?

The conditions for insurability in the context of environmental risks have

11. See http://www.cbsnews.com/stories/2008/06/13/national/main4181049.shtml?source=RSSattr=U.S._4181049.

been examined by Freeman and Kunreuther (1997). Cummins (2006) and Litan (2006) have recently examined this issue in the context of catastrophic risks. The discussion that follows uses concepts from these papers to focus on how an insurer decides whether or not to provide coverage against damage from an environmental risk.

9.6.1   Law of Large Numbers

Insurers are likely to be concerned about the variability of profits from the risks they insure. The ideal risk is one where the potential loss from each insured is relatively small and independent of the losses from other policyholders. As the insurer increases the number of policies it issues in a year, the variance in its annual losses decreases. In other words, the law of large numbers makes it highly unlikely that the insurer will suffer an extremely large loss relative to the premiums collected.

Insurance against underground storage tank (UST) leaks is an example of an environmental risk that satisfies the law of large numbers since losses are normally independent of one another. To illustrate the application of this law, suppose that an insurer wants to determine the estimated loss for a group of identical USTs, each of which has a 1/100 annual chance of leaking and causing damage of \$100,000. The expected annual loss for each UST would be \$1,000 (i.e., 1/100 × \$100,000). As the number of UST policies n increases, then the variance of the expected annual loss decreases in proportion to n. Cummins (2006) considers the case where the insurer is willing to accept a low probability of insolvency ε arising out of a catastrophic loss when insuring a book of business. He shows that for risks that are independent and whose losses are characterized by the normal distribution so that the central limit theorem applies, the equity capital per policy approaches zero as the number of insured policies becomes very large.

9.6.2   Conditions for Insurability

The application of the law of large numbers is predicated on the ability of insurers to estimate the likelihood and consequences of a risk and for the risks to be independent of each other. The risks associated with large-scale catastrophic disasters or accidents are unlikely to satisfy the law of large numbers. The following three conditions can then determine the degree to which such a risk is insurable.

Condition 1 is the ability to identify and quantify the chances of the event occurring and the resulting losses under different levels of insurance coverage. *Condition 2* is the ability to set premiums for each potential customer or class of customers that reflect the risk. *Condition 3* is the ability to make a positive expected profit by providing coverage against the risk. We now examine each condition and raise some questions related to the ability of private insurers to provide coverage.

Condition 1: Identifying the Risk

To satisfy this condition, estimates must be made of the frequency at which specific events occur and the magnitude of the loss. The risk of a leaky UST is one with which the insurance industry is relatively comfortable because there is past data and scientific information that enables them to determine both the likelihood and consequences of such an event. Due to the infrequency of nuclear power plant accidents, it is much more difficult to estimate these parameters for insurance against this risk.

Condition 2: Setting Premiums that Reflect the Risk

Once the risk has been identified, insurers need to determine a premium that reflects the risk while not posing an unacceptably high chance of insolvency or severe loss of surplus due to a catastrophic loss. There are several factors that determine what premiums insurers would like to charge.

Ambiguity of Risk A risk is ambiguous if one cannot assign a probability to it. Insurers (and indeed, decision makers in general) dislike ambiguity. The greater the ambiguity of a specific loss the higher the premium will be. In a mail survey of professional actuaries conducted by the Casualty Actuarial Society, 463 respondents indicated how much they would charge to cover losses against a defective product in two cases, one where the probabilities of a loss (p) was well specified at $p = .001$, and one where they experienced considerable uncertainty about the likelihood of a loss with the same mean likelihood. The median premium values were five times higher for the uncertain risk than for the well-specified probability when the losses from each insurance policy were independent. This ratio increased to ten times when the losses were perfectly correlated (Hogarth and Kunreuther 1989).

In another study, a questionnaire was mailed to 190 randomly chosen insurance companies of different sizes asking underwriters to specify the prices that they would like to charge to insure a factory against property damage from a severe earthquake, to insure an underground storage tank, and to provide coverage for a neutral situation (i.e., a risk without any context). Probabilities and losses were varied. The probability of loss and the size of the claim were either well-specified or there was ambiguity regarding the likelihood of the loss and/or the claim size. The underwriters wanted to charge considerably more for the same amount of coverage when either the probability was ambiguous and/or the claim size was uncertain (Kunreuther et al. 1995).

Adverse Selection If the insurer sets a premium based on the average probability of a loss, using the entire population as a basis for this estimate, those with the highest risk will be the most likely to purchase coverage for that hazard. In an extreme case, the poor risks will be the only purchasers of coverage, and the insurer will lose money on each policy sold. This situation, referred to as adverse selection, occurs when the insurer cannot distinguish between the probabilities of a loss for good- and poor-risk categories, but the insured can.

Moral Hazard Moral hazard refers to an increase in the probability of loss caused by the behavior of the policyholder. For example, providing insurance protection to a nuclear power plant may lead the utility to behave more carelessly than if it did not have coverage. One way to avoid the problem of moral hazard is to introduce deductibles and coinsurance as part of the insurance contract. A sufficiently large deductible can act as an incentive for the insureds to continue to behave carefully after purchasing coverage because they will be forced to cover a significant portion of their loss themselves. With coinsurance, the insurer and the insured share the loss together. As with a deductible, this type of risk-sharing arrangement encourages safer behavior because those insured want to avoid having to pay for some of the losses.

Catastrophic Losses A nuclear power plant accident can produce catastrophic losses. Insurers who cover the risks from such disasters may have to pay potentially large claims to policyholders before they are able to collect sufficient premiums to cover their costs. This timing risk is an important element associated with catastrophic losses (Litan 2006). Rating agencies may also play a role in influencing how many policies an insurer will want to write on risks with respect to catastrophic losses. A recent report by the AM Best Company focuses on the importance of the ratio of annual insured catastrophic losses as percentage of policyholder surplus (PHS). In general, the report notes that the higher the level of loss relative to surplus, the greater has been the financial damage to the insurance industry (Williams and King 2006).

Condition 3: Earning a Positive Expected Profit by Marketing Coverage

In theory, insurers can offer protection against any risk that they can identify and for which they can obtain information to estimate the frequency and magnitude of potential losses as long as they have the freedom to set premiums at any level. However, due to problems of ambiguity, adverse selection, moral hazard, and highly correlated losses, they may want to charge premiums that considerably exceed the expected loss. For some risks the desired premium may be so high that there would be very little demand for coverage at that rate. In such cases, even though an insurer determines that a particular risk meets the two insurability conditions discussed previously, it will not invest the time and money to develop the product.

More specifically, the insurer must be convinced that there is sufficient demand to cover the development and marketing costs of the coverage through future premiums received. If there are regulatory restrictions that limit the price insurers can charge for certain types of coverage, then companies will not want to provide protection against these risks. In addition, if an insurer's portfolio leaves them vulnerable to the possibility of extremely large losses from a given disaster due to adverse selection, moral hazard, and/or high correlation of risks, then the insurer will want to reduce the number of policies in force for these hazards.

9.6.3   Conclusions on Insurability of Nuclear Reactors

The catastrophic risks associated with a meltdown of a reactor in a populated area, together with the release of radioactivity, are unlikely to be readily insurable. The risks are unique and massive, and not well understood. Problems of moral hazard and adverse selection may also be serious. If private insurers were to charge a premium that reflected their risk given the aforementioned features, it is likely to be considerably higher than if there was some public sector involvement. The Price-Anderson Act was passed in this spirit but has not been evaluated with respect to how well it meets society's needs. We now address this question.

9.7   Evaluating the Price-Anderson Act as an Insurance Program

Price-Anderson can provide as much as $10 billion of insurance to cover catastrophic losses. This is perhaps 10 percent of the likely cost of a meltdown associated with the release of radioactivity. The Act cannot provide adequate coverage should there be a severe nuclear accident. The gap between what is available under the Act and what would be needed would almost certainly be filled by the Federal Government. In other words, there is a potential liability by the public sector of $100 billion (or possibly much more) under the Price-Anderson Act. The probability that this liability will be incurred is small, so the expected value of the liability is perhaps in the range of billions rather than tens of billions.

9.7.1   Regulatory Capture

The risk that the government faces with respect to nuclear accidents is not entirely outside of its control. The government has to license nuclear power stations, and the NRC sets safety standards that if well enforced could cut the government's risk significantly. There is a lot of evidence that the NRC suffers from regulatory capture and has performed poorly in its role of safety overseer (Lochbaum 2006). The Federal Government can also reduce the risks associated with nuclear power by influencing the location of nuclear power points to more remote locations rather than major population centers, so as to reduce potential liabilities.

9.7.2   Subsidies Associated with Price-Anderson

Utilities are subsidized under the P-A Act because they are only responsible for damage up to about $10 billion. Canada has a similar cap on damages specified in the 1970 Nuclear Liability Act. The Canadian courts were forced to address the decreased incentive that this limited liability provides for investing in safety measures. In fact, the economist Ralph Winter, in a commentary on Ontario Hydro's behavior, pointed out that the utility is looking for alternatives to investing in safety measures because of the high costs associated with them (Heyes 2002–2003).

Another disincentive for utilities to invest in safety measures stems from the fact that insurance premiums do not reflect the performance and related risk associated with a nuclear power plant. Should there be an outage by a plant, the premiums are not adjusted upward to reflect the higher risk. By not having experience-rated premiums there is a type of interdependence that can be deleterious to all utilities in the industry. The financial vulnerability of one nuclear power plant depends not only on its own choice of security investments, but also on the actions of other agents. Inadequate investment elsewhere can raise a plant's premiums. This concept of *interdependent security* implies that outage in one plant could have financial impacts on all the other utilities operating nuclear power plants. As a result there may be suboptimal investment in the individual components (Kunreuther and Heal 2003; Heal and Kunreuther 2005). The existence of such interdependencies provides another challenge in determining the design of a nuclear power plant insurance program.

9.8   Modifying Price-Anderson

9.8.1   Learning from Other Federal and State Catastrophe Programs[12]

We now review the roles that the federal and state governments in the United States play in supplementing or replacing private insurance with respect to natural disasters and other catastrophic losses. In many respects, the problems faced in these areas are similar to those associated with nuclear accidents: they involve low-probability, high-cost risks for which the likelihoods of an accident are uncertain. Hence, there are lessons to be learned from these other areas. We shall discuss insurance against floods, hurricanes, and earthquakes as well as terrorism insurance.

Flood Insurance

Insurers have experimented over the years with providing protection against water damage from floods, hurricanes, and other storms. After the

---

12. The material in this subsection appears in Wharton Risk Center (2005).

severe Mississippi Floods of 1927, they concluded that the risk was too great for them to insure and refused to continue doing so. As a result, Congress created the National Flood Insurance Program (NFIP) in 1968, whereby homeowners and businesses could purchase coverage for water damage. Private insurers market the flood policies, and the premiums are deposited in a federally operated Flood Insurance Fund, which is then responsible for paying claims. The stipulation for this financial protection is that the local community makes a commitment to regulate the location and design of future floodplain construction to increase safety from flood hazards. The Federal Government established a series of building and development standards for floodplain construction to serve as minimum requirements for participation in the program. The creation of the Community Rating System in 1990 has linked mitigation measures with the price of insurance in a systematic way (Pasterick 1998).

Hurricane Insurance

The need for hurricane insurance is most pronounced in the state of Florida. Following Hurricane Andrew in 1992, nine property-casualty insurance companies became insolvent, forcing other insurers to cover these losses under Florida's State Guaranty Fund. Property insurance became more difficult to obtain as many insurers reduced their concentrations of insured property in coastal areas. During a special session of the Florida State Legislature in 1993, the Florida Hurricane Catastrophe Fund (FHCF) was created to relieve pressure on insurers to reduce their exposures to hurricane losses. The FHCF, a tax-exempt trust fund administered by the state of Florida, is financed by premiums paid by insurers that write policies on personal and commercial residential properties. The fund reimburses a portion of insurers' losses following major hurricanes (above the insurer's retention level) and enables insurers to remain solvent (Lecomte and Gahagan 1998). The four hurricanes that hit Florida in the fall of 2004 (Charley, Frances, Ivan, and Jeanne) caused an estimated $23 billion in insured losses, with only about $2.6 billion paid out by the Fund. Each hurricane was considered a distinct event, so that retention levels were applied to each storm before insurers could turn to the FHCF.

During a special session of the Florida State Legislature in January 2007, the capacity of the FHCF was expanded to $27.75 billion in insurance. However, there would have to be no damaging hurricanes until the year 2024 for the FHCF to pay all its claims from a hurricane with a 500-year return period. If such a disaster occurred before that date, the additional capacity to meet all the FHCF claims would have to come from assessing all property and casualty lines of business, excluding workers' compensation, accident and health, medical malpractice, and flood insurance (Kunreuther and Michel-Kerjan 2009).

Earthquake Insurance

The history of earthquake activity in California convinced legislators that this risk was too great to be left in the hands of private insurers alone. In 1985, a California law required insurers writing homeowners' coverage on one- to four-unit residential buildings to also offer earthquake coverage. Because rates were regulated by the state, insurers felt they were forced to offer coverage against older structures in poor condition, with rates not necessarily reflecting the risk. Following the 1994 Northridge earthquake, huge insured property losses created a surge in demand for coverage. Insurers were concerned that if they satisfied the entire demand, as they were required to do by the 1985 law, they would face an unacceptable level of risk and become insolvent following the next major earthquake. Hence, many firms decided to stop offering coverage or restricted the sale of homeowners' policies in California.

In order to keep earthquake insurance available in California, in 1996 the State legislature authorized the formation of the California Earthquake Authority (CEA), a state-run insurance company that provides earthquake coverage to homeowners. The innovative feature of this financing plan is the ability to pay for a large earthquake while committing relatively few dollars up front. There was an initial assessment of insurers of $1 billion to start the program and then contingent assessments to the insurance industry and reinsurers following a severe earthquake. Policyholders absorb the first portion of an earthquake through a 15 percent deductible on their policies (Roth 1998). However, twelve years after the creation of the CEA, the take-up rate for homeowners was about 15 percent, down from 30 percent when the California State Legislature created the CEA (Risk Management Solutions 2004). It is questionable how effective this program will be in covering losses should a major earthquake occur in California.

Federal Aviation Administration Third-Party Liability Insurance Program

Since the terrorist attacks of September 11, 2001, the US commercial aviation industry can purchase insurance for third-party liability arising out of aviation terrorism. The current mechanism operates as a pure government program, with premiums paid by airlines into the Aviation Insurance Revolving Fund managed by the Federal Aviation Administration (FAA).

As the program carries a liability limit of only $100 million, losses paid by government sources in the event of an attack will almost surely exceed those available through the current insurance regime. In that case, either the government would need to appropriate additional disaster assistance funds as it did in the aftermath of September 11, or victims would be forced to rely on traditional sources of assistance (Strauss 2005).

Terrorism Insurance

Insuring the risks from terrorist attacks has some similarity to insuring nuclear accidents—indeed, one worst-case terrorist scenario involves terrorists causing a nuclear accident. In both cases the probability distribution over possible losses is largely a matter of guesswork, with no historical record to provide a benchmark. And in both cases, government policies can influence the risks. So it is worth spending some time reviewing the extensive recent discussion of how to manage terrorist risks.

Prior to September 11, terrorism exclusions in commercial property and casualty policies in the US insurance market were extremely rare (outside of ocean marine) because losses from terrorism had historically been small and, to a large degree, uncorrelated. Attacks of a domestic origin were isolated, carried out by groups or individuals with disparate agendas. Thus the United States did not face a concerted domestic terrorism threat, as did countries such as France, Israel, Spain, and the United Kingdom.

In fact, insurance losses from terrorism were viewed as so improbable that the risk was not explicitly mentioned nor priced in any standard policy and it was never excluded from so-called "all-risk" policies with the exception of some marine cargo, aviation, and political risk policies. Even the first attack on the World Trade Center (WTC) in 1993[13] and the Oklahoma City bombing of 1995[14] were not seen as being threatening enough for insurers to consider revising their view of terrorism as a peril worth considering when pricing a commercial insurance policy. Since insurers and reinsurers felt that the likelihood of a major terrorist loss was below their threshold level of concern, they did not pay close attention to their potential losses from terrorism in the United States (Kunreuther and Pauly 2005).

Terrorism presents a set of very specific problems regarding its insurability by the private market alone that have similar features to nuclear power. These include the potential for catastrophic losses, the existence of interdependencies, and the dynamic uncertainty associated with the risk. All of these factors increase the amount of capital that insurers must hold to provide terrorism risk insurance coverage. The associated costs of holding that capital increases the premiums they would need to charge. The fact that government actions are likely to influence both the will and capacity of terrorist groups to attack (foreign policy, counterterrorism) and the level of potential losses poses additional challenges. These challenges are closely related to the fact that the Nuclear Regulatory Commission influences the

13. The 1993 bombing of the WTC killed six people and caused $725 million in insured damages. See Swiss Re (2002).
14. Prior to September 11, the Oklahoma City bombing of 1995, which killed 168 people, had been the most damaging terrorist attack on domestic soil, but the largest losses were to federal property and employees and were covered by the government.

degree of acceptability of the risks facing nuclear power plants. The conclusion that emerges from experience with terrorist coverage since September 11 suggests that this risk is not well handled by the insurance market. This was recognized by the passage of TRIA, the Terrorist Risk Insurance Act, which established a role for the Federal Government similar to that assigned to it in the P-A Act.

To more fully understand the losses from September 11 from an insurability perspective, one can compare this event with other types of extreme events that have affected the (re)insurance industry. Table 9.1 presents the twenty largest worldwide insurance losses due to natural catastrophes and man-made disasters from 1970 to 2008. Prior to September 11 losses, the largest loss experienced by the insurance industry was Hurricane Andrew, which devastated the coasts of Florida in August 1992 and inflicted $24.6 billion in claims payments (indexed to 2008) (Swiss Re 2009). When one adds the 6 to 7 billion dollars in payments by the US Federal Victim Compensation Fund to victims of September 11 and their families, the claims from the terrorist attacks are almost twice those from Hurricane Andrew (Congressional Budget Office 2005). Claims from a major nuclear accident could be very much larger even than those associated with September 11.

Table 9.1   **The twenty most costly insured catastrophes in the world, 1970-2008**

US $ billion	Event	Victims (dead or missing)	Year	Area of primary damage
48.1	Hurricane Katrina	1,836	2005	US, Gulf of Mexico
36.8	9/11 attacks	3,025	2001	US
24.6	Hurricane Andrew	43	1992	US, Bahamas
20.3	Northridge earthquake	61	1994	US
16.0	Hurricane Ike	348	2008	US, Caribbean
14.6	Hurricane Ivan	124	2004	US, Caribbean
13.8	Hurricane Wilma	35	2005	US, Gulf of Mexico
11.1	Hurricane Rita	34	2005	US, Gulf of Mexico
9.1	Hurricane Charley	24	2004	US, Caribbean
8.9	Typhoon Mireille	51	1991	Japan
7.9	Hurricane Hugo	71	1989	Puerto Rico, US
7.7	Winterstorm Daria	95	1990	France, UK
7.5	Winterstorm Lothar	110	1999	France, Switzerland
6.3	Winterstorm Kyrill	54	2007	Germany, UK, NL, France
5.9	Storms and floods	22	1987	France, UK
5.8	Hurricane Frances	38	2004	US, Bahamas
5.2	Winterstorm Vivian	64	1990	Western/Central Europe
5.2	Typhoon Bart	26	1999	Japan
5.0	Hurricane Gustav	153	2008	US, Caribbean
4.7	Hurricane Georges	600	1998	US, Caribbean

Sources: Wharton Risk Center with data from Swiss Re and Insurance Information Institute.

Note: This table excludes payments for flood by the National Flood Insurance Program in the United States. In billions, indexed to 2008.

9.8.2   Linking Insurance with Third-Party Inspections
Via Public-Private Partnerships[15]

The Price-Anderson Act needs to be modified to provide a more effective way of monitoring utilities and rewarding those that have undertaken risk-reducing measures. Today there is inadequate inspection of nuclear plants due to limited personnel at the NRC and the lack of incentives by utilities to undertake these measures on their own. Low inspection levels (and low usage of other effective methods for compliance evaluation) may lead to low compliance rates and reduce opportunities for government to find and require firms to correct the sorts of risky practices regulations seek to reduce.

Role of Third-Party Inspections

One way to change the situation is to provide economic incentives to utilities to have their plants inspected. After demonstrating that they are operating safely, they could be rewarded with a lower insurance premium. The combination of private inspection and insurance is a potentially powerful one for meeting and often exceeding environmental and safety regulations. If an inspection reveals ways that a company can reduce its safety and environmental risks, and the costs of undertaking this activity can be recouped in the form of lower insurance premiums that justify the expenditure, then firms will want to adopt these measures.

Insurers have an economic incentive to conduct inspections that focus on risk reduction because they want to reduce the likelihood of paying a claim and the size of their payments. The insurer's economic survival depends on estimating the risk of future losses accurately, not on assuring compliance with government laws. To the extent that regulations are well-aligned with risk-reducing behaviors, insurers are likely to uncover noncompliance problems and encourage their correction.

How Inspections Aid Insurers. Insurance is likely to have greater risk-reducing potential if insurers include inspections, along with other forms of risk assessment, as part of the insurance-rating package. Private insurance inspections can play an important role for several reasons. At the most basic level, insured firms will be more aware of environmental and safety risks as well as regulatory obligations. This promises to be especially valuable in areas of health, safety, and the environment that are plagued by low inspection levels.

Gathering Risk Information. Inspections also enable the insurer to determine how firms investing in risk-reducing measures are likely to reduce their

15. This subsection is based on Kunreuther, Metzenbaum, and Schmeidler (2006).

losses. Insurers can also provide guidance to the firm as to what types of actions would be most profitable for them to undertake to meet or exceed compliance with regulations. If insurers increase their inspections of a firm's safety practices prior to policy renewals, firms will have incentives to comply with the regulations.

Use of Claims Data to Modify Existing Standards. Studying information about claims, incidents, and noncompliance may identify recurring events and high-cost problems calling for new laws or standards. If an insurer has a large enough set of clients and can pool information so as not to reveal identities of firms, then it can provide valuable information to the public sector on the types of claims that have been made. This will enable the public sector agency to modify codes and standards in an appropriate fashion.

Rewarding Firms for Reducing Risks. Insurers providing coverage to commercial enterprises always have the option of raising rates to reflect additional risks that they uncover. Insurers can also bestow rewards on firms that operate at the highest level of compliance and take risk-reducing actions beyond their formal obligations. Seals of approval are valuable to the firm to the extent that customers, employees, and investors make decisions on the basis of safety and environmental records of different organizations. Some commercial partners will see the seal of approval as the designation of a quality operation and favor doing business with these firms.

The firm that earns the seal will have an incentive to reveal its third-party commendation to the public as well as to the government. Regulatory agencies can utilize this information to target inspections to firms that have not had this official recognition; thus, there is a greater chance that those who have not complied with the regulation will be audited by a governmental agency. By raising the probability of a public inspection, more and more firms should adhere to regulations over time.

An insurance commendation is likely to have greater veracity than other sorts of third-party certifications because most third-party inspectors are paid a fee for their services by the inspected firm, and therefore feel a constant tug to keep their customer happy without a strong counterbalancing financial tug to identify risks that may require costly corrections. Insurers, in contrast, have a direct financial interest in reducing risk through their inspections.

9.9   Summary and Conclusions

On the general issue of environmental liabilities, it seems clear that the degradation of natural capital in systems as diverse as the climate system or the coastal barrier island systems can lead to significant social costs that are generally not well-covered by current insurance products. These end up as liabilities of the Federal Government by default, often as a part of the portfolio of the Federal Emergency Management Agency.

In the field of nuclear risks, the Price-Anderson Act transfers significant liabilities to the Federal Government. If there is an expansion of the use of nuclear power in the next decade, as appears to be the case, then these liabilities could increase further. Although it is clear that the contingent federal liabilities associated with P-A are large, it is hard to be precise about them. The probability of a major accident at a nuclear reactor (e.g., a core meltdown) and its costs are ambiguous.

There are, however, certain things that are clear. One is that the risk is to some degree under the control of the Federal Government, via the Nuclear Regulatory Commission, if it enforces safety standards and influences the siting of nuclear reactors in remote areas. There is empirical evidence that the NRC does not aggressively pursue and penalize mismanagement of nuclear power stations, and that the Federal authorities are not sensitive to the increase in potential costs associated with siting near densely populated areas. There is scope for better management of this aspect of Federal financial risks, possibly by the use of third-party safety auditors to supplement the NRC. In addition, the premiums charged to utilities under the P-A Act do not reflect their stations' safety risks: this would be another way of reducing the risk of a disaster. Currently there are few incentives for a utility to improve its safety record.

There do seem to be compelling reasons for thinking that Federal intervention is necessary if the risk of nuclear disaster is to be adequately insured. There are many characteristics of this risk that probably make it uninsurable. But that does not mean that the P-A Act is the best solution. We have reviewed the ways in which catastrophic risks are managed in other areas, such as flood, hurricane, earthquake, and terrorist risks. There has been considerably more constructive public debate about these risks than about nuclear risks. Typical of most of these areas is a first insurance layer covered by private insurance markets, with government coverage of losses in excess of the private risk cap. In the case of the P-A Act, the private coverage is just $300 million per incident, with a pool insurance vehicle covering the next $10 billion. There is no explicit statement of the government's role and liabilities. The figure of $300 million surely does not exhaust the private sector's available capital for covering losses from a nuclear power plant accident. For other areas the private sector provides coverage as high as $10 billion or more. More of the nuclear risk could surely be met through the private sector. This would not only reduce the Federal liability but also provide increased incentives for risk management, sadly lacking under the current regime.

On a more general note, the increased concern with the impacts of climate change on the environment suggests that one rethink the role that FEMA and other public sector agencies at the local, state, and federal levels can play in reducing losses from future disasters. There is a need for innovative private-public sector initiatives to avoid the problems inherent in myopic thinking. For example, in order to encourage residents and businesses to adopt risk-reducing measures with respect to natural and man-made hazards, multiyear contracts such as five-to-ten-year insurance policies and long-term loans should be considered (Kunreuther and Michel-Kerjan 2010). The need for such long-term thinking appears more important today than it did a few years ago, with respect to reducing the catastrophic losses from environmental risks and encouraging a rethinking of the sources of energy that addresses the problems of climate change.

References

Barbier, E. B., and G. M. Heal. 2006. Valuing ecosystem services. *The Economists' Voice* 3 (3), Berkeley Electronic Press, January. Available at: http://www.bepress.com/ev/vol3/iss3/art2/.

Bourne, J. K., Jr. 2004. Gone with the water. *National Geographic.* Available at: http://ngm.nationalgeographic.com/ngm/0410/feature5/.

Congressional Budget Office (CBO). 2005. *Federal terrorism reinsurance: An update.* Washington, DC: CBO, January.

Cummins, D. 2006. Should the government provide insurance for catastrophes? *Federal Reserve Bank of St. Louis Review* 88 (4): 337–79.

Dlugolecki, A. 2006. Thoughts about the impact of climate change on insurance claims. In *Report of the workshop on climate change and disaster losses, May 25–26,* ed. P. Höppe and R. Pielke,

Emanuel, K. 2005. Increasing destructiveness of tropical cyclones over the past 30 years. *Nature* 436 (4): 686–88.

———. 2008. The Hurricane-climate connection. *Bulletin of the American Meteorological Society* 89 (5): ES10–ES20.

Freeman, P., and H. Kunreuther. 1997. *Managing environmental risk through insurance.* Washington, DC: American Enterprise Institute.

Heal, G. 2000. *Nature and the marketplace: Capturing the value of ecosystem services.* Washington, DC: Island Press.

———. 2007. Accounting and the resource curse, (or are oil producers rich?). In *Escaping the resource curse,* ed. M. Humphreys, J. D. Sachs, and J. E. Stiglitz, 155–72. New York: Columbia University Press.

Heal, G., and H. Kunreuther. 2005. IDS models for airline security. *Journal of Conflict Resolution* 49 (2): 201–17.

Heyes, A. 2002–2003. The price of Price-Anderson. *Regulation* (Winter). Available at: http://www.cato.org/pubs/regulation/regv25n4/v25n4-8.pdf.

Hogarth, R., and H. Kunreuther. 1989. Risk, ambiguity, and insurance. *Journal of Risk and Uncertainty* 2 (1): 5–35.

Intergovernmental Panel on Climate Change. 2007. *Fourth assessment report.* Geneva, Switzerland. Available at: www.ipcc.ch.

Johnson, T. 2008. Challenges for nuclear power. *Council on Foreign Relations Backgrounder,* August 11. Available at: http://www.cfr.org/publication/16886/#7.

Kunreuther, H., and G. Heal. 2003. Interdependent security. *Journal of Risk and Uncertainty* 26 (2/3): 231–49.

Kunreuther, H., J. Meszaros, R. Hogarth, and M. Spranca. 1995. Ambiguity and underwriter decision processes. *Journal of Economic Behaviour and Organization* 26 (3): 337–52.

Kunreuther, H., S. Metzenbaum, and P. Schmeidler. 2006. Mandating insurance and using private inspections to improve environmental management. In *Leveraging the private sector: Management-based strategies for improving environmental performance,* ed. C. Coglianese and J. Nash, 137–65. Washington, DC: Resources for the Future.

Kunreuther, H., and E. Michel-Kerjan. 2004. Policy-watch: Challenges for terrorism insurance in the United States. *Journal of Economic Perspectives* 18 (4): 201–14.

———. 2007. Climate change, insurability of large-scale disasters and the emerging liability challenge. *University of Pennsylvania Law Review* 155 (6): 1795–1842.

———. 2009. *At War with the Weather.* Cambridge, MA: MIT Press.

———. 2010. Market and government failure in insuring and mitigating natural catastrophes: How long-term contracts can help. In *Public Insurance and Private Markets,* ed. J. R. Brown. Washington, DC: American Enterprise Institute Press.

Kunreuther, H., and M. Pauly. 2005. Terrorism losses and all-perils insurance. *Journal of Insurance Regulation* (Summer): 1–18.

Lecomte, E., and K. Gahagan. 1998. Hurricane insurance protection in Florida. In *Paying the price: The status and role of insurance against natural disasters in the United States,* ed. H. Kunreuther and R. J. Roth, Sr., 97–124. Washington, DC: J. Henry Press.

Litan, R. 2006. Sharing and reducing the financial risks of future mega-catastrophe. *Issues in Economic Policy, No. 4.* Washington, DC: The Brookings Institution.

Lochbaum, D. 2006. *Walking a nuclear tightrope: Unlearned lessons of year-plus reactor outages.* Cambridge, MA: Union of Concerned Scientists. Available at: http://www.ucsusa.org/clean_energy/nuclear_safety/walking-a-nuclear-tightrope .html.

Miller, M. H., and C. W. Upton. 1985. A test of the hotelling valuation principle. *Journal of Political Economy* 93 (1): 1–25.

National Research Council. 2000. *Watershed management for potable water supply: Assessing the NYC strategy.* Washington, DC: National Academies Press.

———. 2004. *Valuing ecosystem services: Toward better environmental decision-making.* Washington, DC: National Academies Press. Available at: http://www .nap.edu/books/030909318X/html/.

Nuclear Energy Institute. 2005. Price-Anderson act provides effective nuclear insurance at no cost to the public. Available at: http://www.nei.org/keyissues/safetyan dsecurity/factsheets/priceandersonact/.

Pasterick, E. 1998. The national flood insurance program. In *Paying the price: The status and role of insurance against natural disasters in the United States,* ed. H. Kunreuther and R. J. Roth, Sr., 125–54. Washington, DC: J. Henry Press.

Risk Management Solutions. 2004. The Northridge, California earthquake: A 10-year retrospective. RMS Retrospective Report, May.

Roth, R. J., Jr. 1998. Earthquake insurance protection in California. In *Paying the price: The status and role of insurance against natural disasters in the United States,* ed. H. Kunreuther and R. J. Roth, Sr., 67–96. Washington, DC: J. Henry Press.

Strauss, A. 2005. Terrorism third party liability insurance for commercial aviation, Federal intervention in the wake of September 11. University of Pennsylvania, the Wharton School, Center for Risk Management and Decision Processes, June.

Swiss Re. 2002. *Terrorism—dealing with the new spectre.* Focus report, February. Zurich: Swiss Re.

———. 2009. Natural catastrophes and man-made disasters in 2008. *Sigma* no. 2. Zurich: Swiss Re.

Wald, M. 2008. After 35-year lull, nuclear power may be in early stages of revival. *New York Times,* October 24.

Wharton Risk Center. 2005. Insurability concepts and insurance programs for extreme events. In *TRIA and beyond: Terrorism risk financing in the US,* 29–42. University of Pennsylvania, the Wharton School.

Williams, J., and C. A. King. 2006. *2006 annual hurricane study: Shake, rattle and roar.* Oldwick, NJ: A.M. Best Company, Inc., June.

Comment   William Pizer

Key decisions in public policy often come down to efforts to weigh the costs and benefits of various alternatives. In order for such efforts to be meaningful, it is important to include all major sources of costs and benefits—otherwise, what may *appear* to be a reasonable choice can turn out to be quite the opposite when a full accounting occurs. The question would then seem to be, what are the key categories of costs and benefits?

This could be the primary focus of Heal and Kunreuther, who turn their attention to a broad category of such costs and benefits—environmental assets and liabilities—in order to see if there are any lessons for current policymakers. Their chapter breaks down into two parts: first, a review of environmental assets and accounting; and second, a review of environmental liabilities and insurance, with a particular emphasis on nuclear power. Each part offers lessons for improving public policy decisions.

The first section reviews a number of examples where environmental assets have or have not been valued. The Catskills provide significant value to New York City in terms of their ability to cleanse and stabilize the flow of water to New York. Forests offer value in terms of sequestered carbon dioxide that otherwise contributes to global climate change. Oil, gas, coal, and other mineral deposits have very clear market value. Soil provides agricultural productivity. And the climate system, to date, has provided relatively stable climate and weather patterns that have allowed regions to develop and

William Pizer is a senior fellow at Resources for the Future.

specialize—such as Florida's balmy weather or the Rockies' extensive ski resorts. Among these, only the Catskills watershed and mineral resources are examples where natural assets have been recognized, valued, and addressed by economic decisions. Elsewhere, public policy has failed to value these assets with, over time, likely adverse economic consequences.

The second section shifts to liabilities. Some, like the Superfund program and nuclear plant liabilities, are relatively well defined. Others, like the costs of hurricanes and terrorist acts that are not privately insured, are much more opaque. A variety of different approaches have evolved to deal with these liabilities, typically involving some notion of shared public-private risk, as they do not satisfy the conditions for pure private insurability. The nuclear liability program, designed to cover the costs of a nuclear accident and defined by the Price-Anderson Act, is characterized by about $10 billion in pooled private liability. Yet, as the authors show, the potential liability may be ten to one hundred times that—liability that rests with the federal government. Because of the nature of the private insurance, both its size and structure, Heal and Kunreuther argue that plant operators have insufficient incentive to pursue safer operations. In particular, they advocate a system of third-party inspections coupled with insurance premiums linked to inspection results.

In this way, Heal and Kunreuther offer some very specific advice: account for environmental assets and design insurance schemes to properly incentivize behavior. Consider public schemes when liabilities do not satisfy conditions for insurability.

Yet while that advice *could* be the primary focus of the chapter, it is not. The first line of the abstract states "[we] argue that the degradation of natural capital can lead to social risks which ultimately will end up to some degree as the responsibility of the Federal government." A later statement drives home the point regarding Hurricane Katrina: "the public expects the Federal Government to step in and offer restitution in situations such as Katrina." This is a very important point: while the government may or may not seek to take action to preserve natural assets, to avoid liabilities, or to develop explicit insurance programs, it will *always* have liability.

In this way, many public policy choices that may seem to be about action or inaction—for example, regarding climate change—are really about action now versus action later. The same can be said for natural disaster risk, terrorism, or encouraging nuclear power. The latter is a particularly interesting case, as nuclear power itself represents a fundamental risk-risk trade-off—the risk of a nuclear accident versus the risk of climate change (which will be greatly increased without nuclear power). Here, we have choices both about how we will manage the nuclear risk and how we will balance it—through more or less effective public insurance subsidies—against climate change risk.

Climate change, thus viewed by Heal and Kunreuther, remains a catastrophic risk born by the Federal government that should be met with both suitable mitigation and appropriate insurance tools. The ambiguity of risk in this case—concerning both the likelihood and consequence of adverse events—is simply a reason private insurance against climate change will not arise. However, there is another view about the ambiguity of risk in this case. Recent work by Weitzman (2009), and consequent criticism by Nordhaus (2009), take the notion of catastrophic risk a step further—arguing that in extreme cases catastrophic risk can actually throw into question the entire apparatus of cost-benefit analysis.

Weitzman makes the point that conventional cost-benefit analysis relies on some notion that increasingly improbable and adverse events can, at some point, be neglected. Otherwise, our analysis becomes dominated by efforts to estimate the likelihood and magnitude of increasingly rare and super-catastrophic events—efforts that are highly speculative and eventually somewhat meaningless. Weitzman argues that this is precisely the case of global climate change, owing to the unprecedented level and rate of change in greenhouse gas concentrations, uncertainty about the potential of significant positive feedbacks, and no understanding of what a 10 or 20 degree temperature change really means. Nordhaus, meanwhile, argues that we can and should do our best to estimate the likelihood and consequence of various climate change outcomes and use that estimate to inform decision-making. That is, he assumes the probability of increasingly rare events fades more rapidly than the consequences of those events expand.

Weitzman is trying to make an extreme point—that in the case of climate change, conventional cost-benefit analysis is overwhelmed by the catastrophic risk and it is unbounded, with the policy implication that we should do virtually *anything* to contain that risk. This reminds one of a high school debating tactic in the 1980s—the "nuclear option"—where each team would attempt to tie whatever side of an issue they were arguing against to an increased risk of nuclear war. Such an outcome would be catastrophic, and therefore must be avoided. But how does one know how much is enough?

A weaker version of Weitzman's point is one where the cost-benefit is overwhelmed by the catastrophic risk, but is not unbounded. In Heal and Kunreuther's analysis of a worst-case nuclear accident, for example, damages could be on the order of a $1 trillion (what they refer to as "almost unthinkable costs"). Such a risk might be enough to overwhelm the cost-benefit analysis of a $1 billion nuclear power plant, but it is not unbounded.

In some people's minds, this is precisely the calculus—nuclear power is not worth it. Others are okay with nuclear power, perhaps owing to an analyst's calculations that put the expected value much lower, efforts to mitigate that risk through various measures, or a notion that this unknowable risk on the nuclear accident side has an equilibrating unknowable risk on the other side—perhaps the likely environmental consequences from climate change if nuclear power is off the table.

All of this should be a bit humbling, particularly as regards climate change but also more generally for cost-benefit analysis with ambiguous risk. Cost-benefit analysis, and particularly analyses involving catastrophic risk, should not be viewed as a formulaic way to make decisions. It is a valuable part of the decision process—maybe the most valuable part. But, in the end, values and judgment play an extremely important role.

References

Nordhaus, W. D. 2009. An analysis of the dismal theorem. Cowles Foundation Discussion Paper no. 1686. Yale University.
Weitzman, M. L. 2009. On modeling and interpreting the economics of catastrophic climate change. *Review of Economics and Statistics* 91 (1): 1–19.

Contributors

Henning Bohn
Department of Economics, NH 2127
University of California at Santa
  Barbara
Santa Barbara, CA 93106

J. David Cummins
Temple University
617 Alter Hall
1801 Liacouras Walk
Philadelphia, PA 19122

Janice C. Eberly
Department of Finance
Kellogg School of Management
Northwestern University
2001 Sheridan Road
Evanston, IL 60208

Peter R. Fisher
BlackRock, Inc.
40 East 52nd Street, 5th Floor
New York, NY 10022

John Geanakoplos
Economics Department
30 Hillhouse Avenue
Yale University
New Haven, CT 06520

Geoffrey Heal
Graduate School of Business
616 Uris Hall
Columbia University
New York, NY 10027

Dwight M. Jaffee
Haas School of Business
University of California, Berkeley
Berkeley, CA 94720-1900

Howard Kunreuther
The Wharton School
University of Pennsylvania
Philadelphia, PA 19104-6366

Deborah Lucas
Kellogg Graduate School of
  Management
Northwestern University
2001 Sheridan Road
Evanston, IL 60208

Alan J. Marcus
Carroll School of Management
Boston College
Chestnut Hill, MA 02467

Donald B. Marron
5108 Wilson Lane
Bethesda, MD 20814

Robert McDonald
Kellogg Graduate School of
    Management
Northwestern University
2001 Sheridan Road
Evanston, IL 60208

Damien Moore
Congressional Budget Office
Ford House Office Building, 4th Floor
Second and D Streets, SW
Washington, DC 20515-6925

Greg Niehaus
Moore School of Business
University of South Carolina
Columbia, SC 29208

Marvin Phaup
Trachtenberg School of Public Policy
    and Public Administration
The George Washington University
805 21st Street, NW
Washington, DC 20052

William Pizer
Resources for the Future
1616 P Street, NW
Washington, DC 20036

John M. Quigley
Department of Economics
Evans Hall #3880
University of California
Berkeley, CA 94720-3880

Michael Suher
Department of Economics
Box B
Brown University
Providence, RI 02912

Susan M. Wachter
The Wharton School
University of Pennsylvania
Philadelphia, PA 19104-6366

George Zanjani
J. Mack Robinson College of Business
Department of Risk Management and
    Insurance
Georgia State University
P.O. Box 4036
Atlanta, GA 30302-4036

Stephen P. Zeldes
Graduate School of Business
Columbia University
3022 Broadway
New York, NY 10027-6902

Author Index

Subject Index